BALLS TO MS

BALLS TO MS

20 Years of Discovering Your Body Hates You

ANDY REYNARD

First published 2022
Copyright © Andy Reynard, 2022
All photos © Andy Reynard

ISBN: 978-1-3999-1267-9

Cover design by Book Beaver (www.bookbeaver.co.uk)

For further information about the author, as well as further background information regarding this book, visit
www.ballstoms.com

Contents

For all those living with multiple sclerosis. In 2020 that was an estimated 130,000 people in the UK and 2,500,000 across the world.

I salute you and invite you to join me in saying, 'Balls to MS.'

PREFACE

Everything you are about to read happened to me. Some things took place at slightly different times to those presented – I moved a few events around in the service of drama, but really not that much. In addition, I changed one or two names to protect the privacy of certain individuals.

Kate is also not the name of my wife. She didn't want me to use her real name, for deeply considered reasons: "I don't know why, I just don't." As I was writing the book, I amused myself by telling her it's fine, as Kate is a much nicer person than her.

The key point I'm making is that, despite the odd tweak, the following is all true.

God, how I wish it wasn't.

PART ONE

Man plans, God laughs.

Yiddish saying

SOMETIME IN 2002 – THE BEGINNING

The car needs a service. It's just one of those pain-in-the-arse tasks that has to be done. No joy, no retail therapy, nothing that's going to enhance your life. It's just money to part with and for what? So your car keeps running right and you can get to work so you can earn more money to pay for crap like car servicing.

I always use the same garage. This is only partly due to a sense of loyalty and the hope that they will treat me better if they know I will be coming back. The main reason, perhaps strangely, is that I have a habit of embarrassing myself whenever I take my car into Gordons. List of top five incidents at Gordons that I'd rather forget:

1. The time I dropped the car off with a teaspoon-worth of petrol in it. As they were running the engine, trying to sort out some kind of tuning problem, the car unsurprisingly ran out of fuel and they had to tow it to the local petrol station.

2. The present car has an immobiliser that is overridden by a code. On its first visit to Gordons I forgot to give

them the code and they had to push it onto the ramp.

3. Once when I took a car in for an MOT it was pointed out to me that the MOT was six months overdue.

4. During another MOT it was discovered that all four tyres were completely bald. They suggested I was lucky to be still alive.

5. Almost every time I drop the car off, I start to walk away from the front desk before the person behind the counter asks if I might give them the keys before I go.

I'm sure there are countless other incidents that I've blocked from the memory, but you get the idea. You are perhaps left wondering, though, why I continue to go there when I still occasionally let out a pained squeak in bed at night as I recall one of these episodes. My reasoning is simple: my garage embarrassments are currently contained. I hate my visits there but I at least know that the knowledge of my stupidity is limited to a few people. If I start cheating on them at another garage, I will be widening the pool of people knowing what I'm like when I step onto a car maintenance forecourt. Something about it makes me flustered. This is the realm of adults, of men who are men. This is not the domain of a thirty-something man-child who can never remember his reg number.

I park up, take a deep breath and let them know that I've arrived. After I've bid them farewell, then turned back around to give them the keys, I leave for a second time and head to the bus stop. Often on these days, I'll get someone to meet me here so he or she can give me a lift home, but today I've decided not to involve anyone else. I'm going to get a bus into town and then a second bus home. This seemed like a reasonable idea but a quick look at the timetable fixed to the lamppost makes me pine for the comfort of my dad or girlfriend's car. The next one is going to be about twenty minutes. Under my own steam, it's only around twenty into town. I might as well walk it.

The weather's unremarkable today – cloudy and cool. I'm not that keen on walking generally and just thankful I'm not getting rained on. I've never understood why some people seem to get so much from a walk. OK, you might be in a slightly more interesting place than one of the main trunk roads into Wakefield, but really, what's the big deal about this walking thing?

Hang on, what's this? A bit of sunshine. The clouds have parted and suddenly it's unseasonably warm. Hot even. I've been ambling along for around a quarter of an hour and now I'm beginning to feel the thinnest film of sweat forming on my back and forehead. I hate this clammy feeling. Maybe I should have stuck it out at the bus stop. I bet it'll come chugging past any minute and I'll have got hot and bothered for nothing.

I'm distracted from these negative thoughts as I become aware of a strange sensation in my left leg. Pins and needles are dancing up and down most of its length, sharp but somehow more delicate than normal pins and needles. I've not had a heat rash since I was a kid but this feels similar to that, if my memories of it are correct. This sudden sunshine, coupled with all the walking, must have brought it on. It's annoying and also weird that it's only in my left leg but I'm sure it'll go soon enough. At least I'm nearly in town now. I think I'll get a sandwich at a café. A nice sit down beckons.

*

As expected, the pins and needles quickly disappear before I've even taken the first bite of my BLT. Back home, however, I get a call from Gordons. They couldn't help noticing that the exhaust is badly corroded and it'd be foolish not to get it changed today before it falls off. Of course, it has to be a full unit, so with the service and all I won't have much change from two hundred and fifty quid by the time we're done. Triffic.

Car service day is always a crap day.

SUMMER 2003 – WELCOME TO HELL

We're moving house again. Before I met my girlfriend, Kate, I had lived in the same terrace for five years. Another five years have passed since we took our first place together. In that time we've moved on five occasions, including two moves within London because of Kate's job, which were sandwiched between two moves into the same place (the first place we bought). Are you following this? Probably not. Why would you, it's been absolutely crazy.

Now we're shifting our stuff for a sixth time, as she chases her dreams. She made it my dream by showing me a spreadsheet that suggested we could be free of a mortgage in a few months. I had to pretend that I followed her Excel presentation, but I certainly heard the words 'mortgage' and 'free' in close proximity. That's quite appealing at thirty-four.

Less appealing is the fact that it's "a big project". This is Kate's code for 'this is going to turn our life upside down for several months and you'll hate 99% of it.' We've bought a guesthouse in our hometown of Wakefield, which I can only describe as scummy, grimy and seedy (the guesthouse, not Wakefield, though some would say both). The old guy who ran it rented it out to labourers working away from home mostly, so there wasn't much need for airs and graces and Derek stuck rigidly to this business model. This meant that, along with the workmen, all kinds of lowlifes passed through it. The rumour is that he'd even rent you a room for an hour, if that's all you required. I don't think the couples who took him up on this offer just needed a venue for a power nap.

So why are we buying it? Well, it's currently two three-storey terrace houses with a connecting door between them (a door that has the sign 'Dinning Room' on it). We're going to turn it back into two houses, live in one and sell the other. To turn this one shithole into two dream houses, though, is going take a lot of something I'm not at all keen on – hard graft.

*

Work has commenced. I've been in my present job for only a few months, so I've got all that to deal with, then when I come home it's less of the sanctuary one would hope for and more like a building site in hell. I've had to get used to preparing meals in a paint-splatted microwave and eating all food with a layer of dust on it, talking to builder types and trying not say anything that may be deemed a bit poncey and sleeping in a room with sheets for curtains. And that's before I get to this top three list of things that have caused me pain:

1. With spectacular timing, our project manager, Kate, is pregnant with our first child. It's impressive how she's just getting on with it and I know I shouldn't complain when it's her who is actually growing a baby inside of her, but she's never been the most tranquil character. Now, the edge is never far away. Example: I made a dust sandwich for lunch. It was Wimbledon final day

and I watched *three* games while I ate it. I'd normally watch hours of the tournament, but that appeared irrelevant as Kate stormed in and started screaming at me for slacking. I responded by disappearing up the stairs and pulling up the old carpet in an attic room in a proper rage. Sweat was dripping off me by the time I was done, ready for another layer of dust to settle on me and stick fast.

2. I had to hunt down some local kids to warn them not to throw stones through our windows as the place is not derelict, as you may think. Some people, unbelievably, are living there.

3. On a beautiful summer evening, I was outside climbing up and down stepladders as I painted window frames. Drifting up the road towards me I could hear the laughter of people enjoying themselves. As the sound was neither becoming louder nor receding, I imagined they were gathered in the suntrap of a local beer garden, relaxing and enjoying a lovely cold beer, while here I was doing this shit at 9.37 at night.

As if that wasn't bad enough, as I listened to those revellers that funny prickly feeling I got in my leg last year decided to make an appearance again. In fact it's happened two or three times while we've been working on the house. It's always been when I've been going up and down ladders. It *has* been hot like it was the first time it happened, or perhaps I have a trapped nerve somewhere in my foot. Who knows? It's irritating, but in the grand scheme of everything going on at the moment, it's not something to dwell on.

*

While I was at work, a local character knocked on the door. One of our workmen opened it and the guy on the doorstep asked if his girlfriend could come in to take a piss, as she was desperate. Taken aback somewhat by a stranger asking to use the facilities, the workman let the woman in. While she was in the half-finished bathroom, her boyfriend struck up a conversation with the workman.

"You can have her for twenty quid if you like."

"Erm, no, you're all right."

What have we done? Local druggies clearly still think of our new dream-home-to-be as a handy toilet-cum-knocking shop. Could things get any worse?

*

We've been burgled. They somehow smashed through the plasterboard that was acting as a door at the back of the house and nicked a load of tools and, ironically, the burglar alarm that was still in its box and waiting to be fitted. Annoyingly, Kate had nudged me in the middle of the night and said she kept hearing noises. I was absolutely knackered as I'd been playing five-a-side football like I do every Monday and just groaned at her, mumbling that I couldn't hear anything, before rolling over and going back to sleep.

If I'd have just got up like she told me to and pulled back the sheet from the window, I'd probably have seen the toerags unabashedly making several trips through the front door and casually loading up the van.

Worse still, everyone including the police has warned us that they are likely to be back. We've secured that part of the house as best we can with a temporary door and have tried to keep stuff in there to a minimum, but we had to get on with the job, so tools and fittings are again lying around asking to be pinched.

But we have had an idea. We'll soon be needing a baby monitor so we have gone and bought one early. We're going to put it in the empty part of the property and have the parent listening monitor next to our bed. Yes, this is going to help me sleep better. A large part of me, however, still thinks it's very unlikely they'll be back.

*

They're back. It's Sunday morning, 6.20am and someone is clearly creeping up the stairs next door. The monitor, hidden behind some plasterboard, works at least. Not a single breath of the baby is going to get past these parents.

Kate rings the police. I jump out of bed and pull on my jeans in a very sleepy panic. We can hear the burglar taking a full tour of the whole house. We think about all the things he could pilfer while we bite our nails, praying the police are going to turn up quickly.

By now I'm fully dressed and pacing the bedroom. What are the chances the police are going to come soon? They said they would but what guarantee is that? Knowing that he is next door filling his swag bag as we stand around, fully aware but impotent, is too much to bear. Next thing I know, I'm outside. I'm not really sure what I'm going to do, but I take a look down the dirt track that runs along the end of the block of terrace houses. There's a car van parked on it. Hmm, suspicious. I approach it and there's a guy doing nothing but sitting in it. My heart is beating fast but I challenge him.

"What are you up to, mate?"

He tries to stay cool but his reply, "Erm, nothing," would hardly satisfy Columbo.

I ask him if he's all right with me taking a look in his van. They've obviously not put anything in there yet as he becomes more confident. "Yeah, no problem," he says.

Neither of us is covering ourselves in glory here. What I should be doing is taking note of the make and model of the van, the registration, locking his face in my memory. But I've mislaid my police officer's notepad and pen and I've already forgotten what he looks like. *He* shouldn't be saying it's OK for me to peer in his van. He should be saying, 'What do you want to look in my van for? Why don't you mind your own business.'

I make my way back towards the house. Still no sign of the police. The driver's accomplice is going to be out soon and they'll be away with our stuff. I'm going to have to go in. I need a weapon of some sort, though, to defend myself. I raid our current home for something appropriate. All I can find is a tennis racquet. That's going to put the fear of God into him. Bollocks, it'll have to do.

With a bite of her bottom lip, Kate hands me the keys and I head next door. I can hear my heartbeat in my ears now as I turn the lock. What am I going to do when I set eyes on him? Tell him to bloody well clear off, while brandishing my fearsome tennis bat? I'm suddenly very aware how middle class I appear.

The decision is made for me more quickly than I'm expecting. As soon as I push the door open, I'm confronted by a man at the bottom of the stairs who is brandishing a crow bar. He's about six foot, but with the thick metal bar in his grip, he may as well be eight foot two. I'm not conscious of any thoughts entering my head, but I've found that I've immediately shut the door and started to run. However, my legs have given way as I pass my car parked on the front patio. I've always considered it a lame narrative trick when a person trips and falls in a film, just because they're being chased by someone. Now I understand. I've momentarily lost all strength in my lower limbs. I seem unable to run anymore and the only thing taking a thwacking from my tennis racquet is the paintwork of my car as I crumple to the ground. This is horrible. I need to get away from him, but it's like when you're being pursued by someone in a dream and your legs won't respond to your requests to move.

Fortunately, the guy is not taking any interest in the cowering idiot on the ground. He's tearing up the street like a runaway horse. I regain some fortitude and race after him. He's not that far ahead, but far enough for me to have the confidence to call him a few choice names. *I* know and he probably knows too that there's no way I want to catch him. I continue to sprint after him but give up after another few metres, as I fear I may be gaining on him. He piles into his getaway vehicle and is off.

I walk back down the street towards the house, tennis racquet still in hand. It's not a good look to have as, with a stunning sense of when best to arrive, the police show up in a screech of tyres. Also with great timing, the stress of the situation or maybe just the running has encouraged the pins and needles sensation in my legs to return yet again.

As I eye the coppers exiting the car, then across at the skip full of rubble and other shit next to my car, a single thought dominates the many that are spinning around my brain: life isn't fun anymore.

SOMETIME IN 2004 - A ROOM WITH A TERRIBLE VIEW

I have a very boring job. Day after day, hour after hour, staring at a computer screen devoid of anything interesting on it. Kate's eyelids start to droop immediately whenever I try to describe what I do and I expect this would be anyone's reaction.

The monotony is rarely broken but today is one of those rare occasions. Unfortunately, it's not broken in a good way. We have one large window in the studio, around fifteen feet across. When I first walked into this grey room, this prison of the soul, around eighteen months ago it had none. My initial impression on Day One was that of a cross between Hitler's bunker and a sterile hospital, like one of those from 1950s America that appear in US dramas where the nurses are all white stockings and sinister efficiency. But after complaints from the staff, we have a window and not just any window. So the outside world can't peer in and see the sea of large, expensive and very portable Macs that occupy this part of the building, the window is like one of those that feature in crime dramas where the suspect is being questioned in the interrogation room, while interested officers look on in secret on the other side of the one-way mirror. From medical to cop drama with the addition of one window.

The nature of this window provides the primary source of

entertainment while at work. For some unfathomable reason, people assume that nothing is going on behind the glass. The fact that it is set in the side of a large building that is clearly a place of work fails to set off alarm bells. Thus, the window is treated by those passing along the dirt track outside as though it is just part of the wall.

Top three incidents so far as a consequence of this window:

1. A guy parked up right outside the window. He could have chosen many other spots along the perimeter of the warehouse-style building, but he decided this was the best one at which to sit in his car meticulously skinning up a fat one. Most people, like me, thought let him get on with it. What harm is he doing anyone? Anthea, however, in her sanctimonious manner said, "Shall we call the police?" Everyone ignored her and he soon left anyway without smoking it.

2. Some schoolkids were passing on their way back from school. A boy of around fourteen walked up to the window, appreciative of its reflective qualities, and started to preen his hair, smoothing it here, spiking it there and making himself look generally gorgeous. If only he'd known that around thirty people were watching him intently, cheering and egging him on with wolf whistles and cat calls. Hannah eventually took her favourite course of action when someone mistakes the window for a wall – she rapped on the glass, nearly making him jump out of his uniform. He quickly scurried away to catch up with his mates.

3. This one wasn't strictly due to the window being

frosted, but is worthy of note. A football match was going on in the park opposite, contested by mostly middle-aged men. Sometime into the game there was a commotion on the pitch, with concerned looking people standing around a guy who was laid out on his back on the grass. Had he broken his leg? One of the account handlers, Jane, had recently done a first aid course, so rushed out to see if she could help. We watched, somewhat surprised, as she knelt over him and began giving him CPR. Everyone appeared to become increasingly frantic as she pounded on his chest. At times like this, you can't help but reflect on the pointlessness of your job. The ambulance crew soon turned up and Jane returned to work to recommence the pointlessness. We later heard that the guy was pronounced dead before she'd even sat back down at her desk.

And today it transpires that it's time for top incidents of note as a consequence of this window number four. A stubbly bald man of around fifty-five has stepped over to the glass from the road. Between the window and the bushes, he is facing the wall of the building. He glances over his shoulder to make sure there's no one behind him on the dirt track or in the park, leaving me in no doubt as to what he is about to do. Like him, I take a quick look around myself, checking if anyone else is watching the unfolding events, but realise that I'm the only one clocking this, the angle of my desk perfectly aligned with my furtive subject.

I should turn away at this point but it would be easier to stare straight ahead on the motorway when you pass a five-car pile-up. He slips his thumbs into his straining waistband before hooking his jogging bottoms below his scrotum, giving me a thorough view of his hairy cock and balls. A second later, a stream of piss is arcing its way into the bushes and I'm letting out an involuntary yelp, which attracts the attention of my work colleagues.

Suddenly, much of the studio is staring out of the window at this man's crown jewels (though never has that term for what we are observing appeared more inappropriate). Hannah cannot help herself and she bangs on the window. Fortunately for him he's just about finished, judging by the shaking we've all just witnessed, so an obvious streak in the jogging bottoms is probably avoided. The past their sell-by date meat and two veg are away and so is he, the few bits of fluff on his head no doubt standing to attention.

After a chorus of vomiting noises among the workforce, calm soon returns to the studio. I find myself thinking about emptying my own bladder. I seem to find it harder and harder to tell if I need to go or not. Maybe it's an age thing, or more probably it's because I'm always looking for any break from the monotony of sitting at my desk, staring at a screen. Is it time for a cuppa? No, had one ten minutes ago. Lunchtime? No, two hours away. Do I need the toilet? Yes, I think I do. The desperation of that guy has made me think of nothing else for the last ten minutes. Let's give it a go.

In the toilets I head straight to one of the two cubicles. I've never been entirely comfortable with the concept of peeing at a urinal with another man at my side. Imagine if you weren't peeing. Two adult men stand at a wall, each holding his penis in his hand as it dangles out of a hole at the front of his trousers. Eyes focused to the front, though unable to avoid straying every so often to his companion's protrusion. Why does the introduction of piss from the end of each penis suddenly make it OK?

No, I'm into the cubicle without a moment's hesitation, even though the toilets are currently empty. If you ever think I'll just get this over with quickly in the urinal before anyone comes in, you just know that someone will be entering before you've even taken your cock out in a public place (as apparently is socially acceptable). Also, he will probably be someone with the bladder propulsion of a water cannon and you will very soon be experiencing the sensation of sea spray on a breezy day upon the hands, only this is not cooling ocean mist; it's warm urine from another human being.

Not that there is any chance of me getting this over with quickly. On the few occasions in living memory that I've ventured to pee next to someone, my companion is always back out of the door before I've even started. Annoyingly, I've even begun to experience my peeing problems in the cubicle. True, it's worse when there is someone else in the room, worse still again when someone is in the cubicle next to me, but my urination reflex appears to be packing up even when I'm totally alone. As soon as I'm ready, I no longer need to go, or I can feel there's plenty in the tank but it just doesn't want to make its way into the world.

I must remember this frustration and stop going to the toilet at work until I'm good and ready. Through boredom, I must be jumping the gun. Oh great, someone has come in. Please let them go to the urinal. Fuck, I hear the door of the other cubicle being locked and the sound of trousers being dropped. I'm now going to have someone shitting next to me, with all its attendant noises and smells, unless I can push this out in the next few seconds. I move my feet away from the dividing wall so he can't potentially identify whose too shy to pee at the urinal and, it would appear, even unable to pee in a cubicle.

After straining for several seconds to think of my own needs rather than the bowels that are opening a mere yard from me, I hurriedly give it up as a bad job and flush, in order to support my pretence. Back at my desk, with a half-full bladder and newly washed hands, I reflect on Baldy Hairy Balls Man (as he has swiftly become known in my head) and how untroubled he was by the prospect of peeing out in the open air. Trouble soon found him, of course, but that is not the target of my thoughts. There wasn't much to be envious of regarding the episode, but part of me most certainly is. Increasingly I'm being made aware of a bodily function that was entirely without thought until recently. Is this how it's going to be from now on? I've heard that most men start to have prostate problems as they get older, but I'm still in my mid-thirties. It just doesn't seem right.

I gaze dully at the pet food packaging that is back on my screen now that I've moved my mouse and the screensaver has disappeared. I settle on a two-point plan for the future. I won't attempt a number one till it's becoming properly uncomfortable and from now on I will use the disabled toilet further down the corridor. I may feel awkward using it when I'm obviously not disabled, but there will be no chance of my solitude being interrupted, which has got to help. I've never seen anyone disabled round here anyway, so can't see anyone having a problem with this arrangement. Except perhaps me.

CHRISTMAS 2005 - SOME TIME TO CATCH MY BREATH

It's a few days short of two years since my son, E, was born. He's in bed, asleep thankfully, and Kate's out with girlfriends. The house is therefore my own for one evening. If there was shit on the living room carpet (which is a possibility considering we have a toddler), I wouldn't care. I would currently be rolling in it like the proverbial pig, revelling in the quiet, the lack of demands, the absence of stress.

I put on some music. As I have the option, I choose something from my CD collection that Kate doesn't like, which let's be honest, isn't difficult. I pour myself a glass of red wine and sit across the sofa, mainly hearing the sounds that are not present. No crying child, no partner in my ear, no 'play… more… play', no 'why haven't you done that yet'; just my music and my thoughts.

I find myself reflecting on the last couple of years. I know Kate thinks of our life as being pretty regular but I have a slightly different view. It fluctuates between seeing it as being a bit too busy to deciding its fucking mental.

Here's a list of self-inflicted stress since the end of 2003:

1. Christmas 2003 – even though the house was still far

from finished and Kate was eight months pregnant, she was determined that we should have Christmas dinner at ours with all the family.

2. January 2004 – new baby in house. Thankfully our own, but that hardly made it much easier. Being a parent for the first time is *hard*.

3. July 2004 – got married.

4. October-November 2004 – renovated seedy B&B in Blackpool to sell on.

5. April-July 2005 – renovated two terrace houses on the opposite coast of England, in Filey.

6. July 2005 – big anniversary party to mark one year of marriage.

That's just some of the bare facts and they hardly do justice to the turmoil we've put ourselves through. I think a few more details are required.

Back in December 2003, we reached the point in renovating a house where you feel like you've basically completed it, but there are a thousand and one little jobs still to do. The one old guesthouse was now two houses and one of them was on the market. Carpets were finally going down in the one that was to be our home. Unfortunately, within twenty-four hours of getting the new carpet down in the living room, the baby decided to kick Kate's stomach and she threw up all over it. But we managed to lay another one just in time for Christmas dinner and all the relatives came as planned.

Then E was born in the second week of January. Maybe we were short of carpet after the vomit tsunami incident because one of my most vivid memories of those first few weeks of his life was changing him on the bedroom floor, the changing mat lying on a patchwork of underlay. Regular drafts would wind up the stairs and flow unhindered by a fitted carpet under the door, waft across E's nethers and pee would immediately be projected through the air onto my hands and his chest. I wish I could pee that easily now. Despite my best efforts at leaving it till I'm good and ready, I'm still having difficulty. Maybe I should take one of those handheld fans into the toilet with me.

Amidst the psychosis we both suffered due to lack of sleep in those first few months of parenthood, we sold the house next door, so that was one less bit of hassle in our lives. To compensate, our wedding was looming. I obviously decided a regular wedding wasn't emotionally exhausting enough, so decided I would perform a few songs at the reception. I realise that makes me sound like one of those embarrassing twerps portrayed in *Four Weddings and a Funeral* who get the guitar and tambourine out, leaving guests with toes curled beyond repair, but the added tension for both groom and audience was just about worth it. Towards the end of my compositions of heartfelt sentiment two of Kate's friends were crying. True, Kate's face remained untroubled by salt-water, but I'd driven people to tears – and not just with my substandard singing voice. Result.

With stag/hen weekends, a wedding and brief honeymoon out of the way, Kate looked for another way to introduce some anxiety into our lives. She'd spotted another renovation opportunity. This time it wasn't a downmarket guesthouse in Wakefield. Rather, it was a downmarket guesthouse in Blackpool, complete with evocative name – the Casablanca – and gay porn in the cellar. I say cellar but sex dungeon may have been a more appropriate label.

Perhaps I'm furnishing it with more intrigue than it deserved, but there were hooks from the ceiling that looked like they had been added for purposes that had nothing to do with DIY. If we had found a trunk in that room we would have been wary of opening it in case a gimp climbed out, *Pulp Fiction*-style.

After a number of trips to the Lancashire Riviera, usually with a nine to ten-month-old baby in tow, we managed to turn the job around pretty quickly and get a quick sale. Kate's brother and mates who had done most of the work got very ill for a few days in the middle of it all after picking up a bug from our visiting son, but I'm sure they were very pleased for us.

E turned one and life calmed down for a blissful, fleeting moment. But then Kate decided this was boring and bought another house. This one was on the north-east coast and the distance involved and complexity of the renovation meant she went away for days on end while she oversaw the work, leaving me alone with the baby. The planning of childcare would have taxed the military, but at least I was the parent who heard him string two words together for the first time.

This pattern of life went on for around three months but we got through it. We then decided to give ourselves another challenge, however, by organising a big first wedding anniversary party. It was less of a strain than organising the wedding, but I did insist on singing a few songs again, in honour of my wife. I got the distinct feeling that people are less forgiving of this kind of behaviour when you are merely commemorating a wedding that took place a year ago, particularly when it involves my very limited voice.

So that was our last two years. Kate tells me that this is normal, at least if you want to get ahead in life. Is this normal? I've been worked to death, sleep deprived and stressed out beyond belief. Thankfully, the times I get pins and needles in my legs have been few and far between and the bladder problems are just a bit annoying, no more, but maybe I've just been too pre-occupied to notice.

Yes, I have to admit I've got much to be thankful for. I'm getting more sleep now, I'm starting to feel reasonably relaxed again and my wife and child are happy and healthy.

And yes, I'm only in my late thirties and I'm now one of those really annoying people who are mortgage free. Maybe Kate is right. Maybe a load of stress is good for you after all.

4th JAN 2006 – COLD FEET

Driving to your workplace when it's still dark and knowing that when you leave at the end of the day it will be dark again is not a fun concept. The first day back after the Christmas break is a particularly bad example of such a shift. If you have a soon-to-be two-year-old, you'll have spent half your time off cutting through endless bits of wire in order to prise plastic toys from overpackaged cardboard boxes or, once that's done, hunting for batteries. Now I'll have to repeatedly ask or field the question, 'You have a good Christmas?' even though everyone just wants to get their head down and survive the day. There seems to be only one acceptable answer anyway: 'Yeah, it was a quiet one.'

You try to remember how to do your job while contemplating the long grey weeks of winter ahead. I always try to comfort myself with the thought that the shortest day is behind us, but this first day back is always an interminable one. I exit the car and place my key card on the entry reader, grim-faced in the icy blackness.

Trudging towards my workstation, my feet feel peculiar. In fact everything below the knee feels a bit strange. I don't have time to dwell on this as the others on my table are busy asking me and each other, 'Did you have a good Christmas?' Everyone to a man (it's only men on my table) had a quiet one.

It is only once I've turned on my Mac and loaded up a stack of programs that I really become aware again that my feet don't feel normal. They feel numb, like they've gone to sleep. But cold. And there's a strange prickliness to my feet and lower legs, similar to the pins and needles I sometimes get throughout my legs. Did I adopt an unusual position when I was driving here? It's as if I've sat on them awkwardly. Oh well, I'm sure it'll go soon enough.

I always wait till I'm at work before I have breakfast. That's worth ten more minutes in bed to me and it means I get paid for eating my Sultana Bran. With that and a mug of tea inside me, my brain will start its slow thaw. The walk to the kitchen, though, is not the routine one I would expect. It feels like I'm walking barefoot on fine sandpaper all the way, but the sandpaper is really cold and is wrapped tightly around my feet.

This is unnatural. How can my feet feel so numb yet be sending so many different sensations to my brain? Once again I wonder if I have a trapped nerve somewhere. That's what always seems to cause these types of problem, isn't it. I boil the kettle and pour my cereal, shifting from foot to foot, rattling my legs one after the other. I even bend down a few times and touch my toes until someone comes in and almost catches me. Fortunately it's someone who doesn't want to talk about the Christmas that has just gone or indeed talk at all. He's quite a bit older than me so has had to endure the rituals of first day back in January more years than me and his face suggests as much. Bet his feet feel normal, though.

As I return to my desk, it's clear that my minute of exercise has not shaken off these freakily contradictory feelings. It's bad enough being back at work without this. I get talking to my friend

Steve who sits next to me and try to describe what's going on with my lower limbs.

"Are you trying to pull a sickie already?" is his typical reaction.

I change the subject, remembering that we're men and banter is the order of the day, not lending a sympathetic ear to what I guess are fairly minor symptoms of... I don't know what. We have a laugh about a few things before settling down to the tedious tasks of the day. For a living, I check that pet food packaging is going to print correctly – quality control is a rather grander title for it – and I soon get sucked into the minutiae that dominates my working life: should that text be capitalised, is that line 0.2 mm or 0.1mm thick? Bet you're fascinated by this, aren't you. No, neither am I but I have to devote a good portion of my thoughts to it whilst I'm here and so start to forget about the numbness, coldness and prickliness.

I am reminded when I head to the toilet later. I use the disabled one as has become my habit and hold onto the metal support bar as I stand there, hoping that something will happen. Why can't I pee like normal people? Why do I need to concentrate so hard? And I have these weird feelings in my feet to contend with now. Frustration is building from every direction. I'm only 37 and seem to be falling apart. Hang on, I'm finally going, albeit rather slowly. I suppose this wasn't a particularly bad one but it felt longer, standing on sandpaper.

Back at my desk I can't help but complain a little more to Steve.

"My feet still feel prickly. And they feel so cold. Is it really cold in here or is it just me?"

"It's January. What do you expect?" he replies.

"But it's an air-conditioned building. My feet have never felt as cold as this in here before."

"It's the middle of winter. You've got cold feet. Who would

have thought it? Why don't you get some work done and take your mind off it?"

Thank you, Doctor Steve. He makes me laugh and annoys me in equal measure, but I guess there may be some truth in what he's saying. I try to convince myself of this anyway, as I look around for some crumbs of comfort. True, these sensations are continuing for a lot longer than I would have expected as it's nearly lunchtime now, but I can't imagine I'll still be experiencing them by home time. Yes, it'll be dark again by then but at least life will have attained some normality once more.

JAN 2006 – DOCTOR FAT FINGER

I'm at the GP surgery. Nothing has changed below the knee. Prickliness throughout the lower legs, feet cold and numb yet, conversely, I feel like I'm standing on gravel in my socks (I've decided standing on sandpaper isn't quite the sensation). It's been nearly two weeks, so I thought it was time I saw the doc.

He listens patiently but I sense the futility of my visit even as I'm recounting my symptoms. Do you ever feel like you're having an out of body experience as you're talking to someone? It's you speaking but you're kind of listening to yourself as if you're the person on the receiving end of what you're saying. Most times that this happens to me I find myself thinking, 'Who is this nobhead and why is he spouting such bullshit?'

This is one of those occasions. The vagueness of my description makes me sound like a hypochondriac or fantasist. His eyes are staring at me but there's a distance in his gaze that suggests his thoughts have flown somewhere else. Probably thinking about how far behind schedule he is and how he shouldn't have given thirteen minutes to that patient earlier this morning, rather than the requisite ten, or he's pondering what to have for lunch.

Certainly this doesn't sound like something he can easily Google. The medical profession seems to despair of the layman using Dr Google to investigate his symptoms, but GPs generally can't wait to start tapping their keyboards as they grope for a diagnosis. If he entered all the keywords I'm giving him, though, the online medical database would spit out a hundred and one possible explanations and smoke might start to come out the back of his PC. So they'll be no easily arrived at prescription to print off today.

My only chance of progress is if he agrees to a referral, but who would he refer me to? No, as I continue to listen to myself I quickly realise that this is not a possibility. My problems just don't appear serious enough for the NHS to spend valuable resources on me. My mouth finally exhausts itself and I watch as he sits back in his chair, composing his response. Part of me is eager to hear his verdict, a larger part is already resigned to the idea that this is a wasted journey and I'm likely to be leaving here none the wiser.

"I'm not sure, really," he begins, honestly but dispiritingly. "Sounds like you've probably got a trapped nerve somewhere. It should go in time."

I realise that I'm in receipt of the doctor double whammy – being non-committal while falling on exactly the same opinion that I did on the very first occasion this all began, despite the seven years difference in our medical training. The 'go in time' is the real kicker. How much time is 'in time'? A few days, a few months, years?

I mention my bladder problems, I suppose to see if he thinks there might be anything else going on, and his whole demeanour changes. The sparkle returns to his eyes and I can see every part of him cry, 'Ah yes, I know how to deal with this.' I'm lying on my side with my bare arse out, listening to the snap of rubber glove enveloping hand before I can offer any kind of meaningful resistance. I wish my sphincter had acquiesced with similar meekness. He's inside me, knuckle-deep then more soon enough, but the orifice in question is far from happy about the matter. Surely, they are only supposed to insert one finger? Wagging is taking place in my rectum and the words, "Hmm, yes, that's lovely and smooth," are coming from his mouth. I'm of course joking about him introducing more than one digit into proceedings, but it certainly feels like it could be true. He's a large man with, it appears, sausages for fingers. When I booked an appointment to discuss my problematic feet I didn't expect to get a prostate exam, but at least I now know that there is nothing wrong with that. It's lovely and smooth, apparently. That's something to boast about.

Smooth or not, that was more painful than I would wish. As I belt up my jeans once again, a look on my face that can only be achieved by the unexpectedly defiled, the pain between my buttocks is replaced at the forefront of my thoughts by the discomfort in my feet. I'm suddenly conscious of the fact that for the first few wakeful moments in nearly a fortnight I was not thinking about my feet and legs. However, what has just taken place hardly strikes me as an acceptable solution to my ills.

The rubber glove is in the waste bin and I can't help wondering how long it will be till the bin is emptied. Probably at the end of the day, but that means there's a whole afternoon ahead of patients telling the doctor their most intimate problems while a rubber glove sits discarded a few feet away, a thin film of my shit on one of the fingers.

I regard the face of the man who's just been exploring my arsehole. I'm hoping for one tiny nugget of insight into my condition but nothing is forthcoming. All I get is the other medical platitude: "If nothing changes in the next couple of weeks, come back and see us." I suppose this at least provides the vaguest hint of a timescale for my predicament, but I really hope I don't have to take him up on his offer.

FEB 2006 – CHINESE DOCTOR

Every step I take through the local shopping centre is torturing me. It's not that the sensations in my feet are that bad – they're no worse than irritating – but it's the not knowing that is driving me nuts. Not knowing what is wrong with me, not knowing if these sensations will be with me for ever or soon go. They might even get worse, who can say? I just don't know.

Sometimes I forget, while other times I'm all too aware. I'm very aware at the moment. In a strange way, this gives me a little comfort. I don't want this to be the new normal. Being conscious of the otherness of my feet and lower limbs means I'm not accepting of this situation. I'm going to get to the bottom of it if it kills me.

I pass all the usual big names such as BHS and Carlton Cards. Nestled between other familiar brands I spot a shop front labelled Chinese Doctor. There's no other name, just Chinese Doctor. I've noticed it was there before but my attention has moved swiftly on previously. A doctor that resides among other businesses suggests a money-making operation rather than an exercise in health restoration. Besides, Chinese medicine has invariably struck me as something that occupies the mumbo-jumbo category of ailment remedy, somewhere in the vicinity of homeopathy and snake oil. I'll defend the right of anyone to believe whatever claptrap they want to believe, so long as it doesn't hurt anyone. Unfortunately, these purveyors of the hocus pocus variety of remedies do tend to mentally damage those convinced by their dubious claims through relieving them of considerable amounts of cash.

I believe in science. Of course, it doesn't have all the answers but it is the genuine science underpinning Western medicine that means we can cure or vaccinate against a multitude of the common diseases that have blighted human existence for centuries. It's science that has saved millions of lives, not crystals.

Yet here I am, opening the door to the premises of Chinese Doctor. Part of me is interested to find out what they make of my new condition, while part of me is just curious to find out what's inside the shop behind the smoked glass. I went back to the regular doctor three weeks after my initial visit and I was invited to beat my head against the same brick wall as the first time. I was hoping they might be ready to send me for some tests, but Dr Fat Finger was still devoid of interest. At least my jeans stayed on for the duration of the consultation on this occasion.

But it has reduced my options. I guess this is why a lot of people turn to alternative medicine. Regular medicine appears to fail them and they start hunting around for something, *anything* that might be able to help. So here I am. I can see what they have to say for nothing, can't I.

I briefly scan the shelves, inspecting them for any sign of rhino horn or tiger penis. Perhaps this is an insulting myth perpetuated by the Western media in order to discredit traditional Chinese medicine, but it's all I have to go on. The young woman behind the counter asks me if she can be of any assistance and I give a brief description of my problem. She nods politely and tells me to take a seat. Someone will be out to see me shortly.

I sit there staring around the room, wondering what the hell I'm doing here. This is most unlike me. When it comes to anything that requires you to believe in it without any genuine scientific evidence I'm the most cynical person you will come across. But it's herb based, isn't it? Some of them must work. Much of Western medicine is based on substances found in plants and herbs. It's a slim chance but maybe, just maybe, the fact that they're looking at things from a different angle might mean they manage to alleviate some of these symptoms at least, even if they don't manage an actual diagnosis (a diagnosis is what I truly crave). I just need to keep my wits about me so I don't get charged a fortune. I can then walk out of here with my head held high, even if I'm walking out on legs that feel exactly the same as when I entered.

Five minutes later a short, portly old Chinese woman with a warm smile is standing before me and shepherding me into a side room. This should be a doddle. How many people each year are swindled by kindly old grandmas? Not many, I would wager. So I don't think she will be cloning my credit card any time soon. And she's wearing a white coat, which lends the proceedings an air of legitimacy. This is starting to seem more like a good idea.

I take a seat and she invites me to describe what has brought me here today. She listens attentively while taking notes. She nods that nod that suggests she has heard this exact list of symptoms countless times before and knows exactly how to treat them. I feel encouraged. The doctor at my surgery seemed uninterested from the off. This old dear is paying me attention and it feels good. I'm eager to hear what she has to say.

My speech over, she makes some reassuring 'hmm hmm' noises, while she weighs up the best course of action. I'm not expecting a diagnosis that involves names of diseases or conditions that I've heard of, but some fresh and credible insight would be most welcome. She begins to speak. I lean forward.

"There is an imbalance in your body that needs to be addressed," she begins.

To a sceptic like myself, she may as well have just told me that I'm experiencing a case of bad energies. I hear her out, though.

"You see, the body is like machine. One of working parts is not good any more. We need to make it good again."

I can't really argue with that. Seems to be lacking a bit of something, however. Now what is it? Oh yes, science. But she continues on this path.

"The balance of machine means it can't work properly... we need to fix this... we need to restore level..." and so on.

I feel myself zoning out and focussing instead only on her Chinese accent and noting the words and letters that are missing from sentences. I swear she is saying the same thing over and over, but she is on a roll. Her 'diagnosis' is lasting for what seems ages. I'm beginning to feel tired and uncomfortable. These plastic seats are not the best. Could they have not provided something with a bit of padding? And these strip lights – you could locate a prisoner making a break for the wire fence in a gulag using one of them.

There's a brief silence and I realise she has finally finished establishing what is wrong. So what does she recommend, I am about to ask, but she is already telling me.

"For this kind of problem, we must treat it with blend of powerful herbs. This should first alleviate symptoms, then they disappear altogether. But you must use the herbs exactly as directed. They need to be added to water and heated for precise number of minutes. You then drink it like tea. The machine will soon be working again." She writes something down on a piece of paper. "Please take this to counter and they will be able to make you better."

I take the paper from her, all too aware that this is not the NHS and money has not been mentioned yet. I head to the counter, a vague sensation of just being released from an interrogation situation nipping at my heels. I hand over the paper, waiting to see how much it will cost to get this particular machine back on track.

The assistant worryingly is still reluctant to spill the beans. She just begins to grab things from the shelves and place them in a large paper bag. In a moment of clarity, I politely demand to know what the price is for the herbs. She smiles and says she will just check. She taps a few numbers into a calculator, the use of which I hope is just because there are a lot of awkward small numbers involved. She smiles again. I have to say, it's a very attractive smile. She's around twenty-one and I note that she is wearing a thin blouse and figure-hugging skirt.

I'm swiftly snapped out of the unwholesome fantasies that are starting to form in my mind. "One hundred and twenty pounds and twenty-seven pence."

She is still smiling as I grab hold of the counter. I knew it wouldn't be cheap, but it is far worse than I imagined. Over a hundred quid. Are they having a laugh?

"Oh," I say, "that's a little more than I was expecting," angling for the award of Understatement of the Year.

At that moment, the Doc appears behind me like the shopkeeper in *Mr Benn*. "Have you everything you need?"

Something in her tone of voice suggests that she's going to be very disappointed if I don't take the paper bag. "How does that break down?" I ask the assistant, partly as a way of stalling for time. She looks at her piece of paper again. I'm told that it's £65 for the consultation and £55.27 for the herbs.

It's clear that I'm going to be charged £65 whatever. I thought it was just a chat at this stage. Cash was never mentioned. There is no price list I can see. The white-coated grandma chips in again, presumably sensing my resolve to buy wavering.

"This is very good medicine. You will feel better soon."

The assistant begins slowly to unbutton her blouse from the top, all the while maintaining her smile and eye contact. Why brain, why? Why are you making me think that this could be happening? This is not helpful in the situation I find myself. I'm trying to assess the matter in hand here and you are implanting dirty thoughts into proceedings. What am I to do? Pay £65 for the privilege of hearing an old woman say hmm a lot and telling me I'm like a machine that's gone wrong, or cough up the remaining £55 and at least try out this medicine in which I have very little faith? Hell, what have I to lose? Oh yes, one hundred and twenty quid of my hard-earned money.

"I'll take it," I hear myself saying and before I can back out everything is bagged up and my card is in the assistant's hand. After my bank account is significantly lightened, she re-iterates how to take advantage of my purchase.

"Instructions for the medicine are in the bag. Please follow what it says exactly. Heat everything for right amount of time and Bob's your uncle." OK, she doesn't say this last bit, but it would have amused me if she had and deflected some of the discomfort I'm currently experiencing – and I'm not talking about my legs for once. This uncomfortable feeling is more the mild cramping of my stomach as I begin slowly to accept that I've been had.

"If you have any more problems, please come see us," says the older woman. I bet you'd like to see me again, I mutter inside my head. You saw me coming, enjoyed seeing me while I was here and would no doubt delight in seeing me a second time so you could rob me all over again.

Of course, all that comes out of my mouth is a meek, "Thank you."

On my way to the car, what has just happened replays in my thoughts, but now without so much of a fog surrounding my brain.

My GP had nothing to gain financially from my visit. These people very much did and they employed a great portion of the book of con tricks in order to make sure they were not disappointed. As the scales begin to fall from my eyes, all I start to see is a fool. The kindly grandma. The hot young assistant. The failure to tell me that the consultation would cost me whatever, thus encouraging me to spend on the bag of herbs as well. It's a combination that is pure chump nip.

Oh well, it's done now. Let's not consign my bag of herbs to the dustbin of experience just yet. As I leave the car park, though, I'm imagining I am driving away in a second-hand car I have just acquired from an oily man in a double-breasted suit.

*

Back home, I tell Kate about my day and my brush with Chinese medicine. I tentatively opt for the full disclosure option that is generally accepted as the basis of a good marriage. She does her best not to declare that I'm a naïve twit, but her face tells a tale. I disappear to the kitchen with my bag of herbs.

Finding a large saucepan I begin to heat up my 'medicine'. What I am adding to the water looks just like the pot pourri that has mysteriously appeared in every other room in the house since I began to live with Kate, even down to that large star-shaped flower that always seems to be part of the mix. An aroma begins to dominate the air. Who am I kidding, it's a stench, a revolting overpowering stench. It's completely filling the room and quite possibly the house. If this tastes as bad as it smells, as I can only imagine it will, I'm in for a treat.

It transpires that I am wrong. It tastes even worse than it smells. I'd say it tastes worse than it looks too but that would be difficult, even accounting for the acrid liquid I am attempting to sip. How to describe it best? Like something Baldrick has concocted in the trenches, the primary ingredient being mud, with a dash of ratshit. I steal myself for another sip from the mug into which I've decanted this foul brown sludge, but as I tip the trench foot-infused tea towards my mouth, the stench hits me in the guts and I think I might throw up. I push the mug away and rapidly exit the room, heading for the bathroom. The feeling has subsided as soon as I reach the bathroom door but I'm alarmed at the thought of returning to the kitchen, as I now realise that the miasma is indeed beginning to twist up the staircase and its tentacles are no doubt slithering into every room.

There's no way I'm going to be able to down another drop of this hellish brew. How would anyone? I creep back into the kitchen, holding my breath against the reek of a witch doctor's soiled underpants. I pour the brown slurry down the sink, seeing pound signs snaking down the plughole and tip the partially dissolved herbs in the saucepan into a plastic bag. I add the paper bag with the remaining herbs into the plastic bag and tie it securely, as the mush of herbs that have been heated in the pan are still delivering a gruesome punch to the nose. And there goes my experiment with alternative medicine.

"How was it?" Kate asks when I return to the living room. "God it stinks. I hope it tasted better than it smells."

"Much much worse," I reply, a note of horror in my voice, as if I've just returned home from a nightmarish tour of duty.

"Do you think it will do any good?"

"Considering I managed one sip before I started to gip, I doubt it."

"Oh, love." Her tone is full of pity. I curl up beside her and put my head on her shoulder. "What are you going to do?"

All I can answer is, "I don't know." I decide to focus less on my legs and the money I've just wasted and more on the warm affection of a good woman that I'm fortunate enough to possess.

*

Lying in bed, waiting for sleep, the day's events start to turn in my head once again. I try to forgive my own stupidity, as I realise that this is all just an indication of how desperate I've become. I'm losing myself. My legs no longer feel like my own, and now I'm acting out of character too. These sensations, this *otherness* of my own body is driving me to distraction, causing me to make bad decisions, leading me down a path of madness.

I don't believe in alternative medicine. I never have and this episode is unlikely to change my mind. I believe in science. I believe in regular Western medicine. I just wish Western medicine would don its skates and come up with some answers.

APRIL 2006 – TROJAN HORSE

My sister called me last night. She's a dietitian working with eating disorder patients in a hospital, so although she's not a doctor she does have something of a medical background. She's been doing her own research into my problem and asking around at work and she's come up with a theory. She said it might be something called a spinal cord compression, as many of my symptoms match up.

Once I'd put the phone down, I paid a quick visit to Dr Google's Scary Online World of Self-diagnosis. Christine's theory looked a good possibility. Changes to sensations in your body, such as pins and needles and numbness. Check. Having difficulty with peeing, either incontinence or retention. Retention, yes, check. But ninety per cent of people with it have pain. This is often the first symptom and the pain in your neck or back is pretty bad. You can suffer from paralysis of your limbs too. And erection problems. Very much no check, unless you count having to wait frustratingly in the bathroom at four in the morning for one to go down when all you want to do is empty your bladder and get back into bed.

It certainly wouldn't be great if that is what is behind all this.

The cause is usually a tumour on the spine, sometimes benign, sometimes not. If spinal cord compression is suspected, it is treated as an emergency. You're rushed into hospital and first steroids will probably be pumped into you to relieve pressure on the spine. Surgery might be ordered, then radiotherapy and/or chemo.

I'm not feeling it. I've now had this for three months and I've had no pain whatsoever. But there's no denying that much of it fits and the urgency with which you need treatment is a little concerning. I've therefore booked another appointment at the GP's and here I am, the morning after the phone call from Christine, walking into the doctor's room.

Fortunately, it's not Dr Fat Finger on this occasion. It's a woman, which means I don't again have to look into the eyes of a man who's slipped a substantial digit into my anus. I deliver my well-practised speech about the pins and needles, the cold numbness and the difficulty with peeing. But I need her to believe this is a spinal cord compression, even if I don't. Emergency, rush to hospital, A & E. These are all phrases that I read last night and that have weakened my resolve to be totally honest. I'm imagining flashing blue lights, gurneys being wheeled hurriedly down corridors, wires attaching me to expensive machines and teams of doctors standing around my hospital bed, hungry to be the first one to work out what's wrong with me. This is how desperate I am for a diagnosis. I'm even willing to risk it being cancer just so I *know*.

Before my conscience can attempt to put a brake on my mouth, I am therefore now telling her that I've been getting a lot of back pain and sometimes weakness in my legs and arms (weakness was another symptom that was listed that I don't have). I stop short of suggesting I'm having erection problems, but only because I don't want to lay it on too thick. I wait eagerly for her reaction. I don't have to wait for long. She's already reaching for the phone and punching in numbers.

"I'm going to get you an immediate hospital appointment," she says. "We need someone to look into this right away. Are you OK to go up there now?"

"Yes, no problem," I reply. "Why, what do you think the problem might be?" I ask, expecting she will say the words 'spinal cord compression'.

"It might be a spinal cord compression."

"Oh right. Yes I've heard of that."

"There's still a good chance it's not that but we need to get you checked out straight away, just in case."

I don't quiz her any further as I don't believe she'll tell me anything more about spinal cord compressions that I didn't read last night. I let her get on with her phone call to the hospital and enjoy the feeling that I might finally find out what is wrong with me. Nice one, Christine. The last two visits to the GP achieved nothing more than a bored look and a finger up the bum. Now I am being rushed into hospital to be examined closely by specialists. Bring it on!

I leave the surgery with a piece of paper and the warm glow of someone who has achieved their morning's goal. I ring work to tell them that I'll be in later than I thought as I've been sent to the hospital for some tests. I get in the car to make the short drive there, imagining that my Peugeot 307 is in fact a Trojan Horse.

*

I've barely got myself comfortable in my hospital bed before a nurse is forcing a needle into my arm and drawing some blood from me. I have to imagine this as I always look in the opposite direction whenever a nurse is performing a blood test. It's not particularly bad but I'm glad I've had very few over the years. In terms of routine affairs it's somewhere between brushing my teeth and the prostate exam upon which I seem to keep fixating.

It is also not long before my bedside is populated by a doctor. Good old NHS. I can't imagine what it is like when you're having to think not only about your health, but also wondering if your insurance will cover this, or how much it will cost if you don't have insurance.

"So can you describe your symptoms to me," he says, examining the notes in his hand.

I go through my spiel yet again.

"OK, can you remove your trousers and we'll take a look."

I do as he asks and he has a feel of my feet and legs. The examination seems somewhat cursory but he then says something wonderful:

"OK, we've managed to get you in to have an MRI scan. They'll be someone here shortly to take you down there."

'Whoopee, a proper test!' I shriek inwardly. This is what I've been hoping for all these weeks. After the doctor has walked away, I clench my fist like a football manager whose team has just opened the scoring.

I'm soon being wheeled down to the room that houses the MRI machine. This seems a little like overkill. I could easily walk down there myself without troubling a hospital porter, at least once I'd put my jeans back on. But as I acknowledge the glances from people in the corridors who are stepping aside to allow my wheelchair a free run to the MRI department, I can't help but find some pleasure in the attention that I'm finally being afforded. After three months of being fobbed or ripped off, I'm now being taken seriously. True, I feel a little guilty that it has required me to exaggerate the symptoms of a condition that I don't really believe I have in order to get to this position, but I convince myself – rather easily – that this is a necessary evil. It may or may not be a spinal cord compression but it is definitely something. I just hope I'm not shortly sitting at work with a vision of perplexed doctors in my mind and vague notions of a trapped nerve ringing in my ears.

The porter delivers me to the MRI department and one of the staff there asks me to put on a gown. It's one of those traditional hospital ones that fasten badly at the back, which makes me feel even more like a proper patient who has a genuine condition.

"Have you any earrings or other piercings?" another member of the team asks me.

It is explained to me that the MRI machine is basically a huge magnet. If I'm attached to anything metal, that part of me will soon be glued to the machine. The urge to mention my Prince Albert is overpowering. A quick assessment of the situation tells me that they will have heard every such gag a thousand times, but the drive to say it won't leave me alone. I think of Dougal in Father Ted, told not to push a red button under any circumstances. The red button stares back at him and he stares at it till he can stand it no longer and the button is, of course, duly pushed.

"No, nothing," I fortunately hear myself saying, setting me just above Dougal on the Idiot Spectrum. "Just my watch to take off."

I'm given headphones to wear so they can communicate with me and a lead with a button on the end to press – "In case you feel too claustrophobic and need to come out" – and I'm soon being slid into the belly of the beast like a mechanic rolling under the chassis of a vehicle. Only it's me that is being examined and who might require some maintenance.

The tunnel gets darker as I advance further into this polished white tomb. It's not hard to see how some patients would panic. If I sneezed I would bang my nose on the roof. It's about two inches from my face and now the machine is buzzing and clanking away like in a horror film when the air-conditioning ducts decide to chime in with the general atmosphere of impending doom. I close my eyes and pretend I'm lying safe and warm in my own bed.

Even with the headphones on it is acutely loud, yet despite this I find myself drifting off. With everything that has been happening today, I've only had one shot of caffeine so far and I'm feeling sleepy. I guess that means I'm relaxed, which is something. I'd hate to start squealing like a terrified pig, screaming, 'Get me out, get me out!' I occasionally stir as a voice comes through the headphones to tell me which area of my brain or body is going to be scanned next. I then glide further into the machine or I'm drawn nearer to the tunnel entrance. I find myself at peace, feeling strangely safe within my hard-shelled cocoon, protected from the world and its trials.

I finally emerge from the MRI's chamber after what I am informed is nearly an hour. I try to take in whatever else they are telling me as my torpor slowly loosens its grip. The gist seems to be get dressed and await your results on the ward. As my jeans are still on that ward, getting dressed entails nothing more than fastening my watch on my wrist once more. It's then back in the wheelchair, blanket over legs and get out of my way, pretend invalid coming through!

*

The hour I spend back on the ward without news or stimulation makes me feel as if I've been prised from the ample bosom of the NHS and placed in a cold, draughty corridor between the departments of Hope and Anxiety. Overall, I still feel like I'm going to be back in work this afternoon, telling people that they're still not sure what's wrong, or that it's just something minor but it was a little scary there for a while. A small part of me, though, is focused on the fact that someone down at MRI told me that the machine I've just been in cost nearly two million pounds. I'm sure firing it up for an hour's ride is not cheap either. The cash-strapped

NHS is hardly going to do that if there's nothing worth investigating. No, remember they just think it might be a cord compression and they need to be sure. Nothing to see here, move along please.

I look around the ward for some form of diversion. There's an old man in a nearby bed hacking up a lung. He sounds to be in a terrible state. This is confirmed when he spews up down the side of his mattress and onto the floor. He wheezes back into his pillow and a nurse appears. She wipes his chin and ask some questions I can't quite hear. Two minutes later a male nurse arrives with a bucket and mop and a roll of wipes. He pulls the curtain but the gap he leaves means he may as well not have bothered. I can see him wiping up the vomit and understandably, he is not doing it gladly. His huffing and puffing suggest someone who is bitterly regretting his career choices. The fool in me considers pointing out that he's missed a bit, as a way of lightening the mood. This idea is rapidly binned as I catch sight of his thunderous face once more. I don't want to be named beneath the newspaper headline, 'Nurse Sacked for Punching Patient'.

That wasn't the sort of entertainment I was searching for but I suppose it killed a few minutes. I while away the next five half remembering the lyrics to *Help the Aged* by Pulp. 'In the meantime we try, try to forget that nothing lasts forever, something something da da da da da, funny how it all falls away.' I look across again at the old fella. Like the song says, I imagine it is a pretty lonely place he's currently occupying. Always someone worse off than you. Never seems to provide any comfort though. Why would thinking about people going through a shit time ever make you feel better? But thinking about people who are enjoying a better life than you is of no use either. Ah, the human condition. What y'gonna do, as Tony Soprano would say. Focus on what's good in your own life, not on...

The doctor who sent me for the MRI is back by my bedside, cutting short the race my brain has been running, forcing me to focus on that thing I was just telling myself not to focus on. I try to read his face, to see if he has any news of note. He just looks tired and ready to move down the conveyor belt of patients. But now he's pulling up a chair and moving closer. Maybe he has something to tell me after all.

"We have the results back from the MRI," he says, studying the sheets of paper in his hand.

"OK, right," I mumble, filling in the silence, as he's still busy scrutinising those results.

"Yes, well, we can rule out a spinal cord compression. The MRI didn't show up anything that we need to worry about in that regard."

I knew it. It never felt like that was going to be it. It's still a relief though to have it confirmed. I didn't fancy having a tumour on my spine, benign or otherwise.

"So what do you think's going on, Doctor?" I ask in the breezy fashion of someone who's just been given some good news.

"We're not entirely sure at the moment. We need to do some more tests. There's a possibility, however, that it could be multiple sclerosis."

"Oh," is the sound that comes out of my mouth, while my internal monologue says, 'What the fuck!' two or three times. Then my brain chooses the word 'bugger', said in the voice of Unlucky Alf from *The Fast Show*. I almost laugh. Shock mode, I guess. Something in the way the doctor said it may be a possibility suggests that it's much more than a possibility. It's a probability; he's just reluctant to commit to saying it's that.

I scroll through the last three or four years and all the signs I've had that something wasn't quite right. The intermittent pins and needles. The peeing problems. The last three months of constant strange sensations in my legs and feet. Is this what it all adds up to because I never ever gave a second of thought to multiple sclerosis. Hardly surprising as I only have a vague notion of what it is. I know it's not good. Being unable to control your limbs. Crutches, wheelchairs, being bedridden. I've now exhausted my personal font of knowledge on the topic.

What I do know is that I'm a long way from any of those things. I play 5-a-side football every Monday, for Christ's sake. Maybe I am reading too much into this. He says they're not sure, so they're not sure. More tests needed. It's just a possibility at the moment. More tests, rule it out. Yes, let's not catastrophise this. If it was definitely multiple sclerosis they would say, wouldn't they. Just one of many possibilities.

The doctor tells me that they are going to move me to the neurology ward where I'll be seen by the consultant there. "Are you able to make it there without assistance?" he asks.

"Yes, I fucking well am!" I reply. OK, in reality I stop at the yes. It's not his fault there's a possibility/probability/absolute pissing certainty that I have multiple sclerosis.

He draws the curtain. "I'll leave you to get dressed. A nurse will then take you down there."

*

I arrive on the neurology ward. As I'm shown to a bed, my eyes surreptitiously scan the other patients. It only takes one of them staring vacantly into the distance for *One Flew Over the Cuckoo's Nest* to come into my mind. I'm no doubt jumping to conclusions, but I'm not at all sure I want to start batting for this team. There's one guy lying on his side, his head some way short of the pillow. He's lying motionless but unnervingly I see his eyes follow me. Is that woman over there rocking back and forth? Is that screaming I can hear down the corridor? Why can I hear screaming?

Of course, I'm not interested in the middle-aged guy who is happily reading the paper in the chair next to his bed, or the guy around my age who is gently rocking in another chair, but with the reassuring excuse of wearing headphones. These examples of normality are not the ones that grab my attention. But I am now getting onto my designated bed and being left to await the arrival of the consultant. How long this will take is anybody's guess but there's no point in fretting too much till I've spoken to him.

Fret, though, is obviously what I do. I dredge my memory for any information it may have on the subject of multiple sclerosis. I recall a drama I watched several years ago about a guy who had it. *Go Now* or *Go Home* I think it was called. He was a player in a pub football team who's getting worse at the game and he doesn't understand why. Maybe it's just age. (It's certainly what I put the waning of my football powers down to. I mean, I'm not going to be as good now I'm thirty-seven as I was when I was twenty-one, am I.) But then the guy in the story is diagnosed with MS and he's soon on crutches, then in a wheelchair, then he can walk again, then he's back on crutches. I enjoyed it at the time and read an interview with the writer. After being incapacitated with MS, he had found himself watching some terrible TV and thought, I've got to find a new purpose in life and that was when he started writing the screenplay.

Yes, I remember all this because I took a particular interest in his story. It wasn't because of the MS, though. That was a side issue to me. I was just interested in how, as a first-time writer, he had managed to get a drama onto the BBC. I was writing a novel at the time, dreaming of literary stardom. There only one problem with this aspiration: the book was crap.

Shall I call Kate? She'll think I'm still at work. No, she'll only worry. I want the full facts before I call her and besides, I need to be here for when the consultant comes round. I wonder what he or she will say? Will more light be thrown on the situation or will there be additional confusion? Some clarity would be most welcome. How long am I going to be here stewing?

It feels like the consultant arrives a couple of hours later but the watch I've been repeatedly checking tells me it's only been twenty minutes when he pulls the curtain around the bed and sits down on a plastic chair next to my bed. He is around sixty years old with thick greying hair and is wearing a tweedy jacket. Those are the sum total of my observations, as I'm rather more interested in what he has to say.

"Good afternoon, I'm Doctor Leezou."

"Hi."

"How are we today?"

"Fine," I say. Shitting it a little bit, but otherwise tickety-boo.

He examines the notes in his hand. "So you've been getting pins and needles in your legs... numbness... and you're having difficulty passing urine..."

"Yes."

"And how long has this been going on?"

"Well, mainly the last three months..."

I'm about to tell him that I have occasionally been getting these pins and needle sensations over a few years now and that the peeing problems started a while back really, but I get the feeling he's not settling in for a good listen. He says 'hmm' a few times and I'm briefly transported back to the Chinese Doctor's, which was a visit that provided absolutely no answers, unless your question was how do you squeeze a large amount of cash out of an ill and desperate twit. I feel the need to take charge of the conversation and divert it in the direction I want.

"The other doctor said that there's a possibility I could have multiple sclerosis?"

Dr Leezou finally looks up from his notes. "Oh yes, you have multiple sclerosis."

He says it in the most matter of fact manner imaginable and there's even the hint of a smile on his lips. It's as if in his mind I've already had it confirmed to me as an indisputable fact. The smile, I presume, is his attempt at a good bedside manner, as if the unconvincing smile of a sixty-year-old man I've just met is likely to transform this day from one of life-changing revelation into one of shoulder-shrugging insignificance.

How do I react to this news? Apparently by focusing on the wiry hairs that I now note are doing a pretty good job of making a run for it from Leezou's nostrils. I wonder if he asks for a nasal hair clipper every Christmas like my dad but, like my dad, never gets one because none of his family wants to spend a second thinking about father's horrible nose protrusions.

He's talking again and the small part of me that's not floundering in a daze and thinking about stupid inconsequential shit convinces me that I should be concentrating on this.

"I would be confident that you have what we call benign MS, which means we would expect your symptoms to be not as severe as other patients with multiple sclerosis. We usually say with benign MS that you'll be in the bottom twenty per cent as far as severity is concerned."

This is said in a manner that suggests I should now be punching the air.

"We'll need to do some more tests tomorrow, though. We can talk some more then." Another attempt at a reassuring smile. "A nurse will be along soon to give you some information."

With a swish he is gone and I am left to study the pattern on the gently swaying curtains that surround me. I lie back on the bed and marinade in my thoughts once more. I want to speak to Kate but I'm not so sure of phoning her now. This feels like something I need to explain face to face. Besides, my mind is too hazy for my mouth to be able to form the phrases it might require.

A nurse comes to see me shortly, or maybe it was ages, I don't know. Whatever, the storm of thoughts in my head is briefly interrupted.

"I believe you've just been diagnosed with multiple sclerosis. A lot to take in, I know."

Funny really. I've been desperate to have a diagnosis for weeks and now I have one, it doesn't feel all that great. In my wildest nightmares, I never envisaged that this would be the full stop moment. A condition so serious, so infamous. Of course, I know little about it because why would I? It was not something that was ever going to happen to me. Great, not only do I have MS but I'm a cliché too. Why do we never believe it will happen to us? Why would it not? I just imagined that the diagnosis would be a little more... mundane, or uncertain. Maybe they would suggest some physio. After a few weeks of performing the prescribed exercises, these annoying symptoms in my legs and feet might go. And maybe the bladder problems would be unconnected. A mild and easily treatable kidney complaint? Something like that. Not this.

She gives me some photocopies. "Please, have a read through this information. It'll tell you all the basic things you need to know." I take them from her and begin to browse through the sheets of paper. "We'll need to do a lumbar puncture tomorrow. A doctor will be here soon to talk you through the procedure." Before I have chance to ask any questions she has swept back the curtain and I emerge into the world once more, this time as a man with multiple sclerosis.

I make an attempt at digesting what is in my hand but she may as well have given me the instructions on how to deactivate a nuclear warhead. The words seem to be jumping around like I've heard they do for people with dyslexia, but I do manage to deduce that there are many ways that this could go and none of them sound great. I suddenly feel very lonely. I need to speak to Kate, to hear her voice. I still don't think it's a good idea to tell her over the phone though. I'll keep things vague, just tell her that I've been in the hospital all day and they've been running loads of tests. I tell the nurse at the desk where I'm going, so the doc isn't looking for me and I head to the exit.

"Hi, love, how's your day been?" I make sure the initial focus is on her. It enables me to maintain a 'problem, what problem' demeanour.

"Fine. He's been a little bugger, though. He's just fallen asleep. I hope you've not just woken him up."

"Sorry... Listen, I've been in the hospital all day."

"How come? What's wrong?"

I'm going to have to release mere droplets of the truth here. The full torrent will have to wait. "Well you know I went to the doctor's this morning... She thought it might be a spinal cord compression like Christine said so she sent me up here."

"And what have they said? Is that what it is?"

"They don't think so, no. They're still looking into it."

"Oh God!" For a second I think she has worked out that something major is wrong, but then I hear the wailing of a two-year-old in the background. "Are you going to be back in time for dinner, so I know whether to make you some or not?" she asks.

"Yeah, I should be. You know what these things are like though. I'll call you again and let you know."

"K, I've got to go. See if I can calm him down."

"K. We'll talk when I get home."

I thought that last line was quite clever – just put the seed of an idea in her head that there may be something important to discuss as a result of my day but with enough scope to backtrack if she challenged me on it. She probably wasn't listening, though, flustered as she was, but it was still good to hear a familiar voice after listening to doctors and nurses for hours.

Back on the ward, the guy who was lying on his side watching me from an adjacent bed is now sitting up a little. He catches my eye and I gather that he wants me to approach.

"Hi," he says. "MS?"

Inwardly, I shudder slightly with the sensation that I have just entered prison and I am being asked what I'm in for by an old lag. He is certainly a bit older than me and is rather thin and dishevelled. Maybe he's going to dispense some jailbird wisdom like Morgan Freeman does for the character played by Tim Robbins in *Shawshank Redemption*. What was Robbins' character called? Oh that's it, Andy. What are the chances? How many characters in prison dramas are called Andy?

As it turns out, he *is* ready with some advice. "It doesn't have to be that bad," he tells me. "I thought I'd be in a wheelchair by now but I'm still getting around."

I quickly assess what I've just heard out of the mouth of this man who appeared unable to move before I left for my phone call. By 'getting around' does he mean he can explore all four corners of the mattress of his bed?

Should I tell him what I'm thinking? He seems to have set the rules of our engagement to Open and Direct. I feel I can be frank with him.

"To be honest, you didn't look to be in great shape when I first came in."

There is no spike in his quiet monotone. "I just wanted to rest today," he explains.

Wanted or you had no choice? Perhaps he can see the scepticism written on my face because he continues. "I've just gone through a divorce. Stress isn't good for it."

So what you're telling me to help pick me up after receiving my very bad news is that you've split up with your wife, possibly due to the strain that MS has put on the relationship, and instead of coming back fighting, your body has packed up for a bit. This tale is not exactly leaving me feeling reassured.

A doctor appears and he's looking for me. "Mr Reynard?" I nod and he motions with his palm out for me to come back to my bed. I oblige and he draws the curtain again around us, which always strikes me as a strange nod to privacy. Morgan Freeman will be able to hear every word if he so chooses.

"So the nurse has told you that we need to perform a lumbar puncture tomorrow."

"Yes. I don't know anything that's involved though," I reply, honestly.

"OK..."

He patiently explains what will happen to me on this ward tomorrow. I will need to lie on my side with my knees up, so my spine is curved. A needle will then be pushed into that spine between two vertebrae and some fluid will be drawn out. Around this time he says it is sometimes known as a spinal tap. I cheer up a little as I am distracted by thoughts of one of my favourite films. That might be why some of the information he now gives me is not as clear as it might be. Essentially, so I gather, the fluid that they'll be collecting takes a circuitous route via my brain. When they test the fluid it will tell them a little more about what's going on in my central nervous system. Part of the jigsaw that began with the MRI. Before they start and afterwards, I will need to drink lots of sugary pop, as I will be dehydrated. Coke is ideal.

I imagine the schadenfreude of the other patients nearby who are earwigging and crying, 'Hurray, someone else is going to have to go through what we did.' Well they can cheer all they want. I can handle this. I've had a few blood tests in my time. They're not too bad. I just look away and it's all done in two minutes. There's no way I can catch sight of the needle in this case because it'll be behind me. The thought of it is surely worse than the actual deed.

"So if you come in for around 1pm tomorrow."

"To this ward?

"Yes."

With that I'm free to leave and go home to my lovely wife. And tell her that her husband has MS. I make my way down the corridor, the vision of my surroundings rather like that of the lead character in *Lock, Stock & Two Smoking Barrels* – Eddie, was it? – when he's just lost the high-stakes card game to a local gangster and everything starts swimming around him as he realises he is in the deepest shit imaginable. I guess I'm not in as bad a state as him, otherwise I wouldn't now be thinking about Eddie in that film, but still the shit is pretty deep and I don't know how I'm going to have this talk with the woman who I'm closer to than anyone else in this world.

I get to the car and a pin prick in my brain tells me that I'm supposed to call Kate and tell her that I'll be home in time for some dinner. I reach for the phone in my jeans pocket but then I think, 'I'll be home in ten minutes, what's the point.' She might detect something is wrong too by the tone of my voice, now that reality is settling into its space in my brain. I want to concentrate anyway on what I'm going to say to her when I get there. I leave the car park, ready – well nearly ready – to face the music.

*

The music playing when I first arrive home is not the most pleasant tune.

"I thought you were going to call me if you were going to be home for dinner," she says, frostily. "I've not made you anything."

"Well by the time I knew I could come home, I knew I'd be

home in ten minutes," I explain rather feebly. I can tell she's a little frazzled after her day as a mother. I'm becoming aware that I should just have said 'sorry, I forgot' and I've now missed my window.

"Well you know where the kitchen is," she responds.

If I now blurted out, 'I've got MS! Your mundane concerns regarding dinner were not at the forefront of my mind!' I think it would be justified, but I keep my bombshell ticking for now.

The ice melts a little as the fact I've been stuck in the hospital all day apparently registers with some of her angrier emotions.

"What's been said then?" she asks.

"Erm." I wriggle on my hook. "Well, a few things. Can I tell you after I've had something to eat?" I say, trying to make it sound like there's not any definitive news. "I'm starving."

She nods. "I've made a stew." This is very easily deciphered code. There was always enough for me. She just wanted to make her point. Fair enough.

Watching TV while eating one of our regular dishes, everything feels normal. I almost forget. Almost. I'm back in prison again as I stare at the last of my meal, my last meal before the condemned man shares his bad news with Person Number 1 (a list of all the people I would have to tell and in what order had begun to form the second Leezou had so warmly delivered his diagnosis).

"Lovely stew, dear," I say in the voice of John Major when he used to say, 'Nice Peas, dear,' to Norma on *Spitting Image*.

"Particularly the peas?"

"Absolutely." I couldn't live with someone who didn't get at least some of my cultural references.

I take the plates to the kitchen to give myself some breathing space. My heartbeat is a little heightened. Is a part of me enjoying this slice of drama? I have this thunderbolt-size news at my disposal and she knows nothing at the moment. Yes, it's not a piece of me that I'm proud of, yet there's no denying it. But the larger part of me is scared by this power I've been given. How am I going to word this?

This situation reminds me of something. What is it? Ah yes, I know, it's that time when you're preparing to tell a girlfriend that you want to break it off. I'm surprised it's this vivid because I'm pretty sure it only happened once. Numerous other girlfriends must have experienced this moment. Did they feel like this? Probably not. Most had probably been laying the groundwork for weeks and me with my head in the clouds or up my own arse hadn't taken the hint. You're busy again? You always seem to be busy. Oh well, all in the past now. I've got one to stick around and she's in there, with two ears and no knowledge of my plight. I decide to take a leaf out of Leezou's book – *How to Break Bad News for Dummies* – and deliver it in a blunt and matter of fact manner.

"So what's been going on today?" she asks, her female antenna perhaps picking up some negative vibes.

"Waiting, blood tests, questions, waiting, MRI scans, waiting."

Turns out that Leezou's shoes aren't that easy to fill.

"So what have they said?"

OK, here goes. "I have multiple sclerosis."

There's a pause. She scrutinises my face. For what, I don't know. That I'm serious? Maybe she's just stalling. I imagine she's taking a quick look in her store cupboard of knowledge on the condition and finding it only lightly stocked, just as I had when they first started bandying round the term a few hours ago. "Right," she says, finally, after what seemed like a very long two seconds. "Are they sure?"

"They seem to be, yes. It's not all bad, though. They think my symptoms might not develop as badly as other people with it."

Maybe she's just stunned in the same way I was a few hours earlier, because the room is silent again. She just reaches out for my hand, then comes in for a hug. She holds me tightly. So tightly in fact that I can feel the softness of her breasts against my chest. Coupled with the smoothness of her cheek upon mine, I soon sense something stir within me and I begin to wonder if sympathy sex might be on the menu. I imagine she thinks it's the furthest thing from my mind right now. You'd think, wouldn't you, but you'd be wrong.

She jolts me back to the here and now with questions about the thing I'd just briefly forgotten about as my other brain briefly took control. I do my best to answer them with my very newly acquired insights. I tell her about how I've got to go back tomorrow for the lumbar puncture and how it used to be called a spinal tap (like the fact that the procedure gave its name to a cult film is the most relevant thing) and then we're pretty much done. With little more to say for the time being, we watch a bit more TV then go to bed. Just to sleep, worse luck.

*

Predictably, I struggle to drop off. Sympathy sex would have been doubly welcome – post-coital weariness might have just been what the doctored ordered. Unfortunately, what he has ordered, or at least laid at my door, is something rather worse. Did all that really happen? It seems an awfully long time since I walked into the doctor's surgery this morning expecting to be sent on my way again, none the wiser. Is this really serious, or is it a minor bump in the road, something I'll get used to soon enough. I mean, I've kind of got used to the feelings in my feet and legs already. Like the peeing problems, it's manageable. Annoying but manageable. Maybe it won't get much worse. Benign MS. Repeat after me. Benign. A needle will be pushed into your spine tomorrow and fluid will be drawn from your brain. Repeat after me. Oh fuck.

How am I going to tell my family? When should I tell them?

The last three months, as I wondered what was wrong with me, wandering the Earth on gravel-souled feet without a clue where I was heading, now seems like a blessed age. I thought I was desperate for a diagnosis but I realise after today's revelations that much of that depends on what the diagnosis might be. No, in truth I'm still glad I know. I wish it wasn't something so extreme, but I couldn't go on as I was. Hold on to that phrase 'benign MS'. People have to deal with far worse, right? If it contains the word 'benign', surely it can't be that bad.

I hear the cries of E from the next room. As I'm already awake, I go to see him, trying not to disturb Kate. I think he's probably had a nightmare. It's been a day for them for the Reynards. I do the father thing and calm him down.

"It's OK, love. Everything's all right. Daddy's here."

He's still half asleep and with my hand stroking his head he's soon unaware that he was conscious at all. Everything is normal in his world again. This is my normality too. This is what I should focus on. The needle can wait. MS will have to stand in line.

NEXT DAY, APRIL 2006 – THE BRAIN DRAIN

After my sleepless night, I end up lying in till 9am. Pre-kids, I wouldn't have said this was that late, but as I have a two-year-old this is a rare occurrence indeed. Kate has done all the childcare stuff, letting me rest a little longer, allowing my mind and body some extra time to process yesterday's events. I'm eventually woken by E who is downstairs, demanding to know when I'll be up. If you say, 'Want to play with Daddy' at that kind of volume, son, Daddy'll certainly be up earlier than he wants to be.

When I walk in the living room Kate is reading through the information the hospital gave me. E is watching a DVD – just *Postman Pat*, not *Shrek* or some other film unfortunately. As soon as Pat has retrieved his letters again after they've blown away on the windy day, like seems to happen in Greendale every friggin' week, we'll be on the train set and I'll be having to concoct some stories of my own to entertain him. I best get some breakfast down me. Kate picks out some MS related facts whilst I eat.

"There are apparently 85,000 people with it in the UK. They reckon that a lack of sunshine could contribute to people getting it. And diet. If you eat a lot of dairy and red meat."

She explains that she's getting prepared for when we go to the hospital, so she knows what questions to ask. I'm sure Kate's analytical mind will be breaking it all down better than my addled brain was managing last night. She's still reading when E orders me to commence another game of Thomas the Tank Engine nearly runs over Pat's black and white cat, again and again. Either Thomas or Jess or both should be learning from experience here. My son's laughter, though, is bouncing off the living room walls, which temporarily smothers thoughts of needles and hospitals.

*

Kate drops E off at her mother's then comes back to collect me and we head to the hospital together. There's a considerable amount of waiting on the neurology ward but here we are finally, me sitting up in bed in a hospital gown, Kate on a plastic chair next to me and Leezou pulling up another of the chairs to talk to us.

"What causes MS?" Kate asks him.

"We're still unsure," Leezou admits. The suggestions he makes for possible causes have a non-committal nature similar to the vagueness found in the literature I was given. There's talk of diet and lack of vitamin D. There's also possibly a genetic link.

"Is there anything he can do to help reduce the symptoms?"

"There's certain things you can do that possibly help slow down the development of future symptoms."

Interpreting this statement doesn't take much effort. The symptoms I now have I have and there's nothing I can do. Kate obviously hears it the same way because she then says, "So he'll have the symptoms he's got for ever now?"

"No, not necessarily. Symptoms fluctuate. They could easily disappear for a while. That's why it's called Relapse Remitting MS."

Oh. So these symptoms could go for a while. That's something.

"All in good time, though," says Leezou. "I'll get someone to talk to you, about diet and so on."

He's clearly eager to get on with his rounds but Kate won't let him go just yet. "What is the lumbar puncture for?"

"Well, the doctor who will be carrying out the lumbar puncture will be here very soon. He'll be able to answer any questions you may have."

If this was a cartoon there would now be dust and an outline of Leezou hanging in the air. He is already greeting the woman in the next bed. All we can do is wait for the lumbar puncture guy to arrive.

Another hour goes by but something unexpected happens in the meantime – my mum and dad and sister appear, bearing half smiles that betray serious concerns. I cast a loaded glance towards Kate that says, 'I thought we were going to wait to tell them?' She throws a look back towards me that I decipher as, 'They need to know.' I get it. She doesn't want to deal with this on her own.

"What have you told them?" I quickly ask as they approach.

"Just that you're in hospital for tests and can they come in?"

This means I am going to have to think quickly, in order to tell them the situation without alarming or depressing them too much. Thinking on my feet is not something for which I've ever achieved a commendation.

As all the hellos are made, which gives me just a few seconds to get my thoughts together, I decide to give them everything straight. If I drip feed this diagnosis, I'll only be putting off a difficult conversation for later. Even so, I still manage to build a big old ramp towards the news at the top. I tell them that the doctors are not a hundred per cent sure yet, but they think they've got to the bottom of what's going on with my legs and feet and that they think in terms of the severity of symptoms I'll be in the bottom twenty per cent.

My family listen attentively, without interruption, and I take a deep breath to deliver the knockout blow, but the words won't come out. The expectant faces of my mum, dad and sister are looking at me like the panel of a job interview committee. My mind flashes to various interviews I've had over the years, the majority of them disasters. Like the time I'd apparently done OK and they were keen to offer me the job but was then asked when I could start. I wanted to appear eager so without hesitation said Monday, then thought about something I'd been planning on doing on Monday and Tuesday and blurted out, 'Well, Wednesday would be ideal.' What a tit. Or the time I kept saying things like, 'When I start the job/when I begin working here,' instead of, 'If I'm offered the job/if I'm successful as a result of this wonderful recruitment process you're running here,' which clearly got their back up. I saw one of the panel make a couple of sweeps of their pen and not the type of pen sweeps that suggested she was writing down, 'I like this guy, he's got chutzpah.' No, two lines were being drawn through the centre of my name. Double tit.

For most of these silent moments, however, I am reminded of all the times in interviews when my mind simply went blank when I had more than one person looking at me, waiting to hear what I had to say.

But finally the words do come. "I have multiple sclerosis."

My mum throws her head backwards in am-dram fashion. My dad's reaction is so understated that I wonder if he's heard right. Christine stands up and gives me a hug.

"I wish it could be me instead of you," she tells me. I feel the love, but I also can't help reflecting on the insidious effects of popular culture. Something about her sentiment doesn't feel real. It's a line from a film. I have to remind myself that this is real life. This is *my* life now.

There is another pregnant silence. The line it gives birth to is from my dad: "Hmm, your Auntie Gina had MS. She was in a terrible state by the end."

There is another period of quiet whilst we all process what he has just said. As a statement of fact, it's certainly the barest of bare ones. I realise now where I get it from. If there's an awkward pause in conversation, I'll often say something stupid and inappropriate just to fill the gap, like the hole in the communication is worse than coming out with something crass. My early dating days are crammed full of such incidents. Against my will, my mind reaches for some bad memories, but it must be scrambled by the overbearing fruitfulness of the material on offer.

But my mind won't let it rest. It eventually conjures up a worthy example. My younger self was doing it doggy fashion and instead of sticking to the accepted protocol of grunting, 'Oh God, oh yes,' over and over, I said to the woman on the receiving end of the greatest expression of my affection, "Wow, you're the best. You have such a lovely big arse." Suddenly, I was no longer doing it doggy fashion. 'No, I meant it as a compliment,' I spluttered. "It's so lovely and big and curvy." Oh shit, had I just called it big again?

I'm with my family, whom I have just informed I have MS, and I'm thinking back to doing it from behind with an old girlfriend. Christ, get a grip, what is wrong with you? Fortunately, the Doctor who is going to do the lumbar puncture has arrived, snapping me out of it, though the word 'fortunately' here is a double-edged sword.

"Hi, Mr Reynard. I'm Dr Evil." He may have used a different name but I can't help what I hear. Stop it, brain! You need to listen as it's you that's going to be affected by this.

"So you're ready for your lumbar puncture?"

I resist the urge to reply with clichés like, 'Ready as I'll ever be,' and go with, "Yes, but I've not been told that much about it."

"Sure. OK. So your brain is bathed in a fluid and this goes all the way down your spine. We're just going to draw a small amount of this fluid out today, just like letting some water out of a bath."

"Is it going to hurt?" I ask. Key question at this point, I think.

"I'll apply some local anaesthetic which should stop you feeling anything but a little pressure as I insert the needle."

The words 'insert the needle' are already inflicting pain as I picture the area into which the needle is going to be inserted. I resolve to concentrate on Dr Evil's smile, which is one of a man who's done this countless times.

"Maybe a headache and a little soreness in the back afterwards," he adds. "Have you been drinking plenty of sugary fluids, preferably with caffeine, such as Coke?" I nod towards the two-litre bottle of Coke that's on the cabinet next to the bed, already half drunk. "Good. That will help to stave off the worst of any headaches. You need to keep drinking afterwards too."

"How long will it take?"

"Around thirty minutes. Maybe a little longer. That's the difficult part. You must lie very still for the duration of the procedure."

That seems to be an awfully long time to drain a small amount of fluid from me but I can't dwell on it, as Kate now asks a question.

"What's the purpose of the test and when will we get the results?"

"It will just give us a clearer picture of what's going on."

Please, Doc, stop blinding us with science. [*I've since looked it up. A lumbar puncture for an MS patient is carried out so they can look for any unusual antibodies in the cerebrospinal fluid, fragmentation in the myelin nerve coating or an unusual amount of white blood cells.*]

There's a collective shrug from everyone and a realisation that it's time to get this show on the road. Kate and the rest of my family are ushered out of the curtained sanctum while preparations are made. I'm told to curl up in the foetal position and the requirement to stay perfectly still is repeated. What if I don't? Could I have chronic back pain for the rest of my life as well as MS? Could I be paralysed and given a short cut to life in a wheelchair? There's irony in there somewhere.

Let's face it, though, becoming a paraplegic is not my main concern right now. It's not even the thought of the needle being pushed into my spine. My primary focus is that a man has a front row view of my bare arse.

As it is, I don't really feel the needle going in. But he tells me it has been inserted and he'll soon be drawing out some fluid. This is sufficient for me to stop thinking about my exposed butt cheeks and to concentrate on not moving. He tells me I'm doing really well. Of course I am. In 1975 I won first prize in a game of sleeping lions. What a dull game for a children's party. It's one that was clearly invented by a parent who wanted ten minutes of relief from the screaming and E-number-induced hysteria. I wonder if you could get away with it at a kids' party today. Now we're going to play a game where you have to lie down and not move a muscle or make a sound and the one who can do it for the longest wins. What do you mean that sounds like the most boring game ever invented? It's great fun.

On reflection I believe most of the children at the party in 1975 were far from keen when pass the parcel and musical chairs were also on offer. What does it say about me that I wanted to play sleeping lions? That my laziness knew no limits? Essentially, you're pretending to be dead and I was the best. What a talent. Where's my medal? High on my success I seem to remember trying to get a game going at a party only a few months later but no one was interested. Well the last laugh is on you, six-year-old kids I once knew. Look at me now – lying absolutely motionless like a cadaver found in the position of an unborn baby and totally smashing it.

"Nearly there." The doctor's words bring me sharply back to the present. How long was I back in the seventies? I now remember that I'm a lion with a thorn in his back. His words are less reassuring and more alarming. I picture this mysterious fluid filling the chamber of his syringe. I'm sure I can actually feel my brain drying out. Like a toad that's taken refuge from the hot sun in a puddle. But now the hot sun is rising higher and the puddle is shrinking.

A few more minutes pass before he says, "OK, all done." I didn't feel the needle being withdrawn but apparently it has been. He applies a dressing and after a short while he tells me that I can lie normally. I can feel the beginnings of a headache but my back is fine. I've had headaches before, of course, so know what to expect from one. Back pain caused by a needle would be something new to deal with but fortunately that's not an issue.

"You have plenty of Coke left?"

I nod.

"You need to keep drinking. It's very important to keep hydrated. You should be fine then. Keep lying down for the next hour, though."

"When will we know the results?" I press again.

"It's not really that kind of test," he tells me. "It's just to give us a more rounded picture. But sure, we'll send you a summary of the findings in a few weeks."

I'm invited to get under the sheets before he draws the curtain back and departs. My family return.

"How was it?" Kate asks.

"Not too bad. I'm bursting for a pee, though."

As I've been told to lie down for the next hour, together with the headache and developing discomfort in my back, there's no way I'm making it to a toilet. How am I going to do this? Christine wanders off to find someone to bring me a bedpan, whatever that looks like in the twenty-first century NHS. She comes back with a kidney-shaped bowl made out of that recycled cardboard that the vomit bowls are made from. The headache is getting worse and the back is hurting more and more, but most urgent of all is the pain coming from my brimming bladder. I need to go with considerable urgency but know that lying down to do it in a ward full of people, including my family, is going to make this a challenging operation.

I lie on my side and cup the bowl between my legs. I so need to go but of course nothing comes. I'm not comfortable. I adjust my position. That feels slightly better but I'm still straining and nothing is happening. I'm ever more conscious that my nearest and dearest are just beyond that sheet of material pulled around the bed and they're probably doing their best to avoid picturing the scene on the other side to it.

Eventually, a few drops emerge into the bright hospital light. It's at this point that my dad decides he's had enough and says, "How y'doing in there?" I see a hand appear, as if he is coming in.

"I'm not finished, Dad!" I may have started but now the end of my urethra has clamped shut like the airlock on a space shuttle. That's at least another five minutes added to this whole process.

Finally, and with so much effort that I think I might have sweated it out, I succeed in filling the cardboard bowl. I shout to Christine to ask a nurse to come and collect my offering. Soon the nurse with the winning ticket comes to take the bowl away and everyone is able to gather round my bed once more. I can tell it's not going to be long, however, before I'm shooing them out again, as before long I start to feel another significant occupation pooling in my bladder. I'm not keen on chatting. I'm drinking obsessively from my Coke once again as my brain is feeling increasingly like a prune under the nozzle of a hairdryer. I'm starting to realise that this is going to be the headache that gave birth to all the other headaches in the world.

Everyone is struggling to conjure up conversation. What do you say to your husband, son, brother who's got a Coke bottle shoved in his mouth half the time and for the remainder is groaning because his head feels as though it's crumpling like I remember that oil can did when the physics teacher created a vacuum within it in class when I was around twelve.

The awkward atmosphere is interrupted by the appearance of another nurse. "Did the doctor mention having a VEP test?" she asks.

"No, what's that?" I manage.

"It's a test that measures your visual responses?"

"What's that for?" asks Christine.

"I think it just gives them a fuller picture of your MS."

I feel like we've been here before.

"The MS can affect vision in some patients," she adds.

"So when's this test?" I say in sickly fashion.

"There's a slot at 2.15pm tomorrow."

If it could affect my vision it seems like an easy decision. No doubt the headache will have gone by then so I say, yes, I can come in then. Another day off work feels like an acceptable demand in the circumstances.

The nurse bites her lip in preparation to impart bad news. "I'm afraid you'll have to stay in hospital." She explains that this is an in-patient appointment, which means I have to spend the night here. It's likely the first out-patient appointment won't be for three months. I don't want to wait that long to find out if my eyesight is all right.

"You can go home for a bit if you like, though," she offers. "If you're up to it." She may have just clocked the fact that I'm a shade of green that really doesn't suit me.

"What time would I have to be back in?" I'm picturing a burly nurse with a rolling pin standing at the door, swinging a set of keys ready to lock up.

"Well as long as you're back today. Ten, half ten?"

It's only four now. The thought of a few hours at home and the opportunity to see E makes me forget about the pain in my head for a second. "OK, I'll do that then," I croak.

The nurse goes and soon do my parents and sister. It's agreed that only one person is required to listen to my death noises till I feel fit to go home. An hour or so later I manage to peel myself from the bed and shuffle down the corridor at the pace of a sickly snail, holding Kate's hand. I try to move as if I'm carrying a glass of water on my head. They've probably only removed an eggcupsworth of fluid from my skull, but it feels like my brain will bash against bone if there are any sudden movements. It therefore takes for ever to reach the car and I make Kate drive at around eight miles an hour all the way home.

The journey is arduous, despite the short distance. But it feels good to settle into my front room, out of the white and grey building with which I've recently become too familiar. I clutch my Coke like it's my baby. My real baby is across town, still at his grandma's. I wish I could relinquish this bottle and hold him for a bit instead. He'd have to move not a muscle, though, otherwise I might throw up on him. I suppose it would be some kind of revenge for that time when he was only a few months old and ill after his vaccinations. I can still smell the mixture of vomit and Calpol that covered me in my nightmares.

*

Kate goes to pick E up while I lie down on the sofa. I'm

starting to feel a little better by the time they're back but the sound of a two-year-old entering my briefly peaceful domain makes me aware that there is still absolutely no way that I'm going to be able to do anything with him. Kate has clearly briefed him well because he doesn't jump on me the second he enters the room.

"Can't Daddy play with me tonight?"

His pleading eyes burn deep into my soul but I know it's hopeless.

"You've just been playing for hours at Grandma's," says Kate. "Come on, it's bath time. Then I'll read you a story."

"I might be able to manage that," I say, feeling every inch the pathetic invalid. I'm going to give it my best shot, though.

And I do manage it. The bedtime story performance isn't Daddy's greatest – no voices, no acting out scenes like I do some nights – but I get through it. This is partly achieved by pushing him towards a quiet simple story that ends with the sentiment of 'this is how much I love you'. The rest of the credit goes to E, as he's good as gold. Kids, I'm discovering, are very good vibe receptors and except for a couple of moments when he forgets that Daddy's not feeling well, he's the model of the calmness I crave.

I lean over his bed and kiss his forehead but immediately regret it as I experience a swell of nausea in my cheeks. I hurriedly depart for another round of inertia on the sofa.

Over the next couple of hours I enjoy some home cooking and a bit of TV. It is soon time, though, for me to head to my hotel for the night. Kate gets a few things together for an overnight bag while I get my coat and shoes on. I'm actually not feeling too bad at all now. I'm definitely over the worst. The taxi arrives and I kiss her goodbye.

*

"Pinderfields?" the taxi driver asks

It would literally take me five minutes to walk it back to the hospital if I braved the dark alleyway at the end of our road. He's probably wondering therefore why I'm spending money on a taxi. He's also probably wondering why he's copped for this pathetic fare. I start to explain to him that I have to return to hospital to retain my bed but quickly accept the futility of this explanation. Why would he be interested?

Even though we have to take a rather circuitous route by car, the ride is still brief. It's long enough, however, for me to discover that I am very much not over the worst. I can hardly demand that he drive at eight miles an hour and the motion means I have to lie down almost immediately. Fortunately, I'm in the back, otherwise the driver may have found the passenger's head resting in his crotch. I can *feel* the colour of my face – a cartoon green – and imagine the sickly shade rising from my chin to eventually cover my whole face, like I'm sinking down through a sea of bile. Memories of countless early hours' taxi rides in my teens and twenties come to mind. Full of beer and curry, I'd always hold it together till I got out but would be throwing up on the pavement before the driver had even hit second gear. I don't think I ever felt worse than this though.

Mercifully, we have arrived and I wait to hear how much. I prise a note from my jeans pocket and hand it to him, still in my horizontal position. I hold out a hand for the change. I've no idea how much he's given me and I'm not concerning myself with a tip for our ten-minute journey. I manage to haul myself vertical but can't stop myself from groaning as I do. As I open the door, he offers me some words of wisdom:

"If you're that ill you shouldn't have left the hospital, mate."

I tell him to go fuck himself. What the fuck does he know about my situation? I just wanted to enjoy a few hours of normality in the bosom of my family, cos I've just been diagnosed with MS, yes MS, y'stupid cunt.

The mere thought of this fantasy drowns me in another torrent of nausea. Devising a new form of human movement – crawling on two legs – I head towards the big-boned nurse who is jangling a set of gaoler's keys.

NEXT DAY, APRIL 2006 – LAZARUS RISES FROM HIS BED TOO SOON

It's been another restless night. At home, Kate's occasional little snuffling noises are enough to keep me awake, so a ward full of patients suffering from various neurological disorders was always going to offer a challenging sleeping environment. I think some of the people here have forms of dementia, the general mithering of ill people being interrupted at regular intervals by howling. These lunar laments reached such a level of volume and persistence at one point that, when I finally caught an hour or two, I could still hear howling in my dreams.

The ward is now an antiseptic scene of activity. Watching the nurses run around like blue-arsed flies is making me feel even more exhausted. I forgot to bring anything with me to entertain myself, so all I can do is either study their endeavours or stare into space. I must have been engaged in the latter for a moment because I don't initially see the approach of a nurse.

"Morning… Andrew," she greets me, glancing at my notes at the foot of the bed. Andrew is the name I invariably get called by officialdom. And my mum and dad. "How are we today?"

"Fine," I say. I'm sure she doesn't want to hear about how

knackered I am, tucked up in bed with nothing to do.

"You have some trouble with bladder retention?" Before I have chance to answer, she is wheeling a piece of equipment closer to the bed and pulling the sheets back. "We just need to make sure that you're emptying your bladder fully. You've been to the toilet this morning?"

"Yes," I reply, recalling the slow creep down the corridor and my struggles to force my night-time pee to acquaint itself with the breaking day.

"Good. So all we're going to do is use this," she says, holding up what looks similar to the ultrasound instrument they use in baby scans, "to detect if there's a significant amount of urine still in your bladder."

I'm sure there isn't. I have difficulty getting it out but I still have a good sense of when there's anything in there. I can see there's going to be no point in protesting, though.

She draws the curtain. "Can you just lower your pyjama bottoms an inch or two. I just need to apply some gel to the area so we get a good signal."

She's ten to twenty years older than me and reminds me of my Aunt Sheila, but I still can't help thinking of Joanne Whalley in *The Singing Detective* during the greasing scene. The words, 'I'm sorry, I'm going to have to lift your penis now' pop into my head. At the point that Nurse Whalley says this, the Michael Gambon character tries to think of every boring thing in the world that he can. Labour Party conference speeches and the like. I can't stop thinking about Joanne Whalley in the eighties, one of my major crushes at the time, largely due to this particular episode that aired when I was in my late teens and flying close to my horny epicentre. Stop it, brain, stop it! Aunt Sheila, Aunt Sheila, Aunt Sheila, Aunt Sheila, godammit!

Any hint of an unwanted stirring is fortunately quashed by the coolness of the gel and the roughness of her hand. The hand, though, is far too close to my slumbering cock for comfort, brushing my skin just below my belly button. Ms Whalley says hello once again in my mind's eye. She's calling me, begging me to close my eyes so I can picture her more clearly and better imagine her slipping her soft fingers beneath the elasticated waistband of my... No, no! Keep those eyes open. Focus on this Aunt Sheila nurse right here. Imagine *her* naked.

"Yes, all seems normal," she says and passes me a couple of tissues to clear up the gel.

Oh no, it's started again. There's a mess to clear up and it's Joanne that has passed me the tissues to mop it up. Luckily, the nurse has her back turned and is cleaning the end of the sonic microphone thingy because blood is definitely travelling to places now that I would rather it didn't. But the panic is short-lived, thank god. Everything returns to normal very quickly as I catch the guy across the way coughing up every bit of mucous that slid down his throat in the night. I remember where I am.

"Can you grab the attention of a nurse next time you've had a pee," she says as she leaves. "We'll need to repeat it a couple more times."

"OK," I reply, but I have absolutely no intention of doing as she asks, not now I know that Joanne is slinking around in the shadows, ready to pounce at any moment.

*

After another interminable period of focusing on the void before me, I see a very welcome sight. Kate approaches and she's holding E's hand.

"Hey, Terror," I say, and Kate hoists him onto the bed. He climbs into my arms.

Kate perches on the edge of the mattress. "How you feeling?"

I explain how I'm OK so long as I don't move much, how toilet breaks are still a toilsome venture and how certain taxi drivers should keep their mouths shut. I also tell her about Aunt Sheila and her cold instrument of mild torture. I don't tell her about my Joanne Whalley fantasies.

She gives me a quick rundown of mundane occurrences from the outside. E is now off in his own world, experimenting with how loud he can make the doors bang on my bedside cupboard.

"That's really loud," I tell him, as if this is a good thing in a hospital ward where many people are trying to rest. "Why not now try and see how quietly you can close them?"

Manipulating your kids has to be one of the most fun parts of parenting. We've found that introducing an element of competition into any activity is a great way of getting him to do pretty much anything. As we both watch him play, the conversation and mood take a turn I didn't see coming.

"He needs a little friend to play with. He was playing peekaboo with Rabs this morning." She laughs quietly at the memory. "Every time Rabs appeared round the back of the chair he was singing, 'Peekaboo, peekaboo.'

The things mums and dads find amusing about their offspring. Even I'm struggling to locate the joy in this one. But then I'm feeling the weight of the underlying message.

"You don't think a cupboard and a rabbit are enough for a boy?" I say, avoiding directly confronting the thing she is driving at. It's rather more difficult to persist on this path once a single tear begins to roll down her cheek. How does she do that? Her face is serene, her body still, yet here she is, one eye betraying the turmoil stampeding through her head.

I grope for any words that don't have the ring of platitude about them. How can either of us know how this will affect us or what the best course of action will be? MS has smashed any crystal ball into tiny shards of unknowables.

"Well we'll just have to wait and see." What the fuck does that mean? Nothing. That's just chucking a collection of words together in order to avoid saying anything of note. Pathetic.

She wipes away the tears. In the end I count three in total. The conversation then moves back to less contentious issues for the next twenty minutes or so. She then prepares to leave. Only one thing that we talked about is flashing its lights in my mind. Is the purpose of a hospital visit to make the patient feel shitter than when you turned up? If so, she's done a bang up job. At least my headache isn't too bad and she's brought me a couple of books.

"Daddy coming home soon?" E asks.

"Later today," I reply.

"Will you play with me?"

"Hopefully. We'll have to wait and see." Hearing me say the phrase again drives another pin through my heart.

Kate and E go, leaving me with my thought for the day: should we have any more children or not? As they would say in *Blackadder*, it's certainly a knotty one. Best produce another one quick before I get worse. But what if I get worse quickly? What if I stay the same for years and I bitterly regret not taking the plunge because I could only think in terms of worse case scenarios. But do I want to risk my kids becoming carers at a young age, like you hear happening? But but but but but. But we have no way of knowing what will happen or what we should do.

I pick up one of my books to distract myself. I read the first paragraph three times, trying to take any of it in. Nurse/Aunt Sheila pays me a visit, breaking this cycle of dilemma, absent-mindedly reading, dilemma, absent-mindedly reading.

"You're due to have a VEP test this afternoon, Andrew?"

"Yes."

"I'm afraid it's been cancelled."

Apparently, there's a staff shortage or something. Happens all the time. They can squeeze me in Friday. Can I do 3pm?

"Do I have to spend the next two nights here?" I ask, dreading the prospect.

"No, this'll be an outpatient appointment."

"I thought it could be months till you got one of those."

"Well it can be but there's been a late cancellation."

So staying here overnight and the ride of near death with Arsehole Taxis (they so often choose a name that starts with an A) was a complete waste of my efforts. I think I can do 3pm, though Kate may be working. I might have to involve my dad. I tell her 3pm Friday will be fine.

"Are you OK to get home?"

I'm either going to have to call Kate back or could I possibly walk it? It's only five minutes if I could walk properly but that is very much not the case. I tell Nurse/Aunt Sheila yes. I'm sure I can rope someone into collecting me. I slide off the bed and take a couple of steps to check if I can avoid this. My nausea shouts, 'Surprise! Remember me?' Yes, the mother, father and bastard cousin of headaches isn't going anywhere fast, just like me. I feel like my spinal tap is still running. I have to text Kate.

SORRY LUV, KNOW YOU'VE JUST GOT BACK BUT APPT HAS BEEN CANCELLED

Her first reply is one word, although I would argue it's really two.

FUCKSAKE

I probably won't be correcting her grammar immediately. Is

she pissed off at the situation or me? The situation, I guess. I hate inconveniencing her like this. I wish I could just friggin' walk it. Am I going to be saying that a lot from now on?

God knows what E makes of it all but Kate of course comes to pick me up and E gets his second taste of hospital today. My wizened brain doesn't appreciate being forced from side to side inside my skull like a dazed wrestler repeatedly being thrown against the ropes, but I make it to the car and home. I have to go straight back to bed though.

E is not happy about it but this isn't something I can just battle through, like I've done with numerous hangovers during his first two years. This is definitely one that needs sleeping off. Surely by Friday, surely.

*

I awake on Thursday feeling... how am I feeling? Lying here I feel better than crap, which is a start. How would it be if I stood up? Ah, that was a big mistake. I slither back under the duvet.

"Kate!"

My attempt at shouting for assistance has all the power of Rose at the end of *Titanic* when she realises that maybe she should have let Jack on that big piece of wood. I daren't cast any vibrations in the direction of my head but there's no chance that she'll hear my pitiful cries from here, so I try to get back to sleep for a bit. The pulsing in my temples, however, does a great job of keeping me just alert enough to experience every minute of this pain. At least I got some decent sleep last night, far from Bedlam up the road, and no one is now trying to spread freezing cold ointment just above my tackle.

Kate finally comes in to check on me. As a nurse, she isn't a natural but she fetches me something to eat and drink and passes me my phone from my jeans on the chair. I don't need anything else. I know people mean well but I can't stand it when anyone starts adopting that really caring voice and asking me over and over how I'm feeling. There's nothing you can really do so just let me deal with it. I'll grin and bear it and just wait to get better. Oh hang on, I'm not going to get better from this one am I. Just progressively worse. At what pace, who knows, but having you ask over and over how I'm bearing up isn't going to help. Luckily, Kate isn't that type of person and soon departs.

I decide it's time I started informing a few other people. My friends are still in the dark. A group text will get the deed done quickly and should keep a lid on any palaver. I spend a while composing the message. This is what I come up with:

HI EVERYONE. JUST WANTED YOU TO KNOW THAT I'VE HAD SOME BAD NEWS. I'VE BEEN DIAGNOSED WITH MULTIPLE SCLEROSIS. BUGGER.

Unlucky Alf and his bugger catchphrase is always my first port of call whenever I experience bad luck. I've certainly hit the bullseye here. I brace myself for the responses.

SHIT, SORRY TO HEAR THAT LET ME KNOW IF YOU WANT TO TALK

FUCK ME THAT'S A PISSER. IS THIS WHAT WAS GOING ON WITH YOUR LEGS?

ARE THEY SURE? HOW BAD IS IT? I'LL CALL YOU SOON.

ME AND LIZ ARE REALLY SORRY ABOUT YOUR NEWS. SHE KNOWS A BIT ABOUT IT BEING A DOCTOR OF

COURSE. DO YOU WANT ME TO GET HER TO PHONE YOU.

Some of my oldest friends are still to respond. Who knows what they're up to? Maybe they're driving or in the bath. Maybe they're currently skiing down a mountain and the alert has made them lose control and they've just gone plummeting over a ravine like Father Larry Duff after another untimely call from Father Ted.

But then Pete, whom I've known for twenty years, rings me. I was playing football with him only last Monday so this is probably a bit mystifying to him. We exchange some pleasantries that seem over formal to me considering our long history. I suppose that's the nature of the circumstances. He then starts to ask me a few questions about what it all means.

"What have they said about how it's going to affect you?"

"Well they've said there's a good chance I'll be in the bottom twenty per cent as far as symptoms go."

"Oh, God, that bad?"

"No, no, bottom twenty per cent as far as severity goes."

"Oh right. Good. And what have they said you'll be able to do and not do? You know, will you be able to drink alcohol and stuff?"

There's something about this line of questioning that cheers me no end. One of the most pressing issues in Pete's mind is will I still be able to get pissed with him.

"Yes, don't worry," I tell him. "Things haven't got that bad yet."

When I get off the phone to him I'm still smiling. His question was so normal. I guess life *is* still fairly normal. Yes, my legs and feet feel weird and going to the toilet is often a pain but what's really changed? I'll still be heading to work in a few days' time, playing five-a-side on Mondays and living in this Victorian three-storey house with my wife and child.

I decide to make another attempt at rising. As I sit up, my brain ache tells me to lie back down again. 'You're not going anywhere yet, Sonny Jim.'

I'm reminded that, at least in the short term, things are not normal. My central nervous system has been flushed and the cistern is still filling up. The drumbeat in my head has become more distant, though, so roll on tomorrow. Lazarus has shit to do.

*

My dad picks me up at 2.30. I'm still feeling a little delicate but I've managed to get dressed and be ready for him without too much trouble. Things start to go wrong when I walk to the car. My desiccated brain knocks on the wall of my noggin and asks me where all that lovely liquid it used to float in has gone? I haven't the strength to tell it to shut up. I just settle into the front seat and ask my dad to drive as smoothly as possible.

Matters don't improve on arrival at the hospital. We've parked as close to neurophysiology as possible but we may as well have exited the car in Bucharest. The waves of nausea are hitting me like a tsunami as we worm our way through the maze of corridors. I hope my dad knows where we're going because I'm just following his shoes. I'm hunched over as we advance and all I can see is a forest of footwear. I track him along the seemingly endless miles of pale grey flooring. I imagine this is how someone on Captain Scott's expedition must have felt. I'm the straggler who's unlikely to make it, the one who's going to lose the trail of prints in the snow and be abandoned to his fate. If only my original appointment hadn't been cancelled, I could have been pushed in a wheelchair. I feel so vomitous, my head collapsing in on itself like a dying star. How am I going to do this test if we ever get there? I wonder if I can do it flat on my back?

"Not too far now, I think," my dad says cheerily. "Are you going to be up to it though?"

Someone asking me the question opens the door to hopelessness. You know, I don't think I am. But we've come this far. I've got to try. Teeth, it's time to grit. I nod to my dad, which draws on a fresh surge of nausea, but I plough on. I only make it another few feet before I see a seat and every fibre of my being accepts it as an irresistible force. I collapse into it, knowing the game is almost certainly up.

"I feel terrible," I groan.

"I'll go see if I can get someone," my dad says, helplessness colouring his words.

Quite right, Father. I think we need to get a medical professional involved here. They said I'd be fine if I drank plenty of Coke. Did they take too much fluid out of my spine? Have I had a bad reaction? Doctor, please help me! I've never felt as bad as this in all my life.

My dad returns with a woman. I have a vague sense that she's dressed in white. I hope she's a doctor, but she might be a nurse. Let's face it, she could be a cleaner for all I know right now. She shows us into a side room. There's some medical equipment and what's that against the wall? A trolley bed? I've clambered onto it before the doctor/nurse/cleaner can say, 'Would you like to lie down?'

I'm breathing quickly and heavily. The woman asks me a few questions about how I got in this state.

"I had a lumbar puncture a few days ago... my head's still killing. I drank lots of Coke like they said."

I'm only capable of the most limited of communication but that just about covers the most important details.

"And how are you feeling now?"

91

Top of the fucking world, I resist saying. "I feel sick. The worst headache."

"You seem to be having difficulty breathing. Can you try and slow down your breathing?"

Breathing quickly and heavily has become the natural response to my ills. It's helping me to control things, such as not puking.

"You seem to be hyperventilating," she continues. "I think you'll feel better if you can try and slow down your breathing."

I have a go and realise she may have a point. A certain calm appears to be returning to the room as I summon all my remaining strength to breathe like a normal person. Exiting this room at any point soon is absolutely not an option, however, unless it involves me remaining horizontal. I suddenly have another image of being rushed down corridors, the thud of metal against double swing doors. Where am I going? I desperately want to be wheeled somewhere that I'm going to feel better. Can they take me straight to theatre to surgically remove this pain? Failing that, could they push me down the street, up two flights of stairs and tip me into my own bed, the bed I now realise I should never have left.

She hears that my breathing has reduced in speed. "Is that any better?"

"Yeah, a bit."

"I don't think you're going to be able to do the VEP test today, though, are you?"

I manage to focus on my watch for a second. The test is in five minutes. Not likely then, no.

"What I suggest is that you stay in here till you feel well enough to move then go home and rest. Just call up appointments when you can and rearrange it."

I mumble, "K." A full OK is just too much trouble right now.

She goes and it's just my dad and me in this side room off one of the corridors. Somehow I manage to feel a little self-conscious even while stewing in my sickness. I can't really speak and my dad doesn't know what to say. The silence between us is slowly cooking up increasing discomfort. All that can be heard is the sound of my loud breaths as I try to control the pace of them. I'm sure we're both wondering how long this is going to go on for. I already know that I'm going to get up from this temporary bed before I'm ready, thus repeating what feels like the worst mistake I've ever made.

"Take your time," Dad tells me, finally puncturing the leaden atmosphere. "I don't need to be anywhere."

I know his words come from a kind place but it just makes me think all the more about whether or not I can move. I want to be home and beneath my own duvet, but most of all I don't want to be in this isolated room, lying on my side on a trolley bed like a slaughtered goat, with my dad standing over me not knowing what to do with himself.

I'm soon pushing myself back up into the land of the barely living and doing another death march, this time to the car. Somehow I make it without another pit stop. The doors are unlocked and I crawl onto the welcoming rear seats, adopting my presently-favoured horizontal position.

"Can you not sit up?" my dad asks.

I know what the subtext is: you can't wear a seatbelt lying down.

"No. It's only round the corner, Dad." My subtext: I'm dying here! We can break the law for a two-minute journey.

He starts fussing. "If you can just get into the front, the seats go all the way back."

If I had the energy I would scream, 'This is not the time, Dad, to advertise the wonderful features of your Renault Laguna! Just get me home, please!'

Nearly crying, what I actually say is, "I can't move."

He tuts but doesn't pursue the matter. He drives me home – very carefully – in silence.

*

It's three days later. My brain has finally forgiven me for what I put us both through and I'm almost back to square one, if you accept that the square includes all my irritating MS symptoms. I was even able to play for a while with E this morning, though I'm sure he found my game face to be a pale imitation of the usual one. And I'm still off work, which is a bonus.

Kate suggests we get out of the house this afternoon. E is due at my mum and dad's, so it seems like a good opportunity. She suggests a spot of shopping at the White Rose Centre. She needs to take something back and she could do with buying something or other. It doesn't sound like the most thrilling of expeditions but I'm happy to go with the flow.

Just before we set off I get a text from Steve, my workmate. He doesn't know the full story yet, just that I've not been into work and have spent time in hospital. He's clearly smelt that something serious is going on and asks if he can come round at four-ish. It's nice of him to make the effort. This is a developing friendship, not one of numerous years, hence the fact that he wasn't included in my group text. I tell him four will be fine, see you then.

It turns out that I've been over-optimistic with my timings. Once we've dropped E off, trawled round the shopping centre and picked E back up, it's already gone four. My parents only live ten minutes from ours but I know Steve will be there on the dot. Some people are good timekeepers and then there are people like me. I'm on sick leave so being out when he calls isn't going to be a good look.

He texts me at five past, just as I'm strapping E back into the car at my mum and dad's. At least he's not my boss. When I get home I explain that this is the first time I've been out of the house in days, except to go to the hospital. I try not to protest too much, which will only weaken my position i.e. I've been unfit to come into work. Let's not forget, I have a get out of jail free card tucked in my back pocket which I will produce once we're settled in the living room.

I don't plan how I tell him; it just happens. Kate bought a book the other day about MS that tells you all about this new world I have entered. It's face down on the coffee table. It has the words 'Multiple Sclerosis' writ large on its front cover. I toss it over to him.

"Well it wasn't cold feet," I tell him, referring to his blithe diagnosis when I first started complaining about the strange sensations I was experiencing below the knee, back in January.

He turns the book over and reads the title. "Ah," he says.

I immediately feel guilty for telling him this way. I worry that it's maybe a way of saying, 'Makes you look a bit of a tit, doesn't it, the fact that you dismissed my concerns as something trivial.' I've probably watched far too many films and I'm sure the drama of it appealed to me, or maybe part of me wanted to underline the seriousness of the situation as a way of declaring, 'Look what I've had to deal with. Obviously I couldn't come into work.'

Fortunately, Steve isn't the type to feel uncomfortable very easily. He takes it on the chin and asks all the expected questions – are they sure, what does it mean in the short and long term, are there any treatments? I tell him yes, they're sure, but it's early days. This could go in many ways and they've not talked about treatments so far.

The one thing I can tell him with absolute certainty regarding the immediate future is that I'm very thankful I'm finally over the lumbar puncture. I describe what I've gone through the last few days and we have a laugh about it all. It's then time for him to go.

"When will you be back at work then?" he asks in the hall.

"Hmm, I'm not sure. Soon, I guess." This is the first day I've been able to even consider it. In truth, I could probably head in tomorrow, certainly the day after tomorrow.

"Well you may as well get something out of it. Take your time, I say. I'll see you when I see you."

"Aye, see you. Cheers for coming round."

I shut the door and experience a wave of dread at the thought of walking into the studio again. Going back to work after a long holiday is bad enough but going back and having to explain to everyone that I've been absent because I'm now a man with multiple sclerosis is not something that fills my heart with joy. At least it's a wave of dread at a future prospect and not another wave of nausea in a dreadful present.

I sit back down on the sofa and once again open my new book.

I managed to get an appointment to have my VEP test around two months later. I sat at a screen and said if I could see various dots lit up on a board, as they measured my field of vision and the speed of my responses. I received a letter with the outcome a couple of weeks after that. The results were summarised in one word: 'NORMAL'.

Despite some badgering, I never received the results of my lumbar puncture.

LATE APRIL 2006 – NEEDLE PHOBIA

I'm in the Six Chimneys with my closest friend, Dave, who I've known since school. This is my first night out since the diagnosis and everything that went with it. We sit down at a table with our first beers of the evening, him eager to continue hearing about my recent troubles and me eager to keep telling him.

"So what's it like in an MRI machine?"

"I found it all right. You might struggle if you're bad with claustrophobia. The roof is only about two inches from your nose. I just closed my eyes."

"Someone at work had to have one. She said it was really noisy."

"Yeah, it's not too bad. They give you headphones."

This background information is all well and good, but what I really want to get into is my lumbar puncture, the taxi ride to the hospital and the abortive trip for the VEP test. I have a sense of where the best parts of my recent story lie. An MRI scan it seems is a very useful diagnostic tool for doctors but it doesn't have the wincing quality of the spinal tap. And I know the shenanigans that ensued can be spun into a good anecdote.

We're still only halfway down our first pints when I manage to steer the talk onto the episode I'm most keen to describe.

"The worst part was the test they made me do the next day called a lumbar puncture."

"What's that?" Dave asks, swallowing some of his lager.

"Well it's what they used to call a spinal tap. You have to lie on your side and have a needle put in your spine and they take out some of the fluid you have in there so they can test it for... stuff."

His bottom lip heads south-west in that universal expression people make when something is unpleasant or gruesome.

"The needle going in actually wasn't that bad, but I think he was rooting around with it for a good twenty minutes."

Dave laughs but not in a way that suggests he finds this funny. "Can we talk about something else?" he asks, taking another swig of his pint.

I just take this as the type of thing people say to highlight the grisly nature of what is being reported to them. I carry on, ready to tell him about the headache from hell and the rest of my tale.

"So he finally pulls out this big needle…"

"Seriously, can we talk about something else."

I'm now aware that a single bead of sweat has formed on Dave's forehead. It hovers there like a bad omen, despite the room temperature being mild at best.

"You all right, mate?" I ask, in an amused fashion that I hope says, 'Y'big Jessie. I've actually been through this. You just have to listen to it.'

He smiles unconvincingly. "Yeah. Another subject would be good, though." His voice cracks a little at the end of his request and I realise that maybe I need to return to my topic of choice later.

"Fair enough. What's happening with you then?" I inquire, deciding it might be an idea to take this chat well away from the hospital for a while. But he doesn't reply, just downs another mouthful of his lager.

"Nothing much then," I say.

He begins to look anxiously in various directions, like someone about to do a runner on a restaurant bill who is scanning for exits. I follow his gaze to see what he's looking at. The clientele is almost exclusively men, old ones mainly. I'm not expecting him to say, 'Check out the hottie at two o'clock' any time soon.

Finally, he speaks. "Do you fancy some fresh air?"

I don't particularly. We've only just sat down, but I can see that he needs some. "Yeah, sure."

We leave the remains of our drinks and head through the fug from everyone's cigarettes towards the doors. I'm sure he'll be OK in a minute when that cool air hits his face. We are only halfway to leaving the pub, though, when the most bizarre thing happens. His knees appear to buckle in Norman Wisdom fashion and he makes a grab for my shoulder. I grasp him by the waist and can feel that most of his weight is being supported by me, not his legs. Fortunately, he's less than ten stone but this is weird. I thought it was me who had MS, yet here he is experiencing walking difficulties.

"Whoah, whoah! You OK?"

Stupid question really as he's clearly not, but I'm struggling to understand what's happening.

He actually answers me with a, "Yeah, I'm fine," but I don't know who he's trying to prove it to because not one witness in here would believe him. He tries to take another step and his legs go again like those two Olympic marathon runners who had to crawl over the line years ago because they couldn't even walk in a straight line. I have to pull his arm round my shoulders.

"A couple too many?" a nearby grey-haired guy in a long coat chortles.

"Best get him home," I hear another voice say.

"He's not drunk, honestly," I protest. "We've just got here."

Trying to tell the full story is asking too much while I'm carrying nine and a half stone of deadweight. Besides, I don't really know the full story myself. What the hell is going on?

Unexpectedly, he regains some control and walks the rest of the way unaided. He pushes through two doors and, I note, doesn't hold either open for me as I follow him. I'll forgive him, given the circumstances.

Outside, it's surprisingly cold for late April. A fog is even starting to descend on the town centre. We stand on the pavement next to the road, a double panel of those grey metal railings beside us, stopping fools from striding straight into traffic.

"That was a bit strange," I say.

"Yeah, sorry about that."

"What was going on there?"

It's good to see him feeling better. I knew he'd be fine once we were out of the pub. He reaches in the inside pocket of his coat and pulls out a packet of bacci. Yeah, minor crisis, time for a smoke. That figures. Smokin' Dave has been an occasional nickname of his and not because all the ladies swoon when he walks into the room. He opens the packet and I prepare to marvel at how he can build his roll-up standing up without dropping a thing, particular considering how he was a few moments ago.

But then something happens which makes the strange incident inside seem perfectly normal. As he begins to load bacci into his Rizla, his eyes spin in their sockets like the wheels of a fruit machine and suddenly all I can see in there is white. A fraction of a second later he is collapsing like a cooling tower for which the charge of dynamite at the base has just been detonated. On his way down he smacks his chin on the top of the metal railings before hitting the paved ground. It's all happened much too quickly for me to react. I think he may also have hit his head just for good measure as he completed his fall, but like I say, it all happened so quickly that I'm unsure.

All I am certain of is that, with him sprawled out on his back, the bulb lighting the word PANIC in my mind has changed to red. Oh God, are you all right mate? I kneel down. I suppose I should feel for a pulse on his neck first but my instinct is to gently slap him a couple of times on the cheek. It did look more like a fainting rather than a seizure or similar, but he did bash his chin pretty badly on the railings, which ironically probably saved him from cracking his head too hard on the pavement. I'm still majorly concerned here, though. Should I call an ambulance? Should I rush back into the pub and yell out, 'Is there a doctor in the house?' The Six Chimneys is a Wetherspoons, so is it likely? Am I stereotyping? Am I revealing some kind of unwarranted prejudice?

Panic! Remember you're supposed to be panicking. Maybe I'm now in shock. Do people in shock ask if they are in shock? "Dave! Dave! Wake up!"

His eyes open and he quickly stands up, as if he's hoping no one has noticed what happened a moment ago. Maybe he's responded to my cries, like a teenager who wakes from a coma after hearing her favourite song. Whatever, it's a relief.

"Where shall we go now?" he asks. I presume he means for another pint. How can he suddenly be acting like everything is perfectly normal?

"You do know what just happened, don't you? You gave me a right scare."

"Yeah, come on let's get out of here."

Yes, he is definitely attempting to style it out. It's as if he knows exactly what has happened, frame by frame, and his main reaction is one of embarrassment. I see there no point in mentioning that we still have two perfectly good pints in the pub we've just exited, barely half drunk, as he has already crossed the road and is marching up the precinct, leaving me dumb-founded in his wake.

"Wait up, mate!" I call out.

I trot after him and head into the thickening fog.

I later discovered that Dave has an extreme needle phobia. At one time the phobia was so acute that when he needed a routine blood test at the doctor's, he fainted three times and was in there for over an hour.

PART TWO

A taste for defeat sleeps somewhere in us all.

Philippe Djian – 37,2° le matin

JUL 2007 - FEAR AND LOATHING IN WAKEFIELD

This is not good. I can't move. I know that I have to attempt to get up. I have to try and make my legs and body work.

E calls out once more. "I'm awake! Day! Day!"

Shit, he's not put a name on it, so I can't use that one. I nudge Kate in the back again anyway but she is dead to the world, or is at least pretending to be. It was a hot night and she's naked under the covers. I lift the sheet to have a sneaky ogle of her bare arse. Why do I get so horny when I'm hungover? Now is an especially inopportune time, as there is not a hope in hell of her joining me in Lustville. She will be as hungover as me and anyway, there could be a small face at the foot of the bed any second. I summon all my current levels of strength to stand up, which doesn't amount to much presently, and manage to emerge from my pit of post-party gloom.

"I'm hungry," is E's way of offering me a good morning when I push the door of his bedroom open. Breakfast it is then. Let's see what I can manage.

*

E watches an episode of Engie Benjy on DVD while munching on his Crunchy Nut Cornflakes. I spoon soggy mouthfuls of Shreddies into my mouth, slowly and joylessly. I added plenty of milk so that chewing would be an optional extra, one I've so far resisted. I just crush them between my tongue and the roof of my mouth, which seems to be burnt for some reason – a reminder of the chilli Kate made for everyone last night? The milky mush is then sent to the depths of my delicate, gurgling stomach. Who would have thought that out of the two of us my three-year-old son would be the one eating something approximating solids.

An episode finishes. I encourage him to watch another one while I get my shit together. Visions of last night's events materialise in my mind, delivering a sharp, gut-wrenching wince. We had a laugh but my main emotion is one of anguish, which is not great when you already feel like crap. It was our third wedding anniversary. I borrowed some karaoke equipment from a guy at work and set it up in a gazebo in the back garden. We intended wrapping up the singing at around 11 but it started raining as soon as everyone arrived. The upshot was that we only got it going by around 10.30 and we were all pissed by then. Someone shoved the volume up on the mixing desk far too high, but none of us noticed with our ears full of alcohol. Neither could we hear the neighbours who dropped by to offer us their considered opinions on our behaviour.

It was only at around half twelve that we finally caught wind of the rage that was gathering all around us. There was a rap on the back fence after a lively rendition of *Can't Stand Me Now* by the Libertines. I can't remember what she said exactly but it was words to the effect of, 'Would you mind awfully turning it down or perhaps halting proceeding altogether, as my children and I who live two miles away can't get to sleep.' I could smell the burning from the pitchforks that flanked her, as other people from the locality came to lend their support.

We turned it down as requested. It was only then that we realised that Motorhead would have considered the previous noise levels to have been a bit much. We called it a day after just one more track and retired to continue the festivities inside.

Oh, the shame! The pain! The embarrassment! We are not the type of people who when we want to have a party, we have a party and sod the neighbours. We try to be considerate and not upset too many folk. We've properly fucked up this time.

The silver lining is that we're moving again soon, so they'll be rid of us and we won't have to face them for long. Yes, we're rejoining the mortgage club after an all too brief hiatus. Kate spotted a small, dated house across town that sits within a huge garden. A joyful tune played in her head as she imagined all the things she could do with a house on that amount of land and the die was cast.

Of course, my immediate reaction was no, please, I can't go through with moving again. She pointed out that the schools around us are crap. I highlighted the fact that we already lived in a lovely house and, a mere four years ago, its renovation almost killed us. A heated argument ensued and continued for twenty minutes.

In these situations I'm reminded of a quote by the characterful football manager Brian Clough when he was asked how he dealt with players with whom he had a difference of opinion. He said that they would sit down for a while to discuss the matter like grown-ups. Then, after every aspect of the issue had been explored, they would agree that he had been right all along. I am just a team member. Kate is the undisputed manager. The result? We're moving again.

Kate's background is solidly working class. She didn't grow up in poverty, but she did live in a caravan for a while, so maybe it's understandable that she's always striving for the big house and big garden with the good schools. Her dad was a proper Del Boy-type character who was always building stuff, like a house on his smallholding, hence the temporary caravan. He died of a brain tumour when he was forty-five. It was the anniversary of his death recently. I stop my internal griping about the MS whenever I think of him.

As I stare into my cereal bowl, my thoughts are interrupted by E suggesting a game of Thomas mows down some cows on the tracks, cows that are ridden by Postman Pat's mate Ted Glenn. He still loves his train set and will often play for ages on his own with it. Just my luck that this morning he wants Daddy's input. I kneel on the carpet and try to get something going but very soon I start to feel queasy again.

"I'm not feeling very well," I tell him, downplaying the deathly turmoil swimming through every vein. "Why don't we go to the park instead?"

I could really do with the fresh air. OK, the park also means I'll be able to sit and watch him play on the slide for a while, allowing me to sit motionless, contributing no more than words of encouragement. With some reluctance – Ted still has to be knocked off his bovine perch half a dozen times – he agrees.

*

I keep my head down as we move through the park, E on a tricycle, me doing the walk of self-loathing, praying I won't be confronted by an irate neighbour who happens to recognise me. My stooped demeanour today is of course self-inflicted. Most days, I'm getting about fine. The MS has steered clear of any more significant drama. My feet are the same, my legs can get weak, my bladder is often reluctant to empty its cargo, but generally life has settled down into a new order.

There was last July, obviously. I'm generally at home in the sunshine – I love summer – but it was particularly hot. My symptoms seemed to worsen and I felt totally drained. I ended up taking three days off work. Everything calmed down fairly quickly, though.

I've also been informed that I qualify for interferon treatment due to the number of relapses I've had in recent years. So far I've refused it as it involves injecting yourself, which frankly does not sound like fun. It can also affect fertility. Kate and I are still keeping the idea of having another kid afloat but unless Kate pushes it, I know we won't. That's the dynamic in our relationship. There's a stick lodged in the most viscous sort of mud in this marriage. Sometimes it's appropriate for that stick to stay where it is. Other times it needs her hand to extricate the stick like Arthur liberating Excalibur from the stone, so that we can progress in life. That's a rather too involved metaphor to illustrate that she pushes me into things that I'm too scared or apathetic to do myself. With regard to having another child, though, she's currently distracted by thoughts of moving, renovation and turning our life upside down in another way.

I continue to push E along by the long handle that's attached to the back of his trike. I'm feeling progressively worse with every turn of the plastic wheels. Thank god we've made it to the playground. I take a seat as he rushes off to explore. I notice that there are a load of letters being blown around by the gentle breeze. I wonder where they've come from? It's not just one or two that may have been dropped by mistake. There's a whole batch of them, like they've been dumped. I think about gathering them up, but where would I take them? Besides, that would be the deed of a healthy man, not one that is severely hungover.

I'm feeling OK while I sit down but I soon have to get up when

I'm afraid he might fall at the top of the slide. I experience the swell of 5% lager washing across my brain. I'm getting too old to drink like this. I'm briefly transported back to that time post lumbar puncture. It seems ridiculous that I should inflict such nausea on myself out of choice.

E eventually tires of the playground. I have a bright idea of something we can do that will use up more of his energy. I suggest he helps me collect up these letters that are scattered everywhere. He could deliver them back to their rightful owners, just like Postman Pat (I recognise some of the addresses as being nearby ones from previous visits). Needless to say, what I mean by 'help me' is he can do it all while I just direct. He's so excited about actually delivering some letters for real, he's more than happy to do so.

We set off, the letters placed behind him in the pick-up tray of his tricycle. Most of the letters are from one block of flats, just up the way. As we round the corner, we are confronted by a sorry sight. The mystery of why the letters were in the playground in the first place is solved. There is a bank of small metal lockers for the post for all the flats attached to the wall outside. Many have been prised open with a screwdriver or suchlike and are now hanging bent and open. Some ne'er-do-wells have clearly been looking for what they can find among the detritus that now litters the area. Birthday cards with money in them? Identities to steal? Whatever, they must have collected a few then got rid of what they didn't want in the playground.

We're not going to be able to post the letters as planned, as the post-boxes have been properly knackered. I don't remember this episode – *Postman Pat and the Crackhead Thieves*. I find a couple of pieces of marketing crap and give them to E, telling him to post them in a couple of random boxes that remain intact. That seems to head off any potential tantrums. I ask him to search with me for a large stone. I let him point one out to me and I use it to weight down the other letters we have, just outside the entrance to the flats. The residents will have to sort it out from here.

We move on. That bit of excitement distracted me for a few moments from my headache and sickness, but now they're back and this time it's serious. Searching for the stone, bending down… it's all activities an ashen-faced invalid like myself should not be pursuing. My cheeks decide that now is the time to start generating puddles of saliva in my mouth. I know what that means. I had enough episodes of travel sickness as a kid to know that when that happens you've crossed the Rubicon and there's nothing you can do. Just accept it. Get it over with. But where? I'm in the middle of a new housing estate.

I have a quick look around to make sure the coast is clear. It's a peaceful Sunday and not a soul is to be seen. E has his back to me, no doubt wondering why we've stopped. Taking my opportunity, I acquiesce to my body's needs and throw up on the corner of some poor bastard's drive. Yep, I think we've got away with it. I straighten up, a thin streak of puke dribbling down my chin. In this precise moment of something akin to satisfaction and relief, the first moving car I've seen all afternoon peels off the nearby mini-roundabout and heads towards us. Houses and flats are packed tightly together here – there are many drives to choose from – but of course it eases into the one in which I've just been spewing. The tyres at the driver's side narrowly avoid ploughing straight through the pool of Shreddie vomit that I've just violently deposited on the pavement. Oh god, did they see me? They may well have done.

Without looking back (I imagine expressions of dismay, or perhaps disbelief – were we really welcomed home by a man being sick on our drive – on the faces of the driver and his wife) I make a hasty exit, pushing Pat back towards our house. As we go, I see some more crumpled letters being tossed along the path in the light wind like tumbleweed. I half expect one of the envelopes to have my name on it.

AUG 2007 – STINKS OF PISS

My friend Pete has a saying. If there's anything he doesn't like or disapproves of, he says it stinks of piss. That song, how much that ticket cost, his wife's ex turning up on the scene, the train being late, the fact that a politician has been caught lining his own pockets while keeping his own people in poverty – it all stinks of piss.

I'm in the bathroom thinking about this because my piss really stinks. I know what you're thinking – all piss stinks. It's a well-known property of the liquid (hence Pete's saying). No one is making eau de piss perfume. But this properly stinks in a way that's hard to even describe, other than to say it's deeply unpleasant. It's a smell that suggests I'm ill but I feel absolutely fine. Keep an eye on it, I suppose.

*

I should be enjoying this experience. This is how I used to pee – easily and effortlessly. This is something I took for granted and now I'm able to do it again I should be elated. But I'm not.

Trouble is, the process is just a little too free from restriction. I need to go quite urgently when it happens and it seems to be happening quite often, certainly more often that it should be.

This is not good. It stinks of piss. Only it doesn't. It stinks of something far worse.

*

I've just climbed to the top of the house. What do you want, a fucking medal, I hear you say. Your MS isn't that bad, is it. You're still getting around fine you said. True, going up the stairs is not a problem. I only mention it because I've come up four flights wearing only one slipper. I can see the other one on the step way below. I know I set off from the hallway wearing both of them. I must have arrived at the middle floor wearing them both. But then one of them has been shed and I didn't notice at all as I climbed another twenty-odd steps. My feet have been numb since that day in January last year when I walked into work, but never this numb. Not so numb that I can't tell whether or not I'm sporting footwear.

What's happening here? My feet have all the sensation of blocks of wood, my legs feel weaker than they normally would after that amount of exercise and my piss no longer stinks of piss. It's also become a sprint to the toilet to head off disaster. Fortunately, I'm winning that race at the moment, but something is clearly going on. A visit to the doctor's tomorrow, I think.

*

I don't feel good. The pins and needles have now reached my stomach. They've never scaled those heights before, never rising above the level of my thighs previously. I also feel totally devoid of any energy. I'm still new to this, but I'd say with some confidence that I'm having a relapse. Brilliant. I expect I'll get over it in time, otherwise it'd just be called relapsing MS, right? But relapses mean more permanent damage from what I know. I feel like I should be seeing a specialist in MS but the GP will have to do for now. Appointment this afternoon. Let's see what they have to say.

*

I know it's bad because I didn't feel at all guilty about calling into work and telling them I won't be coming in today. I remember saying to Steve only a few weeks before my diagnosis that I wouldn't mind a minor recurring ailment if it meant I could have a few days off sick a year. One of the retouchers, Ben, said he suffered from sinusitis. I'm sure it wasn't fun when it struck but I'm sure he was off sometimes when his nose was in perfect working order. It was just something he could pull out of the bag of sickies when he fancied a couple of duvet days. That's all I wanted. Something I could rely on that was unprovable that could offer me a few days of additional holiday. Obviously nothing serious. Just enough to make watching TV or playing guitar the most effort I could manage that day.

Shortly after my diagnosis, this subject arose between Steve and I again. Be careful what you wish for was his summary of the situation. I couldn't argue with that.

Anyway, here I am shuffling into the doctors. I don't have much hope that they'll say anything of any significance. Looks like I'm having an MS relapse, they'll tell me. Bet I'm just told to go home and rest, wait for it to pass. Who knows how long that will take or what permanent harm will be done to my central nervous system.

"Come in."

It's the woman who sent me to the hospital that day when I convinced her that I might have a spinal cord compression. Good, I like her. I feel like she's listening when I'm speaking.

"How can I help?"

I go through the MS symptoms, both new and old. She nods and notes a few things down.

"When did this all start?"

"Well I have problems with bladder retention. I normally have trouble peeing, but a few days ago it went the other way. I needed to go quickly and it was coming out really fast."

"Hmm, do you need to go more often?"

"Yes, I think so... I'm not sure, yeah, I think so. It definitely smells more."

"OK, just a stronger smell, sweet or like a foul smell?"

"Yeah... unusual. Foul, yes."

She opens a drawer and hands me a little specimen bottle. "I'll need a sample of your pee. There's a toilet a few doors down."

"Right."

I head to the toilet thinking, 'Houston, we have a problem.' I went not long before coming here so God knows how long this will take. However, I hadn't factored in the recent adjustment to my peeing regime. Not that much comes out, but it comes out fairly easily. I manage not to spill a drop too. 'Great cock control there from Reynard,' says the sports commentator who lives somewhere in my head. How do women do it? Are they able to navigate the labial topography and get it in this fairly thin tube without covering their fingers? Do they even know exactly where their pee hole is so they can cup the rim of the bottle around it? I'm fast approaching middle age and I have to admit, I wouldn't be able to collect it for them if, in some strange universe, I was required to. I've never seen it winking at me when I'm in that neck of the woods.

The doctor slips on a couple of rubber gloves before handling the bottle I give her. She holds it up to the light.

"Quite a lot of protein in there I can see."

I'm guessing that's not good. She now unwraps something and dips it into the bottle of yellow liquid, presumably to test it. I stare out of the window through the white slats of the blind while I wait for her to finish what she's doing. Pee. Now there's a funny euphemism. Is it not short for piss? Whenever anyone uses the phrase, 'I need to pee,' or, for example, 'I need you to pee in this bottle,' are the young schoolboy, the prim librarian, the conservative tax inspector or, in this case, the authoritative doctor all really stopping a whisker short of using the word piss?

The doctor sits back down. "We'll send your piss off to the lab," she says. Well, not quite. She doesn't even say 'pee', just 'this', but the imagination has got hold of it now. "I'm going to give you some anti-biotics, though. You've almost certainly got a urinary tract infection. This might be why your MS symptoms have increased."

She smiles and hands me a prescription.

"How long will it take to clear up?" I ask.

She assures me not long. "Hopefully your MS symptoms will settle down then too."

*

It's nearly a week since my visit to the doctor's. The UTI, as I've learnt these things are usually abbreviated to, cleared up quickly like she said it would. I knew it was gone because a couple of days ago I was back to standing over the toilet hoping to piss sometime in the next ten minutes, rather than hoping not to piss myself before I'd got it out of my pants.

Problem is, my new MS symptoms have not gone. In fact,

they're a little worse. Not only has the area of my stomach joined the party, there's now a little bit of tingling in some of my fingers. Is this a sign of things to come?

At least I'm still off work. I just wish it was with sinusitis.

NOV 2007 – OH NO, NOT AGAIN

Yet another visit to the doctors' surgery. They really should give me my own parking space. It's nothing to do with my MS or the associated peeing traumas this time, though. My legs become weak more quickly but the extra tingling has mostly gone after that attack I had back in August and peeing is back to being its normal irritating process. No, on this occasion I've come to have a moan about my eczema.

Eczema has been a curse on my life for over twenty-five years, having first reared its itchy red head when I was thirteen. In my school's wisdom you were given two years to make some friends in your classes. Then they put everyone's name in a tombola they kept in the staff room and marked you down for entirely different classes with boys you hardly knew. The result: you had to make friends all over again. Not something to which a shy, uneasy child is suited.

It began on one elbow. Exacerbated by irresistible, persistent scratching, my whole arm was soon weeping with puss-filled sores. That summer, before the new school year when all this change would happen, I also came down with German measles. As disease had a party in my body, I remember I knocked the scabby head off one of my pustules and green toothpaste arced slowly from the wound. Lovely image, isn't it?

My parents were understandably concerned and asked repeatedly if this rash was a reaction to me being worried about going into new classes. I said it wasn't. The truth was that I had told myself it would be OK. But eczema is a curious beast that seems to bury itself deep within the subconscious, ready to spout forth at any moment from deep-lying anxieties. During several itchy periods of my life I've thought I was fine, but looking back I must have been fretting about something or other because once that episode was over, the rash would die down again. It would never disappear entirely – it has always liked to remind me who is in charge in this relationship – but it wouldn't be nearly as bad.

That first year when I was drowning in teenage angst at school was a nightmare. First it was my right arm, then my other arm joined in. It then spread to my legs, torso and neck. The worst few months, however, were when it ventured onto my face and into my pants. A red rash is really not a great accompaniment to adolescent zit volcanoes, while having eczema on your scrotum is also something I would not commend. I would find myself in places like the dining hall at school, trying to surreptitiously scratch my nuts and hoping no one would notice. Fun times!

It has now flared up again. It's not as bad as it has been at its heights but it's bad enough, hence my visit to the doctors'. You'd think it would leave me alone now when I have MS to deal with but no. I recall Dennis Potter making a similar complaint. He was in his late fifties and dying of cancer but he was still suffering with the psoriasis that had plagued him throughout his adult life. It only left him alone once the cancer had killed him.

The resurgence of my eczema is no coincidence. Our latest house move is imminent. Thankfully, we have been able to extend and renovate without having to live there, so it's not been as harrowing as the last time, but I'm still clearly anxious about moving all our stuff and getting settled in the new place. Sitting in the surgery waiting room now, just thinking about it is making me itch like crazy.

My name is called on the monitor. Balls, it's Dr Fat Finger. Let's all be grown-ups about this. He's had one of his swollen digits inside my rectum but let's remember, he is a medical professional. It's not like he's just a man I met in the street. And at least it's done with now. My sphincter can relax for this visit. I knock on his door.

"Enter."

'Enter' is a bit headmasterly for my liking, particularly as he's probed my a-hole recently. No, stop it, you're fixating again. You're just here to sort out your rash remember.

I explain my problem, he takes a brief look at it, then prescribes me a stronger steroid cream. Sorted. I prepare to leave.

"How are you coping with your multiple sclerosis?" he asks me.

I wasn't expecting that. Most doctors when the issue at hand has been dealt with cannot wait to get rid of you. Perhaps the fact that our interaction took all of two minutes means he wants to take the opportunity to kick back for a while. After all, the next person might want to have a chat with him about their chronic halitosis.

"Not too bad," I reply. "I had a relapse in August though. I had a UTI. That seemed to set it off."

"And how are you with going to the toilet now?"

"Well because of the MS I suffer with bladder retention."

"I see."

Something in his line of questioning is putting me ill at ease.

"Are we sure that this is as a result of the MS?"

What is it with this guy and his obsession with my bladder difficulties? I'm sensing something else itchy besides my eczema and it resides on the end of his hand.

"It could perhaps be prostate trouble."

I knew it! No, we're not going down – or up – this road again. I'm nipping this in the bud. "No, I'm sure it's the MS. I had a prostate exam only last year and everything was fine."

"Hmm, but a problem with the prostate could have developed in the meantime."

Be strong. There is no way I am going to allow him to slide one of his sausage fingers into my anus on this occasion. Absolutely no way.

*

I'm lying on my side on the padded table, listening to the familiar sucking sound of a rubber glove being stretched over an oversized hand. How did this happen? I only came in to secure some cream for my rash. Now my bare arse is out again and it's preparing itself for an unwelcome visitor. Maybe it won't be so bad second time around. Maybe my memory has exaggerated the discomfort.

Wrong. It's still something to be filed in the bearable but most unpleasant category. I picture Kenny Everett on his TV show wearing those huge foam hands for that preacher character. Brother Lee Love, I believe he was called. My pre-teen self used to find those sketches funny. Who's laughing now? Not me, that's for sure. "Great, everything completely normal," says Dr Fat Finger.

No, this is far from normal, I want to tell him. Your eagerness to slide one of your jumbo digits into my arsehole every time we meet is far from normal. All I can manage is a meek, "Good".

I get dressed and he bids me farewell. As I close the door behind me, I attempt to look on the positive side. I have my prescription for a new cream and I'll be joining a new doctors' practice next month. I'll never have to see Dr Fat Finger again. Halleluiah, as Brother Lee Love might have said.

DEC 2007 – PAPA LAZAROU

Recently I was talking to one of my friends who works in the NHS in the West Yorkshire district. He's a physiotherapist, so his department sometimes crosses paths with neurology. He doesn't often work in Wakefield and he's never met my multiple sclerosis consultant, Dr Leezou, but he has heard of him. Oh yes, he has heard of him, and not because of his brilliance or his popularity amongst his patients. In fact my friend laughed when I mentioned Leezou's name. It seems his reputation goes before him, a reputation that extends somewhat beyond the environs of Wakefield.

Remember how he broke the news to me that I had MS? Apparently he is well-known for his bluntness, his total lack of bedside manner, or indeed any kind of empathy for his patients at all. This has garnered him the nickname of Papa Lazarou among some colleagues. Of course, he's not anywhere near as weird or scary as the character from *The League of Gentleman* and much of this has to do with the slight resemblance of his real name, but still, it holds up to some scrutiny.

Senior doctors often display some detachment from the people they are treating, I believe. The person in their care is just a case, a puzzle, an experiment. Someone to patronise, or bamboozle with scientific double-speak. I've read that this demeanour is partly out of necessity, as they need some emotional distance from those in their charge. If they get too involved on a personal footing, what if they have to impart bad news, or see that person die? Fair enough, but Leezou takes aloofness to the next level. I don't think he really sees a person at all, a person who might be trying to come to terms with a difficult change in his life.

Ever since the day I was diagnosed, I've noticed he says everything with a half-smile – some would say a smirk – that I think he's adopted to compensate for his lack of genuine empathy for the subject, or patient as they are generally called. It doesn't make me feel at ease. It is not friendly, as I presume it is meant. It just comes across as demonic, like those preachers that talk of nothing but God, but look like they probably work for the other side in truth. If eyes are truly the window to the soul, the view when I look at him is one of an emotional wasteland.

Here I am, though, in his waiting room, as I don't appear to have much choice in the consultant who is assigned to me. If I was paying for this service, I would immediately search for an alternative. But it's free, so let's not be too negative about the situation. And he is old, which provides two glimmers of light. One, he must have gathered a massive amount of experience in the field. He must really know what he's on about, even if he talks to you as if you're a bothersome child. Two, he might retire soon. Then again, I could conceive that some medical professionals when they're nearing retirement take their foot off the gas. They stop reading the latest papers, cease doing anything but the minimum and begin to speculate on how they can improve their golf handicap rather than how they can improve the lot of their patients.

Whatever the case, I still have little choice. Yes, I know, I could demand a second opinion, but I'm not sure there is anyone else in this department in Wakefield with the same level of seniority, so I'd be relying on someone from a different hospital. How long would it take to see them? Would they be any better? What if I ended up seeing Papa Lazarou from then on, he got wind that I had sought a second opinion and out of spite his treatment of me went even further downhill?

No, he'll have to do for now.

As I walk into his office, he's on the phone. 'Is Dave there?' I hear him say. In truth, he's neither on the phone nor enquiring as to the whereabouts of Dave. This Papa Lazarou daydream is just something to entertain me as I try to ease myself into the surroundings.

"How are you today, Andrew?"

So far, so good, Papa. You're giving the impression of viewing me as a human being, though it would have been a nice touch if you had looked at me. "I'm OK, thanks," I reply, but I don't think he hears, as he's already onto his next question.

"How are you recovering from your recent relapse?"

"Not too bad," I say. I'm about to give him more details, but he's reading from his notes, without looking up at me.

"It was in August, yes?"

"That's ri—"

"And what form did this relapse take?" He finally looks up from his notes. I see the half smile/smirk has been engaged.

"Well, I had a urinary infection and after I'd had that a couple of days, the pins and needles in my legs kind of rose up my body till they reached my stomach and I got tingling in my fingers a bit too."

I want to tell him also how my legs become weak quicker and about the losing a slipper on the stairs incident, but before I can he says, "Let's take a quick look at you. Take your shoes and socks off please."

When he uses the word 'quick', he really means it. I've endured these tests a couple of times before, but he has obviously run through them a million times with various patients and clearly can't wait to get them done. I'm told to walk in a straight line, platting my legs, like I'm a potential drunk driver, then I'm on his examination table. He bangs a tuning fork and holds it to my ankle. "Can you feel that?"

"Yes."

He repeats it on the other ankle. "And that?"

"Ye—"

"Is there a difference in the sensation?"

I don't really know, it was done so rapidly. I need him to do it again in order to give him a true answer, but there's no way I'm going to make that request, so I just mumble, "No, not really."

He moves on to the dreaded pin. This is a highly sophisticated test where he sticks a sharp pin into various parts of my feet and legs and barks at me, "Can you feel that? How about that? And now? Now? Now? Now?"

My responses are all either, "Yes, yeah and ow yeah," but inwardly they are a mixture of, 'Yes, I bloody well can, that hurts,' and tearfully crying, 'I don't know, I don't know, you're doing it so quickly my brain hasn't time to process the information it is receiving. Please stop.'

He proceeds to test the strength in my legs. "Push against my hand. No, upwards, upwards!"

I'm sorry I misunderstood Mr Lazarou. Please don't take me away to the circus.

Once he's finished chastising me with the leg strength tests, I put my socks and shoes back on and he takes me out into the corridor to walk up and down. "How far can you walk usually?" he asks.

My legs definitely become fatigued sooner since the relapse. "For about forty-five minutes." After that duration I generally find I have all the grace of Long John Silver, as my right leg starts swinging about uselessly.

"No, no," Leezou snaps. "What kind of distance can you cover?"

I don't know! I don't take a pedometer with me. "A couple of miles? Three or four?" I'm sorry, I really don't know. All I'm really dwelling on regarding my legs is that I've had to give up football for the time being. I was finding I couldn't run any more from about twenty minutes in and was having to go in goal. I was then even finding it difficult to stand up in goal. It was like weakness had taken an iron grip of all my muscles below the waist. It's what one could call a proper pisser and isn't helped when someone suggests with a chuckle that maybe it's, like, y'know, age catching up with you. No it is not fucking age catching up with me. I'm not even forty. I should be able to stand up without feeling like I'm going to collapse. I wish I could Freaky Friday them, just so they understood.

The tests over, we sit back down in his room. It's difficult to reckon how much he has learnt from them when he rushed through them like that and of course, there's no way he's going to tell me. He does offer me one piece of information, however, and it's not good news.

"You had another MRI on the 20th," he says, peering again at my notes. "Another lesion found in the upper something or other."

Instead of 'something or other' is a technical term not intended for the layman. He elaborates that this means they've detected another lesion in my upper spine, to go with the one already in my spine lower down and the two in my brain.

"This would explain the heightening of your symptoms," he tells me. "Probably as a result of the relapse you had in August."

There's a short pause. I've learnt to take advantage of these when they arrive when I'm in PL's presence.

"Are these new symptoms likely to be permanent or will I recover?" I ask him.

"Impossible to say, I'm afraid."

This is usually the way with my MS enquiries – a big fat shrug.

"So as I mentioned at our last meeting, you have the option of an interferon treatment. Have you given this any more thought?"

Yes I have. Lots. But I'm still no closer to a decision. Injecting myself, whether that be once a week, three times a week or every day, depending on the particular drug, is the first mental hurdle I would have to overcome. Then there are the side effects – flu-like symptoms mainly. They sound horrible. And on top of everything else, it can affect fertility. The way things are, I'm seriously wavering on our original plan to have another child, but in reality, I've gone full ostrich head on the subject. Kate has as well, I think. I have the option of freezing my sperm, but there's no guarantee that my boys will tolerate the cold well and be ready for action as and when. Kate and I really need to discuss it some more, but how can we come to the correct decision when we have no idea what the future holds?

"Yes. I still can't decide," I tell him.

"Well, I would definitely recommend trying one of the different options, but of course the final decision rests with you."

Doesn't it just.

"You have all the brochures on the various treatments?"

"Yes, I'll have another look through them."

"Very good." He passes me a yellow form. "Give this to the receptionist on your way out."

I'm about to leave when he says in a weird, rasping voice, 'Want to buy some pegs, Dave?'

Obviously, he doesn't really say this. It's a line from *The*

League of Gentlemen that has become another building block of my pretend world. Otherwise, this is starting to feel all too real.

CHRISTMAS 2007 – IT'LL BE LONELY THIS CHRISTMAS

I can hear everyone downstairs enjoying themselves. The laughter of relations is rising like a joyous warmth, seeping through the floorboards of the bedroom. E's laughter is the loudest of all. He'll be four in a couple of weeks. I asked him the other day if he was looking forward to his birthday. "I don't want to be four," he said. "I'm having too much fun being three." His grasp of the concept of fun is undoubtedly the most prominent development of his personality. We must be doing something right. I just wish that he didn't want to play constantly. It can be draining and my body doesn't seem to need an excuse to feel drained. But I always try to drink it in. I know he won't see me as the foreman of the fun factory for ever. I have to make the most of it whilst I can, in every sense.

The sounds of the little man having the time of his life come crashing through the ceiling once more. Christmas when you're three – forgive me as I lie here in bed unable to join in, a pitiful wretch approaching middle-age, if the thought crosses my mind that it's all downhill hereon. I can work out from the sounds that he's currently beating up his uncle with the oversized inflatable cotton buds that Santa brought him, dressed up in the little Shrek outfit we got him. Of course he had to change into it immediately and the excitement hasn't ended all day. I smile briefly but then remember that I'm now up here on my own and why that is. Fun is currently something belonging other people.

For the last two weeks or so I've been feeling tired constantly, as well as, strangely, permanently hungry. I get the tiredness – I have MS, what did I expect? But why am I always hungry? I can feel utterly fatigued but then eat something and I start to feel much better. The energy boost doesn't last, though, while often I can't seem to satisfy my appetite. I've become one of those fridge foragers who doesn't know what he wants but knows that he needs to stuff something in his mouth.

Is this really part of my MS symptoms? It must be. I just can't see why MS fatigue would make me want to eat. It's not one of the side effects that I've read about and why would eating make me feel better, if only temporarily? MS fatigue isn't the result of a lack of nutrients. It operates in the central nervous system, not the stomach. All I can say for certain is that chronic fatigue is casting its shadow on my life more and more often. Is it the stress of Christmas, all the extra work? This is probably the first Christmas that E has a chance of remembering. I hope he doesn't remember the absence of his dad.

I want to be part of this. I try to rise from my bed again. It's no use. The mind is willing but the body just won't respond. It's as if I'm lying beneath sheets made of lead; like there's an invisible force field around me that instead of protecting me is holding me down, not allowing me to move. My arms are like paper, pushing against a stiff wind. My legs are made of plasticine. How that little fella Morph used to have so much energy, I don't know. On the other hand, I'm starting to understand that guy I met in the neurology ward the day I was diagnosed, the one who was just lying on his back motionless. 'I just wanted to rest today.' I too just want to rest. No, that's not quite right. I need to rest. I have to rest. I have no choice.

*

"How are you feeling, love?" Kate has come in to check on me. "Are you up to coming down yet? E has been asking after you."

My body twitches as I try not to cry. It's no use. I make the spluttering noise announcing its arrival and suddenly it's pouring from me.

"Love, what's wrong?"

"I just want to play with my son," I croak through the tears. The way my voice cracks, struggling to make the words intelligible, makes me cry harder. I feel so pathetic.

Kate sits on the edge of the bed and strokes the side of my head. "I know," she says. "You'll be better after a rest."

Maybe for a bit, but I'm not going to be properly better ever again, am I. I know this is the snivelling of the self-pitying fool, but when you're lying in bed on your own in a darkened room late afternoon, feeling like a great weight is pushing you down into the mattress, it's an inevitable consequence. The wallowing pit calls your name loud and clear.

She tells me what E has been up to and talks about a few things that people have been saying downstairs. I feel a little better. Expelling some water from my eyes has released some of my misery, which is very weird when you think about it. The human body has some bizarre functions. What other animal cries? And feels better afterwards?

"I'm making some tea and coffee in a bit? Do you think you'll be able to join us?" Kate asks.

"I'll try," is all I can manage. With that she leaves me to my gloom.

One significant relapse and I'm dreaming of getting out of bed for a cup of tea. I think back to those years when MS would visit me with a few mild signs that something wasn't right, then rapidly depart before I'd had chance to take any real note. What carefree days. Going about my business in blissful ignorance. How I long for a time when those were the worst of my MS symptoms. Hindsight, you bastard. Nobody likes you. No one thinks of you except to curse you. Don't be fooled by people saying, 'Hindsight is a wonderful thing.' You're not. You're a terrible thing that can only piss you off when you look at what has transpired.

I think another visit to Papa L is very likely in the new year.

4th JAN 2008 – DEFEATED

I admit defeat. It's exactly two years since I walked into work that day with cold feet, my MS symptoms suddenly accelerated, the first day of my new normal. Now I'm back in Leezou's office, sorting out starting me on an interferon treatment.

I've decided, or at least convinced myself, that I'm not that bothered about having another kid. I'm not the most child-centric sort. Kate had to work on me for years to persuade me it was a good idea. Thank God she did because life would seem pretty empty now if we turned back the clock, but one is tiring enough, particularly when you have MS. Not that I'm brave enough to tackle the subject with her head on, but I get the feeling Kate is coming round to this way of thinking too. She comes from a family with two brothers and had an ideal in her head that we would also have three, but reality is starting to show its hand. It's all the clichés – expensive, knackering, joyful, yes, but also frustrating and worrying. I've decided I can be a better dad to one than two or three, particularly in the circumstances. Of course, if Kate puts her foot down, my best intentions will be trampled underfoot like a feeble flower.

As it is, I'm here discussing the various choices available to me from the range of unpalatable treatments, all of which involve sticking a metal spike into my skin and enduring an array of unpleasant side effects.

"So have you come to a decision, Andrew, on which treatment you would like to begin?"

'Like' is not the word I would use, but I have come to a conclusion on which one I feel will be the least objectionable alternative. "Yes, I think I'll give the Avonex a try."

For this one I'll only have to inject myself once a week, deep into the muscle. The side effects might be more acute, but anecdotal evidence suggests that the headaches, nausea, fever and injection site reactions will settle down after a few months of hell.

"Very good. I'll set the wheels in motion."

If the Avonex can slow down the progression of the MS, all the shit it is going to send my way will be worth it. That's what I have to tell myself anyway. It doesn't reverse any of the damage already done, but it is supposed to reduce the risk of further relapses by around a third. Not great odds or a wonderful new world that I'll be embracing, but it's as good an option as they can currently offer me.

"How are your symptoms generally at the moment?" Papa L asks me.

"About the same. I've been getting one new symptom, though."

I hesitate for a moment. It's in an area that I'm in no major hurry to discuss with another human being, medical practitioner or not. But fuck it. I don't give a shit right now. I'll be sticking needles in my legs before you know it. This will just be a collection of words I'm spilling forth.

"I'm getting a bit of numbness in my anus."

Everything about that sentence is wrong. The sentence as a whole and when do I ever use the word 'anus'? Numbness of the arsehole, Dr Leezou. Is that better? Not really. The one fundamental problem remains – we're still talking about my anus/arsehole.

Leezou doesn't blink. "How does this manifest itself?"

How do I phrase this? "It's just sometimes, like when I go to the toilet, I can't tell if I'm finished or not." I stop short of using the phrase 'anal receptors' that popped into my head. Where the hell did that come from?

"Hmm."

There's another pause in the conversation as we both contemplate my bowel movements.

"Well let me know if this becomes any worse. I would suggest that it is nothing to worry about."

Probably not. It's only slightly numb in that area and it certainly didn't feel that numb when Dr Fat Finger was performing his party trick. Just something to add to my ever growing list of annoyances.

I think we're both relieved when the discussion moves back to the main topic.

"So, I'll arrange for your first delivery shortly. One of the MS nurses will then be able to visit you in your home to offer you advice on injection techniques and so on. Then it's full steam ahead."

Papa L shoots me his patronising/demonic/vacuous half-smile, as he makes another attempt at being a warm human being. As usual, he misses his target, but at least he's trying, I suppose.

"We'll just have to do some routine blood tests first, to make sure everything is okay for you to start on the Avonex. If you take this and head up to phlebotomy now." He holds a form out to me while looking at his computer screen instead of me, in that dismissive way that he has perfected (unlike the half-smile he keeps attempting). Normal service has resumed.

I take the form from him. I've resisted the needle for long

enough. I'm in your hands, Mr Lazarou.

'You're my wife now,' is the phrase that chimes in my ears as I leave.

FEB 2008 – MY BODY HATES ME

Another day, another appointment, another department. Endocrinology this time. It's not something I'd heard of till the other week, but here we are, leg two of my tour of the NHS.

I'm due to meet one Dr Amalia Gonzalez. I roll her name around my tongue and try to picture her. Undoubtedly, she has a sexy name. With little else to kill the time while I wait to see her, my mind sets off on a little fantasy. She's around thirty-five, slim but curvy and is wearing a figure hugging white lab dress (is that a thing? – it is now). She's olive-skinned, with dark brown hair, mostly tied up but with a couple of strands falling down at the front, framing her high-cheekboned, full-lipped face. Of course, she's wearing glasses because she's super-intelligent, but removes them to talk deep into your soul about medical shit and stuff. Stop it, Andy. This is not a good idea. You are setting yourself up for inevitable disappointment. And besides, is this fantasy not, more or less, just Kate dressed up in lab gear with the cunning disguise of a pair of specs? How unimaginative.

I guess I'm trying to distract myself from why I'm here. I'm still yet to pierce the surface of my skin with a single needle and this is why: back in January 2006 when I was diagnosed with MS I had some blood tests. Amongst other things, the results showed that my thyroid levels were as they should be. However, two years later, when I really need them to be normal so I can start injecting Avonex into my body, they've decided to head off the scale. Thyrotoxicosis it's called apparently and I'm here to look at ways of sorting it out. With Dr Amalia Gonzalez.

Is it worth acquiring yet another medical problem so I can meet her? Of course not, but it's a nice line in compensation, even if the reality will surely trounce the fantasy.

My name is called. I find myself automatically adjusting my hair, but Dr Sexy will have to wait. I'm just led into a side room by a stout nurse. I sit down on her instruction in a weighing chair. First, she takes my blood pressure. Does anyone else worry that something will go wrong with the machine and the armband thingy will keep tightening around its prey to the point where it starts to crush muscle and finally bone? The nurse is frantically trying to turn the evil contraption off but it's having none of it. I start to scream but it's too late. My arm is squeezed so hard that the arm is severed and the lower portion of it falls to the ground with a thud.

Of course, it stops inflating just at the point at which it starts to become uncomfortable, like it does every time. The nurse announces the reading, which as ever means nothing to me, but then says, "Good, totally normal."

Well that's a triumph. One part of me that's working as it should be.

She notes down my weight. Though I'll be forty before the year's out, it's the same as when I was nineteen – 10s 5lbs. I come from a long line of skinny bastards. All that eating I was doing over Christmas doesn't seem to have had any effect, so far anyway.

The nurse tells me I can take a seat back in the corridor. The doctor will see me soon. Dr Amalia Gonzalez. We will soon be alone together at last.

*

I'm playing a game of golf on my phone when she opens the door. I look up and I see her and... (cue Leslie Phillips voice) hello! Of course, she isn't wearing the outfit of my fantasy and doesn't quite match the description conjured up by my adolescent imagination, but she's young and attractive and I definitely would – if I wasn't devoted to Kate obviously and Dr Gonzalez had any interest in me other than treating me for thyrotoxicosis. It's certainly a nice change from Papa Lazarou.

I take a seat and she has a look through my recent medical history on screen. "I just need a quick read through your notes," she explains.

Leezou would just be making me sit there in silence, not acknowledging my presence. 'I like your accent,' I hear myself say. Fortunately, I only hear myself say this in my head. Neither do I say out loud, 'You have beautiful eyes. They're dreamy.' I content myself with trying to decide from which country she may hail. Spain? Rather route one. Portugal? Or maybe somewhere in South America. Brazilian? Yes, let's go with that. More exotic. For a moment, I've forgotten why I'm here and about my other medical problems, but then she speaks again in her sexy Brazilian accent.

"So, your readings are rather high..." She talks a little about levels of T this and T that, which is way beyond my sphere of knowledge, but I'm still enjoying the conversation.

'Have you ever thought of straightening your hair?' I ask.

'Sometimes, yes,' she replies, running a hand through her brown curls in the fantasy branch of the chat.

"So options," she says, back in reality. "The letter from the MS

Co-ordinator states that you want to start beta interferon treatment… Yes, we'll have to get your levels closer to the normal range first. I think we'll put you on Carbimazole first. We'll see how you are on this in a few weeks."

"Are there any side effects?"

"No, not really, a very very small number of people have side effect, but your readings are rather high. I'm not sure it'll bring the levels down sufficiently."

I'm hoping that she's now going to offer me a range of other options, but I'm happy to wait while I watch her push away from her desk a little and turn to me. I can now see the whole of Dr Amalia Gonzalez once more. She's wearing trousers but that's probably just as well.

"One of the most common treatments in these kind of cases is radioactive iodine," she tells me. The phrase really shouldn't make me swoon, but I've properly gone now and I'm just enjoying hearing her voice. "It's not without its complications, though. I read in your notes that you have a four-year-old son."

"Yes," I manage.

"The treatment is perfectly safe, but you will have to keep your distance from him for a couple of weeks afterwards."

For the last five minutes, I've been wondering how soft her skin might be, but her last statement has jolted me out of my reverie.

"Why? What's involved?" The notion has crossed my mind that I'm not at all sure of a treatment that means I have to keep away from my child for a fortnight. What is this shit?

"OK." She warms up for her explanation by, I can't help noticing, clasping her hands together between her thighs. Impure thoughts rush from brain to crotch. My remaining thoughts maintain their rapid circling trajectory in my head. "The radioiodine is a small capsule that has a low level of radioactivity.

The dose is taken up by the thyroid, reducing the levels of hormone that the thyroid produces." She gives me a reassuring smile. I have to say it tramples all over Leezou's efforts. "You would be perfectly fine to have contact with adults immediately afterwards, so long as they are not pregnant. But children, because they are still developing, it is recommended that you keep some distance for two weeks.

"Maybe the Carbimazole will be sufficient to bring your levels down, but if you wish to start your interferon treatment soon, I would suggest you seriously consider the radioactive iodine treatment."

Could I stay away from E for that amount of time? Could he stay away from me for that long? No playing games together, no wrestling on the bed, no big hugs.

"Well, I'll have a think about it. Are there any other side effects with this?"

"There is a very small chance it could affect fertility. Certainly, you should avoid unprotected sex for a while."

Oh God. Dr Amalia Gonzalez is sitting three feet away from me and talking about sex, talking about me having sex. Is she imagining me having sex? Almost certainly not, but I let her words hang there just for a couple of seconds, just for the hell of it.

"I think we've decided we're probably going to stick with one," I say. Of course, in truth we've just buried the decision under a great mountain of sand, but it's certainly starting to seem like the odds are against us. MS may mean looking after another kid will be a challenge. Treatment for MS may cause infertility. Treatment I probably have to go on before I can start treatment for MS causes, guess what, infertility.

My poor boys and I, what are we to do? Under attack from all sides. And after my meeting with Dr Amalia Gonzalez, some more unfortunates are likely to be discarded when I get home.

Andy Reynard

MAY 2008 – SHIT SUPERHERO

Carbimazole has reduced the torrent of hormones that my thyroid is producing but nowhere near enough. I'm already becoming familiar with needles skewering my body as blood keeps being taken from my arm for testing, but if I want the privilege of injecting myself every week, I'm going to have accept the radioactive iodine challenge.

I enter the endocrinology department, resigned but also hopeful. The hope though has nothing to do with the treatment I'm about to undertake. It's just the potential to see Amalia again that is helping me to deal with this (in my fantasy, we are now on first name terms). I'm shown into the main corridor and see the nameplate Dr A Gonzalez on one of the doors, but I'm directed to the end room. Maybe she'll be in there.

No such luck. The only medical person I can see is a male nurse. There is one other guy and three women. Patients, I presume. They are sitting around in a semi-circle like some kind of support group. Are we going to have to introduce ourselves and tell the story of why we're here? 'Hi, my name's Andy and I have an overactive thyroid. I have no control over it. I need help.' Cue crying. Fortunately, there is nothing more than a casual acknowledgement of each other's presence before the nurse begins to speak.

"OK, looks like we're all here now." He presses his hands together and smiles. "My name's Simon, by the way."

I now feel as if I'm at some kind of works away day. Unlike the training days I've occasionally been sent on by my employer, I guess I'll have to stay awake for this one.

"I'll be explaining how we're going to do things today and how to take your medication." He takes a seat at the front of the class. "So, the radioiodine is contained in a case that we'll bring in shortly. The case contains five sealed containers similar to a test tube with a capsule in each one. You'll all be getting slightly different doses, but the method involved in taking the medication will be the same for all of you. When you are ready, you remove the seal from the tube and swallow the capsule immediately. It's important that you don't hesitate before you swallow the capsule, as once the seal is broken, the tube can't be resealed. So, open the tube and immediately pour its contents into your mouth, then swallow some of the water in the cup provided. Any questions?"

Is everyone sitting on the same question? What happens if the seal is broken and you don't swallow the capsule? Why is it so important that this stuff isn't left lying around in the open air? What the hell are we putting into our bodies here? Of course, no one says anything.

Nurse Simon grabs a wad of A4 paper and starts to hand out sheets to each of us. "First, I need you all to sign a waiver form agreeing that everything involved in taking the medication has been explained to you fully."

I skim through the form. It doesn't seem to contain anything that I haven't already been told, but like every person ever faced with a waiver form, there's not the slightest chance that I'm not going to sign it. I give it a cursory scan in order to follow the accepted social rule that has been written in stone, then scribble my signature at the bottom.

He collects all the forms. "Good. OK, everyone ready?" he says, beaming reassuringly in our direction. I have the sudden sensation that we're all cruising in a small plane and are preparing to experience our maiden skydive. The sliding door has just been opened.

He brings in the box that I have to remind myself only houses five vials of medication. I still can't stop my cinematic senses from searching our surroundings for a laptop. I picture Simon tapping in the nuclear codes before the lead-lined case can be opened. As it is, there are just a couple of metal clips between us and nuclear armageddon. The lump of uranium casts a green glow across the room.

I shake off these unhelpful daydreams, but then have a genuinely worrying thought. I have difficulty swallowing tablets. What if it gets stuck in my throat as large tablets sometimes do and it consequently fails to dissolve in my stomach acid. What if all the radioactivity fixes in my neck rather than flowing into my bloodstream and my Adam's apple starts to glow red. It sounds like the storyline of a crap comic – The Birth of Shit Superhero.

He hands out the tubes to everyone. When he gets to mine he says something that adds to my concern: "Biggest dose for you, Mr Reynard." He looks down at his form again. "My, those are pretty high, aren't they."

Wahoo! Shit Superhero wins the Battle of the Thyroids. Of course, I have no idea how my hormone levels rate against my fellow skydivers. I'll have to take your word for it, Simon.

We all wait, ready for instruction.

"OK, remember, as soon as the tube is open, you need to ingest the capsule. Ready? If everyone opens their tubes now. Good. Now tip the capsule straight into the mouth."

Everyone does as he says and happily, mine sinks straight down. I picture the capsule travelling through my body like the submarine in Fantastic Voyage. My radioactive crew wave to my thyroid, shouting out, 'We'll be back in a bit,' before they descend my alimentary canal to the lobby on the middle floor.

How did all this happen? I've more or less come to terms with the fact that I have multiple sclerosis. I did not expect to have a radioactive cherry on top of this particular cake. Have I offended a higher power, the Fates? No, remember you follow the teachings of the wise philosopher who said that shit happens. Shit happens to good people, shit happens to bad people and it happens to everyone in between (my people).

Capsule swallowed, there is not much else to do. Nurse Simon tells us to wait a while and reiterates the necessity of maintaining some social distance from women we don't know in case they're pregnant and, of course, from children. Inevitably, I think of Little E. It's going to be hard for both of us, but we've talked it out and he seems to understand. He understands enough anyhow to know that our separation is not out of choice. We'll get through it. And at least I might get some rest from the playing... the endless endless playing.

I can handle it so long as it works. Come on thyroid, play ball. I need you to calm the fuck down so I can move on to Chapter Two of My Shit Year.

OCT 2008 – THE NEEDLE AND THE DAMAGE AVERTED

It's the last stretch of the motorway before I peel off at my junction. Work today was not particularly taxing, if you don't count the superhuman effort it required to crawl out of bed at least an hour before I was ready, but there's no time to relax when I get home. Not that there ever is these days. I always have a four-year-old demanding playtime as soon as he hears the front door opening. Today, though, he's going to be missing out. The MS nurse is paying me a visit in about twenty minutes and by the time she leaves I'm going to be in no fit state for any demanding games.

It's been a mixed bag since my venture into the radioactive world nearly six months ago. First, the bad: I had another bladder infection in June. Fortunately, I managed to avert much damage being done, as I rushed to the doctors' followed by a cloud of dust at the earliest onset of any symptoms. Having it before made it easier to spot the signs and I was taking antibiotics before the infection could get its claws into me. Still, my pins and needles were a little heightened and made an appearance in my fingers again, but happily it all settled down soon enough.

The good news is that the folk at Endocrinology contacted me to tell me that my thyroid levels were back to normal, so the radioactive iodine was clearly successful. The two weeks after swallowing that charged capsule were difficult, but E took it in his stride and the hug I was able to give him at the end of our period of social distancing was one of the best I've ever given anyone. And the result is that Papa L is happy for me to finally begin injecting myself with my chosen interferon treatment, Avonex. That's the purpose of the MS nurse's visit. She's going to talk me through how to do it and whatever else may be involved. I can't say I'm looking forward to this new chapter – who would – but the alternative is risking my body failing further, in a more rapid fashion. If they can't fix me, this is the best option available. I've had long enough to wait, long enough to come to terms with it. I just want to get it started now.

As I arrive home, E attacks me in the hallway. Fortunately, I avoid a punch to the balls as happened once recently. His Power Rangers DVDs have a lot to answer for. Kate has taken the first syringe out of the fridge this afternoon, as I requested. You have to keep it refrigerated but it's supposed to attain something close to room temperature before you inject. Having liquid with a temperature of three degrees swimming through your blood is not something anyone is going to enjoy. I turn the thin plastic pack around in my hand, as I wait for the nurse to arrive. She's on time, so I don't have to sit in contemplation for too long. Conversation is here to distract me.

"Do you prefer Andrew or Andy?"

That's a good opener, Nurse Janet. I hate it when someone launches straight into calling me Andrew without a second thought. I always think it makes you sound like a precious wanker if you correct the person and say, 'Actually, it's Andy,' so I appreciate you asking and giving me the opportunity to say, "Andy." Andrew reminds me of being told off as a child.

"How are your symptoms at the moment?"

I try to avoid sighing. I recognise that it's an appropriate question, but it's one I'm always having to field. "They've not really changed in the last year. My legs get weak after a while, you know, when I exercise. I can walk for around forty-five minutes, sometimes an hour before my right leg starts swinging around. I can run about for... well it's a while since I did any running, but I could probably play football for around twenty minutes. If I rest for a bit, though, I can then do a bit more."

"Oh, that's good."

"Yeah, one of the worst bits, though, is my bladder problems. I sometimes think they're the worst part of it."

"Do you need to go really urgently, or do you find it difficult to go?"

"It's difficult to go. And difficult to continue going when I've started."

"Yes, very common, of course. There are a few things you can do. Have you thought about a catheter?"

Woah, woah! This little chat has suddenly changed gear.

"It's not as bad as people imagine," she continues. "You just insert a thin pipe into the end of the penis and up into the bladder."

Before my brain can stop my mouth, I find myself blurting out, "You want me to shove a pipe up where? Are you serious?"

"Well, it's worth considering if you're having a lot of trouble. You wouldn't have to use it permanently, just when your symptoms are at their most severe."

OK, I've considered it. The answer's still no fucking way. I strain to keep matters polite. "It's annoying, but I don't think I'm ready to go down that route."

"OK. Well another option is there's a device you can get that can agitate the bladder. It can help to get things started."

"What's that?"

"It's just a small thing that you hold in your hand that vibrates, rather like a… well it vibrates and you hold it against your bladder. The agitation can help to stimulate the urination reflex."

Kate and I exchange glances. It's plain that the medical professional in our midst was, as Junior Soprano would say, a cunt hair away from likening a medical instrument to a vibrator, particularly as she clearly suppressed a giggle. I'm guessing this thing buzzes like a vibrator as well. I decide to embrace the moment. We're all adults here. Let's not pretend we don't know what we're all thinking.

"Yes," I say, "I can see how well that's going to play at work when they hear it buzzing away. Why does Andy keep disappearing into the toilets with a vibrator?"

We all laugh and Nurse Janet now seems to be out of painful or totally impractical solutions to my bladder problems. After a brief discussion about the spectre of bladder infections, the conversation turns to the main reason for her visit.

"We advise that you take painkillers prior to injecting, around half an hour before. Just a couple of Paracetamol and two Ibuprofen. That should offset most of the side effects."

"Yes, I did that as soon as I got home," I tell her.

"Ah, OK, good." She fishes in her bag. "So I've brought some syringes and sponges for you to practise on." She hands one of each to me.

The sponge has apparently been made to replicate human flesh. She takes me through the procedure for sticking the needle into it. It's all pretty boring, but obviously stuff I need to know: wash hands, have clean toilet paper to hand for mopping up any blood, check batch number and use before date, remove cap, tap syringe to remove any bubbles.

I stare at the syringe, upright between my fingers. Even though this is just going to be pushed into a sponge, I think I know where my friend Dave would be at this juncture – lying in a heap unconscious on the floor. I tap the syringe, enjoying the sensation of being a doctor in one of those medical dramas that we've all seen, even though there's not actually any liquid in this dummy syringe. I then turn the syringe over and hold it just above the sponge, imagining that it's my leg. My heart beats a little harder as I begin to push the metal point downwards. The sponge is surprisingly resistant and as the needle makes its slow descent, unpleasant feelings rush through me, like the ones I experience whenever I pull cotton wool apart. I push the plunger down to complete my practice run, trying to blank out the thought that I'm going to have to do this for real very shortly.

"How did that feel?" Nurse Janet asks.

"Weird. I don't know if I'm going to be able to do this."

"I know it takes a bit of getting used to but you'll be fine. Do you want to have another practice?"

I have a sudden surge of resolve. Let's stop fucking around here. It's been months. No turning back.

"No," I say. "Let's do this."

APR 2009 – INJECTION OF POSITIVITY

Bathroom scales, impart good news like you used to do. Bollocks. Still showing that I've put on more than a stone between my first visit to endocrinology in February 08 and now. Can I use that traditional excuse that it's my glands, because of my thyroid problems and the fact that I was always hungry back then (the pie-glands as some people call them, due to the over-riding urge of the sufferer to eat lots of them). Or is it the lack of exercise due to the MS, or perhaps just the beginnings of middle-aged spread? Probably all three.

I'm half an inch off six foot (the bastard half inch as I think of it, though it is never mentioned when I tell people how tall I am – I'm six foot, goddammit) and I'm now 11st 7lbs. I imagine you're thinking that seems like a reasonable weight for your height, but after so long being 10s 5lb, it has been a bit of a shock. I certainly don't have the desire to take a delivery of any further timber. I don't want to be hauling my corpulent frame around on crutches.

Hopefully, now that my thyroid is back to normal, I can start shedding some pounds or at least maintain. I had an appointment at endocrinology in March and was told that everything was still fine with my bloods. Still no sign of Amalia – it was some bloke – but the news was all good. Looking back causes me to wonder what has been going on with my body for these last eighteen months. When I was feeling totally drained I assumed it was due to the MS, but having done extensive research into symptoms associated with an overactive thyroid – okay, ten minutes spent with Doctor Google and a couple of questions aimed at the endocrinology guy – I now realise that many of the symptoms cross over, so it's difficult to separate them. The lack of energy, the feeling of being completely washed out, the inability to move – it could have been as much because my thyroid levels were going nuts as because I have multiple sclerosis. The fact that these horrendous feelings generally improved once I'd eaten something certainly suggests that it was more to do with the thyrotoxicosis. The constant hunger definitely was.

I'm just grateful that this episode appears to be over. My constant cravings for food are no more and although my energy levels would still shame a sloth, I can at least get out of bed now when I want and get around fine. It's going to help fuel my determination not to expand any more. I don't want to be one of those guys in his forties who looks like the hose of a foot pump has been shoved up his arse and someone has said, 'Are you ready to look your age?'

I move over to the toilet, pull down the lid and take a seat. I pick up the plastic packet containing the syringe and prepare myself mentally. It's twelve months since the radioiodine treatment, six since I was easing a needle into a sponge with some trepidation, prior to the main event. Injection night is now just another part of the new routine, like brushing one's teeth, if you brushed them only once a week, it involved a significant amount of pain and some blood emerged from your mouth afterwards. I still experience a frisson of fear as I peel the packet open. I stare at the needle. Every time, I have to indulge in estimating how long it is.

An inch and a quarter? Inch and a half? Some interferons only need to do their work just beneath the skin, as you inject them every day or three times a week. This has to go deep into the muscle, as it has to stay in your body for longer.

The next obstacle is the dreaded bubbles. The liquid we're dealing with here could accurately be described as gloopy. If a bubble appears in it, it can be sizeable and getting rid of it can be a nightmare. The thrill I enjoyed the first time I tapped the chamber to burst them, pretending I was a hotshot doctor, has long gone. Now it's just a pain in the arse when all I want to do at this hour is get it over with and slither into bed. You flick it, your target pops, but the movement involved creates another bubble. I try now and sure enough, the big bubble has gone but it's given birth to three smaller ones. I try again and again and again, achieving a similar result each time till I'm no longer staring at three smallish bubbles – I'm back to staring at one big one again. Bastard bubbles. How I hate you so. I'm not even sure how important it is to get rid of you. Nurse Janet seemed to think I should involve myself in this tap dance, but I've heard elsewhere that it would take a hefty-sized bubble to kill you. Asking the question is on my to-do list.

The solution I am about to push into my body is finally clear of air. Time to choose a spot. It's one leg one week and the other leg next. You'd think I'd forget which leg got it last week, but somehow I always have a clear recollection of what I did on the last occasion. Right leg – prepare for pain. I give it a rub to warm up the muscle. At least that's what I tell myself, but it's probably just a delaying tactic really. I wet the hair in the area I'm going for, so I can part it and not push a hair into the needle hole like some kind of organic needlecraft. It's probably bad clinical technique to be spreading saliva on the area but I've not had any problems with it so far and saliva has antiseptic qualities, right? Okay, I've no idea really, but that's how I justify it. The needle looks extremely sharp as it hovers over my white skin, skin which looks extremely soft. I hope it's a good one. Sometimes it hits a spot where the flesh seems dead. Pain is minimal and there's not even a spot of blood when it comes back out. Other times the flesh seems to be composed purely of nerve endings, every one screaming, 'Why the fuck are you doing this to us?' For these performances, you can be sure that there'll be a mini geyser of blood once the needle is extracted.

OK, here goes. I take a breath and push the point against the surface of my skin, so it first depresses and is then broken. I may be in luck. The needle may be entering a dead zone. No pain yet, but I still edge the point further and further down at a funereal pace. I'm sure a nurse would be shaking her head if she was watching me, as I proceed to force the needle to disappear at pathetically slow speed. But I get the job done – it's now fully submerged in my leg and all I have to do now is get the Avonex into my system. I adjust my hand slightly so I have a proper grip under the lips either side of the chamber and begin to ease the plunger down towards the pointy end. This I also do in pitifully creeping fashion, but this time it's accompanied by a non-descript tune. I don't know why, but I always mouth some nonsense or two-note melody as the medicine goes down. I can't help it, but it somehow assists the process. "Do do do do do do do do do, boo boo boo boo boo boo boo boo boo boo." I pull the needle out, carefully but rather more quickly, and wait to discover how much blood follows. One small drop that I dab with a square of toilet paper. That should dry up quickly, no bother.

And that is that for another week. Well not quite. I can look forward to tomorrow when I will either have a banging headache all day, accompanied by some nausea, or more usually, a headache for a short amount of time accompanied by a single rush of nausea once when I stand up too rapidly. As I was advised, I always do the deed just before bed. If I get to sleep without any problem, I can avoid the worst of any side effects, as I'll be immune to the pain of the waking world. By the morning, we're coming down the other side of the mountain.

Yes, jabbing myself with this needle every week is working out okay. I don't think I'll ever look forward to it, but it's something I can handle. Let's be honest, you can handle most things if you have no choice and in everything that has happened to me in the last few years, my choices have been very limited.

One definite plus point is the effect it has had on my working hours. Tomorrow will be a day off, like all Wednesdays, which isn't the case for most people at my place. I just got shafted by MS. My colleagues all got shafted by our employer.

Let me explain. A few months ago, they told us that they wanted to make a big, exciting change to our working practices. They made us all convene in a cinema, lowered the lights and proceeded to make their momentous presentation. After a number of tedious slides, they finally reached the part of relevance to us all. We would have the option of flexible working hours. If we wished, we could compress our work time and, so long as we reached our total hours, could have a day off each week. Longer days, but a four-day week.

Most people were pretty enthusiastic about this state of affairs, but wondered what the company wanted in return. Surely they weren't doing this just to make us happy. Then the kicker arrived. Casual as you like, they dropped in a slide to say we would be moving from a thirty-seven and a half hour week to a forty hour one. For no more pay. Everyone went, 'Ah,' and were understandably dubious about whether they were prepared to hand over this pound of flesh. However, the lure of having a day off each week was still too great to resist for most people, even if you would have to work ten hours a day to take advantage of it. The deal was done.

Those that signed up to the scheme were like ducks in water, pigs in shit, hogs in heaven. I resisted for some time as I couldn't face a ten hour day and the attendant early start, but those with a day off each week talked so enthusiastically about their new working life that eventually I too put my snout in the trough. Everyone agreed that the new arrangement was a tremendous leap forward.

Well, not quite everyone. A mere five or six months later, the company gathered us for another tête-à-tête. They had thought long and hard about the situation and, unfortunately, they had decided that the compressed hours thing just wasn't working. Sorry, we're going to have to knock it on the head. A brave soul edged their hand into the air. Does that mean we'll be going back to a thirty-seven and a half hour week again too? Oh no, that bit's working a treat. But I thought that was the agreement. We move to forty hours but we can have a four-day week. Oh no, the hours thing was nothing to do with it. Anyway, no more questions? Great, see you Monday.

To say people we're pissed off is an insult to the phrase 'pissed off'. But I was one of the lucky ones. Part of the reason I had signed up to the devil's contract in the first place was because I was preparing to start my Avonex treatment and having a day off the day after injecting was something of a clincher. I told my boss this and, with the power of a chronic condition at my shoulder, they agreed to let me stay on the compressed hours. And because I have MS, none of my fellow drones were allowed to resent the fact.

So here I am slipping into bed with the happy prospect of a day off tomorrow. True, I may find myself feeling a bit rough at times, but it's still better than breaking out of my duvet-shaped cocoon way too early and shuffling off to work. Thrusting that spike into my leg once a week is never fun, but it's given me this advantage over my co-workers, so let's embrace it as best I can.

I lie on my back, my hands across my stomach. I start to think about my weight once more. It's about time I started exercising again. I want to play football above all else. The fact that I can think about running round a football field is another aspect of my circumstance for which I should be thankful. For some people with MS, the first sign they have it is a sudden paralysis of one of more limbs. How do I get to play again, though? The short months of compressed hours for everyone meant the regular Monday night games at work died a death. Too many people off on Mondays. No one has taken it upon himself to start it up again and anyway, the pace might well be beyond me now. There are some decent players in the company with a few youngsters i.e. people in their twenties added to the mix. I need to be playing alongside old, preferably slightly disabled people like myself.

It will require some thought. I give my lovely wife a quick kiss goodnight – I need to get to sleep before the Avonex starts kicking in – and roll over into a decent place.

OCT 2009 – GREAT ARSE, SHIT NEWS

I find myself singing the 1982 England World Cup song in my head. 'This time, more than any other time, this time.' The reason is Dr Amalia Gonzalez. Her name was on the letter I just handed in at reception. I've learnt that this does not necessarily mean she will be the one I see. I've been disappointed previously on my visits here to endocrinology. Then there was that other appointment where the letter suggested our paths would finally cross once more which was cancelled at the last minute. Then I missed the re-arranged appointment. Then the next as well. Just completely slipped my mind. I'm sure this had nothing to do with the fact that on those occasions I was due to see Dr Saag, a man and very much not a sexy woman.

The result of my forgetfulness is that I'm finally here five months later than I should have been. Please, Amalia, show thyself. I'm beginning to feel that you may be someone I conjured in a dream. Of course, you are merely balm to a battered soul, a distraction from the shit thrown my way. But an appearance would be most welcome right now.

I'm summoned by a nurse to the room at the end where they keep the weighing chair and the blood pressure monitor. She makes a note of my weight but doesn't tell me what it is, like it won't be important to me. I'm not going to waste the results of some proper scales and so ask her what the mighty weighing chair has announced.

"Seventy-three kilograms."

I know from my night-time visits to the bathroom scales that this is around 11st 7lbs. So, at least I've not become any heavier. Hopefully, I've peaked. A little exercise and I should be able to get it down easily. I've not got around to organising any football yet, but it's near the top of my current priorities. Next, the blood pressure test. Repetition must have weakened its mental grip on me. I think I treat it like everyone else now i.e. as if it's nothing at all. As usual, everything is normal.

With all the routine tests out of the way, it's time for the main event. I've barely sat back down in the waiting room when Dr Amalia Gonzalez is opening her door and calling my name. She offers me a warm smile as I rise. Does she give everyone that smile, or is there more to it? Does she recognise me? Does she ever so slightly... no, don't be stupid. Of course she smiles at everyone like that.

I take a seat and Amalia says, while looking through the notes on her screen, "So you were due to see us in June."

I sense a little admonishment in her voice. I'm sorry for missing the appointments Amalia, but your department did cancel one as well. Please don't shout at me. But then the warm smile returns and she asks me, "How have you been recently?"

"Fine," I tell her. "I feel myself again." Feel myself? Does that sound like I've fallen back into my regular pattern of masturbation?

She tells me that my bloods were fine when I had my last test a couple of weeks ago and talks about levels of this and that. At this point I'm afraid I'm just watching, rather than listening, assessing her hotness. Not right perhaps, but true. She's still the most attractive doctor I've come across, though absence may have allowed the heart and head to elevate her to a slightly higher plain than my personal taste warrants. She's certainly no Kate and let's face it, hailing from Brazil (or Spain or Portugal, certainly not the UK) her command of British comedies of the last thirty years is going to be basic at best. Mr Bean and Fawlty Towers won't cut it. Will she ever have heard of Father Dougal, Swiss Tony, Malcolm Tucker or their ilk? I don't think so. That's a third of my conversation gone.

I'm still enjoying being in her company. I feel like our meeting will soon be over, given that everything remains as it should be, so start to try and think of ways of extending the conversation. I know I should think of something regarding my thyroid but all that comes to mind is the question that's been occupying me recently – what causes an itch? I don't mean like with my eczema, where the skin is dry and flaky. No, what causes an itch when it is isolated and appears out of the blue? You're just watching the TV, perfectly relaxed, when suddenly the end of your nose itches. Just in one small spot. What reaction is taking place that makes it impossible to ignore it and why does scratching get rid of it?

Does Stephen Hawking consider this question on a daily basis? If he gets an itch on his nose, it must be really bad news. Amalia's a scientist. Could I drop this topic into our exchange? Maybe she'd think it was charming, or would the more likely reaction be, what's wrong with this weirdo? Doesn't he realise I'm busy?

Perhaps fortunately, the opportunity has gone. She says she wants to examine me. I shift in my seat a little as she moves towards me. She is now arm's length away from me and is feeling my neck. I don't know why she needs to prod my thyroid – yes, it's still there – but I'm glad she does. She's standing right in front of me, her breasts only a few inches from my face behind the thin shield of her blouse. And she's touching me. Admittedly, only because she has her hands around my throat, but all the better for imagining we are married in my alternate universe. She makes some grumbling noises like she can't get a good grip of my recently tamed gland. Maybe my Adam's apple is getting in the way. I've always hated it. It's more like Adam's grapefruit, or more accurately, Adam's pet vulture's beak. I hope her sighs of dissatisfaction are not because she can't fathom what she is touching. 'Sorry, in medical school we never encountered such a... an unusual... neck.' Of all the places of mine for her to stare at first. My neck is thin with this great, angular protrusion in its centre. It has to be in my top three worst physical features. I should have seen this coming. My view is considerably more agreeable.

But she is now asking me to change positions. This puts me in mind of only one thing. Frankly, this could not be going better. What's that, Amalia? You want me to turn around and put my knees on the chair? And do what with my head? Although I appreciate you ordering me about, I'm not sure what you mean.

She is now demonstrating what she means. I promise I have not engineered this – I really wasn't sure what it was she wanted me to do. But suffice to say that when I said this could not be going better, I was wrong. She is now in the chair, facing away from me, with her shapely Latin arse sticking out. Her fawn-coloured jeans are tight. She looks over her shoulder in my direction to complete the picture.

"Like this. If you can raise your head back a little." In what must be a sudden realisation of how this appears, she lets out the cutest giggle. I too laugh, but in truth it's just an effort to conceal the immoral thoughts that have now taken a firm hold of my entire being. I can literally feel the blood rushing down between my legs. Surely this shouldn't be happening. You don't enter a medical examination room and expect your doctor to adopt a highly suggestive sexual pose that begs the question, 'Would you like to fuck me now?'

The moment is fleeting, but one I'm not likely to forget. However, now it's my turn. I'm doing my best to copy what Amalia has just shown me. She is behind me. Oh no. That is not helping. I feel what I assume is her groin briefly touch my skinny backside. I'm now glad that what is happening in my lower regions is out of her sight. I tilt my head back as she told me to and she places her hands on my neck once more. The front of her jeans touch the back of mine again. I'm not sure what position this would be, but it's still charged with sexual electricity. OK, only for me, but still. She is rather more concentrated in trying to get a good feel of my thyroid.

Without warning, her whole demeanour changes. I can't quite ascertain what it is about her alteration in manner, but it's definitely detectable. She makes some concerning noises – I'm not quite sure why they seem concerning but they certainly don't sound like positive ones. She asks me to turn back around and she places her fingers on my throat again in various positions. I wonder some more about what she has found, while being more than a little conscious of the semi aimed at her.

"I'm just going to fetch one of my colleagues," she says. I would ask why but she is already dashing from the room. Dashing! That's not a good sign. Stop looking at her arse as she leaves! Concentrate on what might be happening. I think of Hugh Grant when he was caught having an intimate chat with Divine Brown in a car on Sunset Strip. From what I recall, he's supposed to have said, 'What's going on?' when the cop turned up and tapped on the window. I'm similarly aroused and bewildered.

I have little time to gain any composure, as Amalia returns with an older man I've not seen before. I now feel like the Elephant Man being passed around Victorian London's medical community, as he too is now prodding my neck. I hope she hasn't just asked him in for a laugh at this freakish Adam's apple I'm sporting. To be honest, there doesn't seem to be a great deal of mirth flying around the room.

He turns to her and says, "Yes, I agree. Get it booked in," or something very similar. He then departs, almost as rapidly as he appeared.

If this was Leezou, he would probably start banging on his keyboard without acknowledging anything out of the ordinary had just happened. Fortunately, Amalia has a human side. As she turns her chair towards me, her hands disappear into the tight space between her thighs like they did that first time we met. I try not to think about anything other than what she is about to tell me.

"So, we're a little concerned about your thyroid today. There feels to be a small lump on it."

She stops there. Is that all you're going to give me, Amalia? Maybe she's just choosing her words very carefully. I jump in with, "OK, what does that mean?"

"Well, we're not sure at the moment." She pauses again. After my recent dealings with the medical profession, I'm used to being given non-committal answers. "But it could be cancerous."

I suppose I should have seen that coming. Non-committal seems an awful long time ago already. A lump in my throat. Wasn't that the title of the book by one of Nigella Lawson's former husbands who had cancer? An entertaining read that was made into a TV screenplay. Spoiler alert – he died a few years after the lump was found, but not before a chunk of his neck and tongue had been removed, from what I remember.

"But we can't be sure at this stage. We need to do another test."

"What does that involve?"

"We need to perform a biopsy."

Sounds fun, like you're going to put on a play about my life.

I'm guessing it's not fun but tell me more.

"We use a fine needle to draw material from the area so we can analyse it further."

Things start to get a bit hazy as I picture a needle being pushed into my throat. I've become used to having injections through the self-administered ones of the last few months and the endless blood tests of recent years, but in the throat! That's a whole different level. Where next? My balls?

I force out a couple of questions about the future, questions that assume it is cancerous. Surgery is mentioned and also the promising prognosis associated with thyroid cancer. Still cancer, though, isn't it. But she is making me feel a little better in the aftermath of the immediate shock. She continues to talk and I try really hard to take it all in, but the pull of creating a league table of medical problems with attendant disability and my place within it is too great. The thyrotoxicosis was clearly Championship level. Probably trying to avoid relegation to League One, to be honest, but it certainly doesn't feel like it when you have it. And the treatment where I had to be radioactive for a while and couldn't even hug my son definitely sent me on an unbeaten run to the play off positions. That all aside, though, I have surely been Premier League material for the last few years on account of the MS. That's top half of the table stuff, pushing for Europe. No doubt I've lost a bit of ground, however, as I'm not particularly disabled with it. I can even run, up to a point. Yeah, for a while I might have qualified for the UEFA Cup or Europa or whatever they're calling it now, but the lack of genuine disability might have caused a loss of form.

Now though, cancer has entered the sporting arena. That has surely projected me into the Champions League places, along with such as the blind and those with serious heart disease. From what Amalia is telling me, I'm clinging to coattails, the Arsenal of the clinical world, but I've still played a blinder in this period of the season.

OK, I think it's now time to stop this. She's been on the computer sorting out this biopsy thing but has now turned back to me.

"That should go through to the receptionist. If you can check please when you leave. You should get an appointment through soon."

"How long?" I ask.

"It should be within seven days."

As I said, Champions League now. This is the NHS operating on a different level to the one to which I'm accustomed. I bid Amalia farewell.

*

Having checked that the receptionist is fully aware of the situation and what needs to be done, I walk through the hospital grounds back to the car. Well, I didn't see that coming, but who ever does hear the creep of cancer as it tip-toes towards you? What do you think about it all, Unlucky Alf? I feel his presence alongside me, the tap of his cane on the pavement almost audible.

'Bye 'eck, lad. You're an unlucky so-and-so, aren't you. I'm an old man now and beside a bit of trouble with m'waterworks, I guess I've been pretty lucky w'me 'ealth.' He chuckles to himself. 'Who'd 'ave thought it, eh? Me, a fitter fiddle than you! Mind you, see that ambulance yonder? Knowing my luck I'll be run over by one of them things.'

Sure enough, when another ambulance passes us, Alf catches a foot on the edge of the curb and stumbles. He falls into the road and the ambulance drives straight over his head, crushing it to a mushy pulp. Just as the wheel mounts his skull, I can hear the faint strains of one word coming from Alf's mouth: 'Bugger.'

I wince as this scene plays out. That's an ironic way to go, Alf. I'm sure you'll be back, though.

I pass the main entrance to the hospital, hoping to spot my favourite type of ill person. There are a few folk in dressing gowns fagging it outside. They're my second favourite type. I admire their commitment to their craft. Ah, brilliant. Here she comes, stepping slowly from the confines of the revolving door. Also dressing-gowned, she is wheeling her friend alongside her, one of those saline drip stand things. I don't know for sure that it's a saline drip – that's probably just something I've heard on a TV show – but you know what I mean. There's a bag of some liquid that's attached to her arm by means of a tube, pumping something into her body. But the fact that she's hooked up to this thing and she's resident on some ward that could be deep within the bowels of the building hasn't stopped her from indulging in the most essential activity of the day – receiving her regular shot of nicotine to the lungs. Fair play, madam.

I put my hands in my pockets. Despite the death row of puffing mannequins outside the hospital suggesting otherwise, there's a definite chill in the air. But not to worry, I'm soon back in the car. I stare through the windscreen and try to stop the noise. Cancer. I say it again to myself. Cancer. What am I going to tell Kate? Should I even tell her yet, or should I wait till I've had the results of the biopsy. Yeah, there's no point in worrying her unnecessarily. Amalia was insistent that there was a good chance that it might be benign. Why share my concerns when it might be nothing? Yeah, I'm sure she'd understand my position. Cue Irish accent: 'That sounds like a grand idea, Ted. I've never been so sure of anything in my life.'

Looks like the noise has risen again. Father Ted one minute and now, as the word cancer announces itself again, I'm in one of those emotional dramas where the central character has just received the worst news imaginable. Would the actor be breaking down at this point, his face on the steering wheel, tears rolling down his cheeks? Probably, but nothing is coming from me. It just doesn't feel real, like much of my life. I'll be heading to work as soon as I start the engine and I know that I won't be brooding endlessly on the tiny limpet that has attached itself to the gland in my neck. No, I'm much more likely to be recreating the image of Dr Amalia Gonzalez kneeling backwards in that chair, pointing her great arse at me and giggling in sudden awareness of the beautiful image she has just offered to me.

OCT 2009 – THE PEDESTAL IS ERODED

It's one of those lovely bright October days where the cold bites in the shade but the sunshine pours down from a cloudless sky making it all OK. I'm sitting on a park bench in full view of that huge star, millions of miles away, observing a couple of squirrels as they prepare themselves for the winter months ahead. I'm not entirely sure what they're doing – I'm no naturalist – but I'm sure it's something to do with nuts. They've been hopping around for a while now and I'm still not bored of watching them. I have the park pretty much to myself as it's early morning. Positioned up here on a hill I can see over the trees in the distance, which are still in their full autumn dress of reds, golds and browns, and beyond them the city shimmers in the sparkling light. It's one of those scenes that makes you glad to be alive.

My mind casts back again to Dennis Potter's last interview. Riddled with cancer and in full knowledge that he would soon die, he talks of 'nowness', appreciating what is right in front of you and which may be taken away from you at any moment. The plum tree below his window has the blossomist blossom imaginable. It's as if he's seeing it properly for the first time. I focus on one of the squirrels. Is that the bushiest bushy tail I've ever set eyes upon?

I still haven't told a soul. That is why I'm in the park at this hour on a work day. I left at my usual commuting time, but I'm not due at the hospital for a while. I've found it quite easy to be honest. Parking news I'm not yet ready to deal with is one of my talents. I've pushed fears of what may reside in my body down a hole in my brain like a magician poking a handkerchief into his fist. Keeping shtum is much easier when you forget about it yourself. I realise this is probably an unusual response. I recall when my aunt was told that she might have cancer. She was on the phone at once and my mum and dad dropped everything to head straight over to see her, even though there was still the possibility it was nothing. My fourteen or fifteen-year-old self found everyone's reaction false and over-dramatic, though this may have been partly because I was busy adopting the eye-rolling demeanour of Holden Caulfield, as I negotiated my adolescent morass.

Anyway, turned out it was cancer and she was dead from it around eight years later.

Whenever this cancer thing has briefly reared its head in my mind, I've mainly reflected on the missed appointments. If it wasn't for my forgetfulness, would the lump even have begun to show itself? Would Dr Saag have had a feel of my neck (probably, nay hopefully, without attendant erotic poses) and said, 'Yes, everything's fine with that.' By the time I had another appointment and the lump had gone through a growth spurt, might it have sent out a few scouting parties to have a look around some of the other regions of its host? Maybe the lump's friends would have started to set up home in these comfortable places they had discovered. Who knows, but it's only a centimetre across at the moment. I don't know how quickly these things develop but I can't imagine it had been there long. Whatever the case, one thing is certain: if someone was going to discover a potentially cancerous growth in my neck, I'm glad it was Dr Amalia Gonzalez.

I check my watch. It's time to go and face the needle. Even the pull of the Brazilian belle isn't sufficient to make the journey one I take eagerly. I'm guessing she won't be doing the deed anyway. There was certainly no indication on the appointment letter. Just the thought of what's involved gives me a nauseous feeling in the stomach. All that cheers me up when I picture what I am about to experience is thinking once again about Dave and his needle phobia. I wonder if they'd be able to do it still if he was out cold.

I trudge to the car, thinking of squirrels curled up and cosy in their dreys over winter and trying my hardest not to visualise sharp rods of metal being forced into my neck in the manner of that other magician's trick – sliding swords through the black box containing the soft flesh of his lovely assistant.

*

Well what do you know, it's Amalia who's welcoming me into the room where I gulped down that radioactive pill last year. The older guy who she fetched for a second opinion when she first detected something might be amiss is also present. I'm invited to take a seat.

From their interactions, it quickly becomes clear that she is the junior partner in this operation. He is there in an observational/supervisory capacity. That makes sense as he is a lot older than her, but now I worry whether she knows what she is doing. Much as I'm happy to be close to her again, I'd be even happier if I knew this wasn't her first time. As he's telling her exactly where to insert it, I have the awful feeling that it is. As she bends down towards me, needle in hand, I try to concentrate on the breast area. It's not something I've ever had to put much effort into before (in fact, trying not to stare in that direction has generally been the greater battle) but soon even this diversion is denied me as I'm instructed to lift my head. I can only see the top of hers now. Then it hits me. Coffee breath. All over my face. Oh, Amalia! How soon the pedestal is eroded. Coffee breath is the worst. At least it's not mixed with fag breath. If that was the case, the pedestal would now be languishing in a skip.

There's another circumstance that is cooling my ardour – the tiny detail that she is about to force a needle into my throat. I hope she can't smell the sweat that is running from my pits. She feels my neck once more, presumably to confirm the entry point.

"OK, please, try to relax," she says.

She must have sensed that I'm a little tense. Perhaps the fact that I'm doing a decent impression of an ironing board gave the game away. Or is the odour emanating from under my arms as overpowering as her coffee breath?

"You may feel a little discomfort, but only a little."

I find these words, said by her in her very soft Brazilian accent, comforting and I try to calm myself. The shortest route to distraction is of course more impure thoughts about the woman in front of me. I apologise Amalia, but needs must.

I'm drawing a blank on the fantasies – hardly surprising considering my situation – when I feel the sharpness of the needle. It's only the briefest moment, then it's just like a having something stuck in the throat, only this time it is not a piece of meat or potato that's gone down the wrong way. She's really close now. Her lips must only be two or three inches from mine, but the thought is only a fleeting one. All I can still see is her hairline, while I'm suffocating under the weight of second-hand coffee fumes. I imagine being given a survey afterwards, asking for my opinion on my experience today. Sharpness of needle – 5; Hotness of medical practitioner – 5; Freshness of medical practitioner's breath – 1.

The voice of her expert coach comes from over her shoulder. "If you enter here now." I feel the needle being withdrawn and, after a tortuous thirty seconds of anticipation, going in once more. Is it a different needle? Not a particularly pertinent question to be honest. I'm sure they're all the same. I only have one neck, that's for sure. It's not been too bad so far – the thought of it has been worse than the actuality – but it now feels like she's twisting it in all directions, as if she's decided that I'm coping with it too well and I should be more uncomfortable. From my voice box, which must be really close to the needle right now, I let out an uncontrolled groan.

"I'm sorry," she says, "we just need to collect as many cells as possible."

No problem, Amalia, but would you mind awfully hurrying the fuck up? I pray that we're on the finishing stretch. The needle is withdrawn again. Are we done? Please tell me we're done.

I hear them in discussion but can't quite make out what it is they're saying. Have we tortured him enough? Shall I fetch the electrodes and the nipple clamps? Then I hear some unwelcome words.

"OK," says Amalia, "we just need to take one more sample."

Noooooo! Enough already. How clampy are these nipple clamps? Maybe I'll give them a try instead.

She's in for a third time. Repetition is most certainly not making this easier, quite the opposite. I have the impression of a long screwdriver being thrust down my windpipe and she is now twirling it in all directions like she is stirring a pot of paint. I'm making those moany noises that you make when you're in a dentist's chair and he or she is doing something unspeakably unpleasant to your teeth. Amalia, I used to like you. Why are you doing this to me? Oh yes, because I might well have cancer. Why did that sudden remembrance not make me feel any better?

Finally, the two of them seem satisfied that the paint is fully mixed. "All done," she says.

She places a soft hand on my cheek. 'You were really brave.' The soft hand on the cheek is in truth just a small dressing being applied to my neck and the brave bit is merely implied, but I'm so relieved now that I forgive my childish inventions. Released from the grip of my squeamishness, I'm so high on happiness that I struggle to take in what I'm told about analysis and results, but the general gist seems to be that they should have a clearer idea of how concerning my little lump is within the week. I will then be told what's what soon after that.

So, a few more days of keeping my counsel. Shouldn't be a problem. Compartmentalise, bury whatever I don't want to deal with and seal the lips. It's what I do.

NOV 2009 – BOSS FEIGNS CONCERN

The cat food packaging on the screen in front of me is failing to hold my attention. At my new workstation in the studio I'm a lot further from the single window than previously, but still I stare off into the distance through the glass at the park beyond. The conversation I had with Kate several nights ago is playing on a loop in my head. "I can't believe you haven't told me," was her initial reaction, words which laid bare the inner workings of her mind. I could see her straining at the reins of her anger in order to avoid giving me too hard a time. I have cancer after all. Can this guy not get a break?

Once her incredulity had subsided – at both the fact that I had cancer and that it had taken until it was confirmed before I told her – her ire moved on to another target. "Don't you think it's strange that you got thyroid cancer a few months after they gave you the radioiodine?" It seemed a fair point. I believe thyroid cancer went through the roof in the area of Chernobyl after the disaster. But I pointed out that they had been using this treatment since the 1950s, so there would be plenty of evidence about whether or not it was dangerous. I had to admit, though, it was notable that they kept prodding my thyroid afterwards, as if they were checking to make sure no lumps had developed.

"The survival rate is supposed to be very good," I continued, trying to steer talk back to the most pressing issue. What's done is done. They told me it was a very low dose and perfectly safe. Who am I to argue with their years of medical research? I'm just glad they've found it in plenty of time. I've even seen the surgeon already. The NHS displayed its Champions League capabilities again when it comes to cancer by giving me an appointment within a week of the results of the biopsy. Kate came with me to see Mr Frewitt – a nice man, even though he is one who is going to cut my throat soon. He told me that there is every chance that I'll make a full recovery. He was very reassuring and very posh. So posh in fact that I couldn't stop thinking about the two surgeons in the Harry Enfield sketch show while he spoke. I hope it didn't appear as if I wasn't taking this seriously, as I occasionally suppressed a snigger while I thought of Sheridan and whatever the other fella is called.

Anyway, since meeting him I've pretty much stopped worrying. I just want to get it over with. Kate's calmed down and my mum, dad and sister have also been told. I've now had the date through for the surgery, so there's one last person on my list that I have to give the news to – my boss.

Ian Book is his name. Short on name, short on personality. I realise it is predictable for an employee to dislike his boss, but he's the fourth one I've had in my time here and I have to say, the others were fine, decent and fair even. Book, on the other hand, is a complete and utter wanker.

Five solid reasons to hate Ian Book:

1. He likes to be known as Booker. I don't know where this comes from, but I imagine he thinks it enhances his reputation as a badass leader of men, like it makes him

sound like a no-nonsense New York cop or something. Steve and I refer to him as Booksy and encourage anyone around us to adopt this nickname, hoping it helps to undermine his self-image by giving him a soft cartoon edge.

2. Often he positions himself in his office doorway at the far end of the studio surveying his domain, like he's a General conducting a righteous war. What he's actually doing is just watching what we're up to, hoping to catch us engaged in non-work-related chat. The fact that he is just standing there doing fuck all doesn't seem to set off the irony alarm. He's also been known to say things like, 'There's too many people here who think they're owed a living.' What does that even mean? We turn in every day to an unfulfilling job, do it to the best of our ability and go home. Yes, it would be nice if, in return, the company gave us some money.

3. There are three main categories of packaging that we deal with – cat food, dog food and human food. A few weeks into his tenure, he gathered us all for a presentation that you would have thought was a United Nations address for all the import that was attached to it. He told us that he was going to divide us into teams that specialised in just one of the categories. These were to be called 'Purring', 'Barking' and 'Belching' for – as he put it – want of a better phrase. Well, Booksy, you've been working on this grand plan for ages, have you not had time to come up with any less cringeworthy names than that?

4. He wrote a long email to someone in the technical department once. A guy on our team helped him to decide

on the topics that needed to be raised, which is how we know what happened next. After the email was completed, Booksy read through it again and said he wasn't entirely happy with its content. He proceeded to remove every instance where he had written the word 'please'.

5. He seems to collect hangers-on who view him as some kind of power broker who will give them a leg up the career ladder. They're in and out of his office every two minutes, licking his arse clean. They also laugh heartily at comments he makes in presentations that I didn't even realise were supposed to be funny. I'm not sure Ian Book understands why they're laughing either, as he's a humourless automaton with little understanding of human interactions.

I'm not looking forward to this. For reasons such as the ones I've just given, I try to avoid him at all costs, but I need some time off work and therefore have no choice. I've been working up to it for a couple of days and now is my chance. He's paid a visit to our table, probably to kick some ass in his mind. I call him over and ask if I can have a word in private. The proofing room behind me is empty, so we head in there together.

I want to get this done as quickly as I can, so I just spit it straight out. "I've had some bad news about my health. I have thyroid cancer."

Booksy closes his eyes and throws his head back. "Oh God."

There is something fake about his reaction. I immediately see it for what it is – a response built on how he thinks people behave when faced with this situation. I'm always fascinated by people with a barely-developed human side floundering as they try to establish what is the correct conduct in a particular emotional scenario. For most of us, what we say or do comes naturally, but there are a surprising amount of people like Booksy and Leezou who struggle to join the dots. They're usually in a position of authority too – another signifier of a messed-up world.

"Isn't that one of the worst ones as well?" he asks, referring to the type of cancer I have.

I can't pretend that a part of me isn't enjoying seeing him squirm as he attempts to display some empathy. I'm tempted to confirm that it is one of the worst ones, just to watch him writhe some more like a freshly-salted slug, but I tell him no, it's one of the better ones to have.

"They've found it early too. I should recover OK. I need to have it cut out tout de suite though." Tout de suite? Why the fuck did I say that? What's wrong with 'as soon as possible'? Maybe they could cut my tongue out while they're at it. "I've had the appointment through. That's why I needed to tell you 'cause I'm going to be off for a least a couple of weeks, possibly more."

He mouths all the right things – yes, take as much time off as you need/hope it goes well/ anything you need, just let us know – but without the weight of authenticity behind his words. They're just lines from the HR handbook, but I suppose he's trying at least. I'm sure I've said exactly the same about Leezou before. I guess it's not their fault. There's just something missing from their DNA.

Anyhow, mission accomplished. Everyone who had to be told has been told and all that's left to do is wait for December 4th. Here's to an early Christmas present where everything goes back to normal. Except for the small matter, of course, of multiple sclerosis. That's the thing about cancer – it can make other worries seem trivial. Bet not many folk get to say that about MS.

DEC 2009 – STUPID SOCKS

I feel like a prize berk and a hungry one at that. I've not been allowed to eat anything since yesterday evening and now I'm stuck in this waiting room wearing a hospital gown and stupid socks. Apparently, when you have an operation involving general anaesthetic there is a danger of deep vein thrombosis, so they make you wear these tight stocking type things that go all the way up to the knee. Obviously I want to avoid having a blood clot, but who made the decision to make them bottle green? Could the NHS not have chosen a colour that drew less attention to them? I hate to think what I look like in my baby blue smock and green stockings, but I take comfort from glancing around at everyone else here who will soon be heading to theatre. They all look daft and nervous. It's like staring in a mirror.

"I must look a right tit," I say to Kate, complaining about my garb once again.

"You've worn worse things," comes her reply.

Our top banter is interrupted by the arrival of Mr Frewitt. After the brief hellos, he explains a few things about what is going to happen this morning.

"So we'll take you up there very soon now and we'll get that thyroid whipped out. Did I explain about the parathyroid glands?"

My face contorts into quizzical, I can't quite remember pose. He explains, probably for a second time, that there are tiny glands attached to the much bigger thyroid that produce calcium. He will try to avoid damaging any of these but this is not always easy.

I nod. "OK."

"So first you just need to have a scan, just to make sure it has not spread to your chest."

Excuse me? What are you on about, 'make sure it's not spread to your chest.' Who said anything about the possibility of it spreading? That sounds like proper cancer, not this pretend type I thought I had. You told me the survival rate with this kind was nearly 100%. Why are you springing this on me now?

He moves on before I can start pacing the room like Corporal Jones shouting, 'Don't panic!'

"How are you feeling?" he asks. "Are you ready for today?"

"Yeah, fine," I say. The truth is, I have been perfectly calm about the operation till about one minute ago when you talked about scanning and spreading. I glimpse Kate's expression and detect a similar note of sudden anxiety within it.

"How are you today, Mr Frewitt?" I enquire, searching for extra assurance. I imagine the well-being of the surgeon isn't often considered, but I want to make sure that he didn't have a heavy night with Sheridan and his other mates at the country club. He might try extra hard as well if I'm nice to him.

"Yes," he laughs, "I'm very well, thanks."

He then departs and I'm left with the feeling that this just got a little more serious.

*

Time to head to the front line. I'm hoping for a secret

passageway to take me to the operating theatre but am disappointed. A nurse ushers me into one of the main corridors, past people in their civilian hats, coats and scarves. I wish I was dressed in similarly warm clothing. We're close to the doors that lead to the outside world here and it's freezing. I feel like a soldier injured during the Russian campaign being marched to the field hospital, about to have a piece of troublesome shrapnel removed from my neck. Of course, in such circumstances my wife would not be by my side, but we are now told to say our goodbyes. My assumption that this would just be a formality crumples as I see tears begin to meander down Kate's cheeks. Maybe she's just clocked how ridiculous I look again. Tears of embarrassment? Yes, this is your husband. Smock and green stockings. What's your problem? I think it's something that'll catch on.

Until she started crying, I was only a tiny bit afraid. True, our meeting with Frewitt raised some additional concerns, but I've already hidden them in the old brainbox and labelled that box with the words 'Not To Be Opened'. Kate doesn't appear to know this trick.

"Why are you crying? It'll be all right," I tell her, giving her a hug. I hate to see her upset like this.

"I'm just worried about you," she splutters.

I gently dry her cheek with the back of my hand. "It'll be fine," I say, I suppose as much to myself as her. "Everything'll be fine."

And with those words, I'm led away to face the knife.

*

"Andrew, Andrew." Click, click.

Mum, is that you? My eyes slowly flicker open. The light is sharp. It's not my mother before me. It's a nurse.

"Hi, Andrew. How are you feeling?"

"Hmm, what?"

"You've had your operation and you're back on the ward now. I'm told that everything went well."

"Right."

"We'll leave you for a while to come round. OK?"

She departs and in my solitude the fog slowly lifts from my brain. A picture of me holding Kate, a cry of, "Ow, y'bastard," as he spiked my vein with the tube that would carry the anaesthetic to my brain. Then the counting backwards, "Ten, nine, eight..." That's pretty much all I recall. How incredible is modern science, that I knew absolutely nothing else. You're put into a temporary coma but kept safely alive. My neck's been cut and opened up, a gland I've been living with for forty years has been removed and my neck has been sewn up again. All with no knowledge of it whatsoever. I wonder what my acquaintances down at the Chinese doctor shop would make of it. Would their first words be, 'Hmm, hmm, how much did it cost? No money? No good!'

I feel like I've been beaten up. Not surprisingly, my neck is sore, inside and out. I've been told they stick a breathing tube down your throat while you're under, which can't help matters. But everything above the waist aches too. What it feels to be normal is only a vague memory. I'm still not allowed to eat anything either, which must be contributing to my overall weakness. Not that I'm particularly in touch with my stomach and its current desires. If it's craving food, I wouldn't know. As it is, all I'm given is a small cup of water with ice chips in it that I'm told to sip/suck.

Boredom soon raises its familiar head. I try to entertain myself by watching the comings and goings on the ward, but with little success. There's nothing much out of the ordinary happening. I manage with some difficulty to grab my bag from the bedside cupboard. I don't feel up to reading. Instead I pick my iPod and headphones out and listen to some music, but that too fails to relieve the tedium. I'm not in the mood for much of anything.

Somehow I need to pee anyhow. I've only downed a shard or two of ice but can feel a significant occupation in the bladder. Without moving, I can tell it is going to be a major procedure just to reach the bathroom. I haul myself up and push my legs over the side of the bed. I lower myself cautiously till my feet hit the cold floor. Thankfully, my slippers are ready and waiting and I begin the slide down the corridor. I edge along, keeping everything on the level. I think back to the lumbar puncture. I've done this walk more than once. I'm light-headed, yes, but fortunately nausea is not one of my primary symptoms this time around.

I arrive at my destination, enter the cubicle and prepare myself. I straddle the bowl and push on my bladder. I can feel it in there, but how the hell am I going to deliver it into the toilet? The reflex required seems to be completely absent.

Ten minutes go by and I'm not even close. I pull the seat down and slump onto it. I feel weak and that's as much standing as I can bear. My thoughts cast back once more to three years ago – lying in bed after the lumbar puncture, bursting with Coke, trying desperately to pee in a cardboard bowl. That was a bad one but this feels even worse. As I lay there then, despite the struggle I knew that I would get there eventually. Now I'm losing hope. I know I need to go, but the physical impulse to is simply not there. I've heard this is a thing after you've had a general anaesthetic. Add to the mix my usual shy bladder syndrome and it's a recipe for sitting depressed and alone in a chilly hospital toilet cubicle.

Pins and needles are developing in my legs. I stand up again for a bit, rub the back of my thighs, try to piss like a man. I just want to be in bed, but I know that I have to do this if I want to get any sleep tonight. It's no good. All senses in the vicinity have been quashed. I sink onto the seat again, my chin resting in my palm. I

191

push. Nothing. I try to relax. Nothing. I force a hand down on my bladder again and shake it. Nothing. I wait and wait and wait. Nothing. I push some more. I start to sweat. Now I feel close to tears. Are my eyes going to start shedding liquid before anything else does? Am I going to be here all night? Should I speak to a nurse about a catheter? No, I will not be that guy. This is going to happen the natural way, I promise, though absolutely nothing feels natural about any of this business.

*

I shuffle back to my bed around, by my best estimate, an hour and forty minutes later. Even when I eventually squeezed a few drops out, the remainder was still happy to stay where it was for ages. But I don't care how long it took now. I'm too busy revelling in the sensation of relief. I'm exhausted though. Having anaesthetic still swimming round my body in addition to my lavatorial exertions mean unconsciousness beckons her finger with considerable allure. I ease tentatively onto the mattress, trying not to jerk my neck at all, comforted by the knowledge that I have nothing to do tomorrow, other than continue my recovery from having my throat sliced open.

I roll gently onto my side, close my eyes and look forward to the impending deep sleep. However, another bodily function that should come effortlessly appears primed to deny me. Every time my thoughts begin to fade away, I'm jerked back towards awareness of where I am by the sound of nurses going about their business as if it's the middle of the day. Their kitchen or common room or wherever is just down the corridor and the reception desk is just outside the double doors of the room in which resides my bed, along with those of three other patients. Inexplicably, the doors are propped open, so if it's not laughter or general chit-chat assaulting my ears, it's the sound of a nurse typing, rustling sheets of paper and banging down folders and clipboards.

Why did I not pop some earplugs in my overnight bag? Oh yes, because I was rather focused on the surgery and not on its aftermath. That must be why I made the unfathomable decision to pack a round-neck T-shirt to wear in my hospital bed. What an absolute plank! It's undoubtedly the worst thing I could have chosen. It's not even a loose round-neck. I keep pulling it down at the front, but it persistently rises and rubs against my fresh scar. The constant commotion and the T-shirt are conspiring to engender a sense of despair and hopelessness similar to the one I experienced during my visit to the bathroom. What a night. Crying while perched on the toilet, swiftly followed by a desire to whimper while lying here, staring forlornly at the ward ceiling.

I can stand it no more. There's not much I can do about the noise, but I can at least affect some pain relief. There's only one thing for it – I'm going to have to ask a nurse to cut my T-shirt.

I prise myself from the bed again. There's no nurse currently on the front desk but I don't think I'm going to have much difficulty locating one. I creep like a snail close to death towards the sound of gossiping nurses that is escaping unhindered from the room down the corridor. I interrupt their midnight rave with a light knock on the door. They stare at me, clearly wondering why I am bothering them. Surely I should be enjoying a lovely, restful sleep. Resisting the urge to ask them if they might turn the chatter the fuck down a notch, I explain that I'm here because I'm a complete idiot. Could they get some scissors and cut my T-shirt so it stops digging into my poorly neck?

"We can give you a pyjama jacket to wear if you like," one of them suggests.

Right. Yes, if one's available that would be a much better idea.

Five minutes later I'm lying back in bed wearing a pale blue

NHS-issue pyjama jacket under NHS-issue bedsheets. I don't own a pyjama jacket at home but if I'd known how much better an option this would be, it would have made sense to purchase a pyjama set prior to today. Now I just look like I should be eighty years old. I wouldn't be surprised if a geriatric patient had died in this jacket. Stylish it ain't, but it's doing a much better job than the T-shirt, so let's at least applaud the decision I made to speak to the nurses about my predicament. Finally, time for sleep.

Wrong. Time for more ceiling gazing, more listening to the nurses have a lovely time either side of playing a game of who can be the loudest secretary in the whole friggin' world. Not that my fellow wounded soldiers seem to be worrying about it much. Added to this infernal mix are three varieties of snoring – deep and droning, squeaky and irregular and wheezy deflating balloon. Hopeless despair pays me a third visit. I reach for my iPod again as a way of neutralising the torture of my surroundings. Let's dive into another world, far from this one.

I select *Felt Mountain* by Goldfrapp. The otherworldliness of the opening track, Lovely Head, should do a decent job of transporting me away from here. Ethereal is an overused word in music, but it could have been invented to describe Alison Goldfrapp's voice, while the music has a space age quality to it. I close my eyes and let the song do its stuff. No more snoring, babbling or noisy admin. Just a dreamlike sleep-inducing soundscape.

Only problem is, I remain resolutely awake. I've never been one to fall asleep watching TV or, for that matter, listening to music. Tonight, I just find myself sinking further under the spell of the instrumentation and that voice. Alison is inducing nothing other than an onrush of melancholy. Why does her singing have to be so beautiful? And why is its beauty making me so sad? Is it the inevitable result of perfection rubbing up against my shitty day and even shittier night? Is that what's happening here? No, don't you dare set me off crying. You complete and utter cow.

I just about hold it together. As the album moves through its paces, I find myself thinking about my close circle of friends. A warm rush of affection ploughs into the wall of negative feelings that is currently being built around me. Maybe that's why, like a prisoner, a list of what I'll do when I get out of here quickly begins to take shape. I'll be in touch with the guys more often. We have to see each other on a more regular basis. I know we would never say it, but I love you all. We need to show it more often. Who knows where life will take us and when? We shouldn't take anything for granted.

I become aware of talking bleeding into the world I have created for myself on Felt Mountain. I open my eyes a crack and see silhouettes moving. I try to ignore the intrusion, but it's proving impossible. I make it to the end of a song and then give up, removing my headphones. I have to find out what's happening. A bloke I haven't seen before is in discussion with one of the nurses. Why they have to do it here, I don't know. Is there not a side room somewhere that's, say, more than ten feet away from three patients who are either a) sleeping b) were once sleeping but have now been woken or c) not sleeping but trying to escape from the chaos that seems to surround him, even though it's past 3am.

The latest cause of my pain appears to be a burly sort but the type that has a high-pitched voice that seems ill-matched to his size. He has a big fat catalogue of complaints that the nurse is doing her best to listen to patiently as he rifles through it. Even in the half-light, I sense her exasperation. If you can have something wrong with your body, Pogo Patterson here has it. Stomach problems, bowel problems, blood pressure problems, heart palpitations, headaches and more besides. Is there anything not wrong with you, I want to shout out. The nurse attempts to interrupt him a couple of times, but his flow is full and he has a lot to get off his irregularly beating chest. The radar that detects over-indulgent mothers is bleeping. Eventually, and no doubt relieved to palm him off on someone, the nurse manages to scurry off to find a doctor.

Medical history's greatest mystery sits down on the one spare bed in the room and mutters to himself. In the absence of anyone else apparently conscious – I'm certainly not about to let him know I'm awake – he seems to be reciting his thick file of ailments to himself. When the doctor arrives ten minutes later, he's delighted to be able to unload once more and I'm left wondering a second time why on earth this is taking place in here.

"I've got this pain in my stomach and my heart's beating really fast. I keep getting this pain up my bum as well. I saw the doctor about it last year, around February, no March, no it might have been February. He said it would probably go soon but I'm still getting it and I always feel sick and I keep getting these headaches..."

On and on he goes. I zone out as I imagine the doctor has also done. I just catch the words, "My mum said I should go to casualty if I'm that bad..."

I knew it. Mother has her mention and the guy finally runs out of breath. If he managed to calm himself down a little, he would perhaps feel an immediate benefit. The doctor starts to run through his many troubles, but the upshot is that they'll have to do some tests tomorrow when, you know, it's not the middle of the friggin' night. Patient X keeps interrupting, but we finally get there. The doctor runs off screaming and the sickest man in Britain is left to get into bed. Great, if I ever drop off, I'm going to be waking up to this guy. I'm going to put any energy I'm able to summon tomorrow into not catching his eye.

*

I remember 4am. Next I knew it was around half seven. The first thing I saw through my morning haze was the guy who came in bleating like a sheep about to be slaughtered in the early hours of the night. Fortunately, he was sitting up facing the bed next to him, so eye contact was averted. I fixed my stare on the light fitting above me till I was ready to haul my arse back to the scene of my near two-hour nightmare yesterday – the bathroom.

My neck is still sore, of course, but I can live with it. I'm more concerned with how well my morning pee is about to go. The anaesthetic must have mostly worked its way out of my system because it's just the normal problems now, not the deluxe ones. I get back into bed, have something to eat finally, then sink back into my pillow, suddenly feeling like someone who only got two or three hours sleep last night. I drop off I think, which is an indication of just how tired I am as there is, predictably, even more going on now. I have a vague sense that I'm in a hospital, but my thoughts are those of someone who is allowing his fantasies to take control. Joanne Whalley appears over my bed, a look of whatever you want me to do, I'll do it on her smooth-skinned, doe-eyed face. A shadow has fallen upon me. I feel her presence. My eyes open.

Instead of Nurse Whalley, Pogo Patterson is at the foot of the bed, just staring at me. I avoid a dramatic visual jolt, but it's certainly a shock. What does this creepy man-child want with me and why is he watching me sleep? Is this how he wakes his mum every morning?

He doesn't say anything. It's down to me to say, "Hi."

He continues to stare then finally says, "Hi. What are you in for?"

No pleasantries, no exchange of names, just straight in there with the personal medical questionnaire. I'm sure if I'd murdered several people and was a lifer, I'd be afforded a little more decorum by my fellow inmates.

"I had my thyroid taken out yesterday. It had a cancerous lump on it."

"What's a thyroid?"

"It's a gland that's in your neck that controls your metabolism."

I'm braced for more questions: what's your metabolism, what's a gland, where's your neck, but I soon realise that he was only asking so he could tell me all his problems. Not only do I have to hear again about his stomach, bowel, blood pressure, heart, head and every other part of him complaints, but I have to pretend that I've not heard it all before. I let him get it out of his system. Not that I have much choice. He doesn't draw breath, just like last night when he was explaining his situation to the nurse and doctor.

He does add one detail, though: "They're talking about sticking a camera up my bum. Have you ever had that done?"

Hi, I'm Andy. I'm a quality controller. I'm married with a son. Pleased to meet you. Are we bypassing all that boring stuff and going straight for the topic of 'have you ever had a camera shoved up your rectum?'

"No," I tell him, just Dr Fat Finger's sausage digit up there for me – twice. "It's not too bad, though, from what I've heard," I say, choosing to be reassuring, as I can see the worry in his pin eyes. "Someone I know had it once. I think they give you a sedative to relax you and you don't really feel it."

His face loosens a fraction with that news, but then I can't help myself from adding, "Of course, it depends what you've already had up there."

He smiles, but it lacks depth, like it's an involuntary reaction. I see another side to him, one that doesn't sit comfortably with the persona of a daft, naïve but essentially harmless lad that I've given him. Suddenly, I could imagine a switch being flicked and him beating someone e.g. me to a bloody pulp. I now see him as having the potential to be the muscle to some short-on-arse but long-on-nasty gangster. Pogo here would be the heavy-set sidekick with the learning difficulties and big fists who without questioning why puts people in A & E at his master's behest.

Instead of pummelling my head deep into my pillow, my comment has the happy effect of getting rid of him. He turns and heads out of the ward. I look around at the other three guys in their beds. They're all looking at me. I feel a need to say something.

"Your turn next."

The guy in the corner who I'd say is around sixty says, "You did very well."

I feel a small bond has formed. It's comforting to know that it's not just me. Pogo is a strange one with whom you don't really want to get stuck in a conversation if you can help it. I see recognition of this in my fellow patients. I slip on my headphones, even though I don't put on any music, ready for when he comes back. Whether this will ward him off when the fact that I was asleep did not is hard to say, but I have to try something.

*

The rest of the morning is dull and uneventful but there's the match to look forward to this afternoon. It's an early kick off and I don't want to miss the commentary. I can't remember, however, exactly when it starts. I think back to late last night as I pictured all the things I would do with my friends going forward. I decide to send a group text to four of them to ask them when it starts, as a way of getting the ball rolling with my new commitment to greater contact. At the very least, it should generate a conversation to distract me from my boredom.

I wait for some replies. Five minutes go by. Another five go by, more slowly this time. Ping. Finally.

NOT SURE 12.30 I THINK

For fuck sake. That's not taken me any further forward. If I was to write my thoughts down in a text, that's precisely what I would have written. But I haven't got access to the Internet on my crappy phone. Was it too much effort to spend a second checking. Ping.

EARLY ONE INNIT. COME ON THE BOYS!!!

Double fuck sake. The other two don't even reply. Neither is there anything about my operation from anyone. Have they forgotten? The fires of my affection have just been introduced to a bucket of piss. I suppose I shouldn't be surprised. We're not the type of friends who lean on each other all the time. Since we've all hooked up with wives and had kids, we've been busy getting on with our lives. When we get together on our ever rarer nights out, though, it's like we've never been away from each other. The clock spins back twenty years and all is good. Then we part ways again.

Oh well, my family will be here soon. They have to show an interest in my op. Then there will be just one more night in purgatory before I'm off work for ages. That's a definite silver lining to this business. The most welcome of full stops.

Yes, they'll come through those doors soon and I'll get to see and hold the thing that I crave above all else right now – my ear plugs. OK, it might be nice to get a kiss and a hug off Kate and E and see the loving faces of my mum, dad and sister. Ah, here they come, right on time.

CHRISTMAS 2009 – YOU COULDN'T MAKE IT UP

It's over three weeks since my operation. Christmas Day is behind us and we're now in that strange hinterland where we await New Year. It was great to have two weeks to prepare for the big day. I remember pre-Internet Christmases. Three of four trips into town and you were done with the gift purchases. Decisions had to be made. These days you may avoid the pushing and shoving, but the temptation to spend hours researching products and comparing prices between sites is too great for feeble-minded tightwads like me. To put it another way, previously you just had the shops in your locality from which to choose presents. Now there's the whole world to explore. Throw into the mix having a young child for whom you are desperate to make Christmas special and you are left with the notion that you will have to book two weeks off before Christmas every year. I just hope it's for the benign reasons outlined above in future.

I have to confess, I did go into work for the last few days before the holidays. I don't suppose many people would have. Friends and family thought I was mad and even Booksy said to me, "I didn't expect to see you before Christmas, Andy." What was going through my head? I'm not entirely sure myself, but I think my reasoning was two-fold. One, I hate that first day back after a long absence from work. If I went in for those few days, I could acclimatise without having to do that much. A relaxed atmosphere for three and a half days, prior to another long break, thus diluting the depression that will inevitably descend upon me on the morning of January 3rd. The second motive probably reflects badly on the man: a part of me that I didn't even want to admit at the time was looking forward to seeing people's faces when I walked into the studio. Hey, what are you doing here? I thought you had cancer? You must have balls of steel. Well, thanks for mentioning it. Yes, yes I do.

As it was, my unexpected appearance was barely acknowledged. Most people, I guess, want to avoid talking about cancer at all costs, if possible. Or maybe they thought I wanted to carry on as if everything was normal, hence me showing up just two weeks after surgery. Well, you'd be wrong. I would have been more than happy to discuss my balls of steel.

I'm busy showing E how to die repeatedly playing Super Mario Bros. The five-year-old in the room keeps taking the Wii controller from me and saying things like, 'It's so easy. See?' while I look on bemused, wondering how they pop out of the womb with these abilities fitted as standard. I'm about to receive another lesson when Kate pushes the door open and says, "Can you come in here a sec?"

"Yeah, just a minute," I reply, desperately trying to reach that bloody flagpole without falling to my death yet again.

"It's important," she says. From her tone of voice, I can tell it is, so I reluctantly tell E I'll be back in a bit.

I watch him effortlessly negotiate a section I think of as impossible as I back out of his playroom. "Yeah, what's up?" I ask Kate, wondering if it really is important or if she's dragged me away from the fun/frustration for nothing.

"I've just noticed this in the mirror. That's not been there before, has it?"

She points at a sizeable lump on her neck, near the centre below her chin. "What the ..." I peer in for closer inspection. "No," is all I can say.

"It feels... pudgy."

"Does it hurt at all?" I ask, thinking I'm pretty sure that's in almost exactly the same place as the thing I've just had cut out of me.

"Not really, no." She pokes it. "It feels soft." The lump moves when she presses her finger on it. It looks like whatever it is involves fluid.

I try to allay some of her fears, working from a base of next to no knowledge. "It's probably just some kind of cyst or boil that needs lancing. I doubt it's anything sinister." But my mind can't help casting back to that time after I had the radioiodine treatment and was told to keep away from E for a fortnight. I continued to sleep in the same bed as Kate, having been told it was fine. Sex was off the cards, even from behind – she didn't accept that keeping my neck that far from her was a legitimate argument and anyway, how would she get in the mood without any kissing – but I was still regularly in close contact with her. Was this safe?

"You're probably right," she agrees in response to my assessment, rather uncertainly.

"Just make an appointment at the doctors' tomorrow. They should be able to tell you pretty quickly."

My words are said with a breezy confidence out of step with my inner tension. I'm struggling to come up with anything to add. Kate sinks onto the sofa and stares straight ahead.

"Daddy! Daddy!" comes the cry from the other room.

I wonder what the correct course of action may be. Kate shrugs in a way that indicates I should go to him, so I head back to Super

Mario World. E hands me a controller. "Your turn, Daddy."

I was hopeless when I was focusing so now I'm just embarrassing. "Daddy," E groans, his tone one of exaggerated pity. You see, Kate, this is why you should keep bad news to yourself until you know for sure that it is bad news. A worry shared is a worry doubled. The remainder of the Christmas break is now ruined. Will there be any more untainted joy with E? Will you and I be able to utter the phrase 'happy new year' with any conviction at midnight, as we head into 2010? Yes, it's most likely nothing, but I'm no medical expert. What if it's not? How the hell could this have happened? It's as if her neck has sprouted this growth as some kind of sympathetic reaction. A symptom of the anxiety she's been carrying? Are we this closely entwined? I know in truth it's just a coincidence, but as coincidences go it's a belter. I'm actually due to see a woman in oncology at St James in Leeds in a couple of days' time. That's how much of a coincidence it is. The aftercare for my brush with cancer is still going on. Would it have been too much to ask for us to get that out of the way before this reared its head? I mean, once I get the all clear, I'll only have multiple sclerosis to deal with. I'm sure I could have coped with my beloved potentially having cancer without breaking sweat if I was swimming in those calm waters.

Now stop it. Let's reclaim our grip. You know in your heart that it's likely to be something easily resolved. That thing in her neck doesn't have the hard consistency of the thing that Dr Amalia found during the Arsegate episode. And you're seeing an oncologist in less than forty-eight hours. That could be the ideal opportunity to quash any sense of panic.

I need to relay my plan to Kate. E has sensibly taken back control of Mario and is so concentrated, his little tongue poking out the side of his mouth, that I think he'll hardly notice if I leave him to it for a moment. I slip back into the living room where Kate is sitting in the same position, now watching TV, though somewhat vacantly.

"I've had a thought," I begin. "I'm seeing Dr Fisher on Tuesday. I know I said there was no point in you coming along, but why don't you? We can casually point out the growth in your neck and get her to take a look."

"She won't do that. You know what they're like. They won't look at another patient if they don't have an appointment."

"I know they don't normally, but it's worth a try."

Kate scowls, clearly marking it as a crap idea in her head.

"I know she won't give us a full diagnosis but she might at least take a quick look and give us an idea of what's most likely. What's she going to do, refuse us point blank? You'll have to turn on the waterworks if she does."

Kate continues to be very doubtful but agrees to at least come along to the appointment. She wanted to all along to hear what Dr Fisher had to say about me, so she doesn't take that much persuasion. I know we'll probably get told to go through the proper channels, but having a plan helps to alleviate a portion of my feelings of impotence.

I glance at Kate's face, her beautiful olive-skinned face, down at her neck with its recently installed squatter, then back to her face. Her eyes look a little glassy. I imagine mine do too. Kate, my love, what have I been putting you through these last few years?

LATE DEC 2009 – SHIT SUPERHERO SET TO RETURN THIS SUMMER

Time feels like it's paused these last couple of days, but here we are finally at St James, more than ready to see Dr Fisher. Will she say anything to ease our anxieties or will she follow strict protocol and let us stew a while longer? First, though, it's my turn in the spotlight.

"So how have you been since the operation, Andrew?" she begins. I'd estimate that Dr Fisher is in her forties. She has an air of experience and efficiency about her but with just enough warmth for me to feel comfortable in her care.

"Yeah, fine, thanks." I've already seen Mr Frewitt since the surgery. He told me that the scar was healing nicely and he thinks there's a good chance he managed to save my calcium producing glands, though this remains to be seen. They'll have to keep a close eye on it.

"That nasty growth is still with the lab. I've not heard back yet whether or not it was cancerous." She gives an apologetic smile. "Christmas, of course."

So it wasn't definitely cancerous? I thought that was all established. Might I have gone through all this for nothing?

"We have to assume, though, that it was. I should have the results back soon. We'll have a better idea of how to proceed from there."

Proceed? Are we not done?

"The priority now is to keep your thyroid hormone levels as such to keep you healthy. You'll be seeing the specialists in endocrinology soon?" I nod. "So they will be able to discuss it with you further, but we need to keep your thyroglobulin levels very low to reduce the chance of any thyroid growing back and the cancer reappearing. There may be a few thyroid cells left, you see, providing a base for regrowth if we don't get our levels right."

I try to take all this in but I can't help thinking about the lump in Kate's neck instead. I'm drifting in and out as Dr Fisher continues to outline how the next few months are going to pan out.

"With this in mind," she says, "you will need to visit us again in a few months' time. I see from your notes that you had radioiodine treatment in… May last year. We'll need to repeat this a second time as we try to kill any remaining thyroid cells."

Oh for fuck's sake, not again. My focus is very much back. Will I have to stay away from E again?

"This needs to be a higher dose so it'll require a hospital stay."

I guess that's a yes.

"What's involved?" Kate chips in.

"So you will be given another radioiodine capsule with, as I say, a much higher dose than when we were just trying to reduce the hormone production of your thyroid. You will then need to be kept in isolation for a week in the specialist unit."

Bloody hell. Images of people in white hazmat suits staring at me through a porthole in my lead-lined door spring to attention. What's radiation on this scale going to do to me?

"Your pee will need monitoring," she goes on, "to make sure no radioactive urine is present in the bladder."

Is this the return of Shit Superhero? This time his piss is radioactive!

"We'll do a CT of your chest at the time too."

There they go again, talking about checking for cancer in my chest. I wish they'd stop it.

"There may be a small possibility of external beam radiotherapy too. We'll decide on that nearer the time."

I'm clearly not out of the woods yet. Dr Fisher checks something on her computer screen while I glance at Kate and roll my eyes. I detect a certain look of resignation on her face.

"It's quite a good setup in the nuclear medicine ward," says Dr Fisher, turning back to us. "There will be a DVD machine in your room and an exercise bike, I think. A private bathroom, of course…"

Nuclear medicine! Those Hazmat suits heave into view once more.

"Have you any children?"

"Yes, a son."

"Have you any intention of extending your family?"

I look in Kate's direction and mutter, "No, not really." Not really? How non-committal can you be? Kate remains silent on the subject that dare not raise its voice.

"Well, because of the nature of the treatment, you may wish to consider having some of your sperm frozen if you have any intention of having further children."

My poor sperm – news of another incoming attack. Like a sportsman who's been battling a series of injuries for years, the boys may as well admit defeat and retire.

The doctor offers a few more details of what the future holds for me as she begins to wrap up our meeting, but I'm struggling to concentrate on anything she tells me as I'm busy searching for an opportunity to introduce Kate's problem into the conversation. I don't want to bottle it until we're on our feet and almost out the door before I turn back around Columbo-style and say, 'Just one more thing…'

My opportunity arises when she says, "Have you any questions for me?"

"We do have one major concern, yes," I say. Dr Fisher is all ears. I hope she's going to be receptive. "The other day Kate noticed a lump on her neck. Kate leans her head backwards and points at it. "I know it's not the normal way of things, but could you possibly give us your professional opinion on what you think it might be. I know it's difficult without proper tests but…"

She's straight up on her feet and coming over to take a closer look. Kate raises her head again and Dr Fisher runs her fingers over it.

"It's soft, like it's full of fluid," I say. "Do you think it's just a boil or cyst?"

There's a pause while she runs her fingers over it again. I'm grateful that she's being so accommodating, but these seconds are far longer than I would wish.

"Hmm, yes, it does feel like it's mainly fluid. I would expect it's just a cyst, yes. Without the necessary tests, I can't be certain but that's certainly my feeling. Go and see your GP as soon as you can and they will be able to refer you to someone who can examine it properly."

The clouds haven't lifted completely, but things are looking much brighter. "Thanks so much," I say. "We really appreciate you taking a look."

"Yes, thanks," Kate chimes in. "We always thought it was probably a cyst but you know, lumps on the neck…"

I can almost feel the sweat in my pits drying up. In truth, I think I was probably as worried about asking Dr Fisher for this favour as I was about Kate's health. A clear frailty of the human soul –

almost elevating my awkwardness at the potential situation that could arise from raising the topic above concerns for my wife's well-being. A clear frailty of my soul anyway.

We stand to go. As we leave and head down the corridor, I notice Kate is carrying herself differently to how she has in recent days, her back somehow straighter. I'm suddenly looking forward again to midnight on the 31st.

FEB 2010 – MORE FOOL ME

Just a run of the mill Tuesday. I pick up a new job to check and sigh. A flexo bag. Mixed screening. I won't bore the world with an explanation of what this entails, but suffice to say it's as bad as it gets – brain-meltingly complicated and ripe with potential for error. I'm just reading the brief, wondering how I got myself into this industry, when I get a text from Kate. The boiler's on the blink at one of the houses she renovated a few years ago in Filey, one that we now rent out. Great. Hassle, expense, another problem that I could really do without.

Rather than face up to calling boiler engineers, hoping that one can get round there this month, my mind sets off thinking about that lump on Kate's neck again. Not long after seeing Dr Fisher, the lump was no more. As we suspected, it was just a fluid-filled cyst. She saw the GP the day after our visit to oncology and a specialist not long after that. He drained it there and then. Apparently the little bugger that had caused us so much unnecessary worry nearly filled a sizeable syringe with its delightful contents. But with that my stolen thunder was returned to me and a certain happiness returned to the Reynard household. For her at least, everything was back to normal. Case closed.

I'm just considering whether to sneak onto the Internet for two minutes to check out boiler engineers on Yell.com when Baker marches over and tells me that Booksy requires my presence in his office. It's clear that Baker is revelling in his role as Booksy's primary henchman. Dogsbody would be a better term in my opinion but whatever, the sense that the big mafia boss has summoned a minion for a potentially violent reprimand is undeniable.

As I enter, Booksy is sitting at a table with various print-outs on it. This isn't good. I don't suppose he's invited me in to tell me how well I did to spot one of the two dozen major errors I find every week. No, it's no doubt regarding the one from the last six months that I must have missed. I sit down opposite him and quickly assess what kind of job it is. Gravure. Fucketty fuck. If gravure cylinders have been engraved and they need to be scrapped, it'll be expensive. Worse still if the job has been printed and the product is already on the shelves of the supermarkets. An empty space opens in my stomach, ready for Booksy to inject a wedge of his righteous wrath.

"Hi, Andy."

Pleasant enough greeting but this is what he does. Bet he loves *The Godfather*.

"We've got a slight problem with this job. He pushes the printouts closer to me, though I can see them perfectly well without his power play move. I stare at them thinking, 'You bastard. Couldn't you just tell me up front without forcing me into this pressurised test to see if I can work out what's wrong from the evidence before me.' I hurriedly scan the various images, praying that something leaps out at me. Yes! That panel is in four process colours. It should be out of just one pantone.

"Ah," I say, acknowledging the mistake, but deliberately avoiding saying what it is, partly just in case that isn't in fact the problem, but also as my own little power play. Ha, Twatface, I'm going to make you spell it out anyway. Over to you.

"I don't understand how this one has got through," he says cooly, but unaggressively. Classic Booksy. What he really means is, 'How the fuck have you missed that you knobhead. What are we paying you for? A simpleton could have stopped that from going out the door.'

I note that he is still refusing to confirm what the problem is, so I will have to assume we are talking about the same thing. Admittedly, I really should have picked up on it but as I always say, they all look easy to spot when you've been told that something is wrong. It's a bit trickier when you're onto your tenth job of the day, you needed around three hours more sleep that morning and you're contemplating jacking it all in and trying to convince your other half that you'd make a great househusband.

I really can't be arsed with this. I could try to argue my way out of it like Steve does. Slippery Steve I call him, as no shit ever seems to stick to him. He would probably make a good defence barrister. He could convince a jury that a man kneeling astride a mashed in skull holding a hammer had in fact just been doing some DIY, tripped and fell hammer-first on the victim. That kind of thing is not my forte. Even if it wasn't my fault, I would probably manage to implicate myself in screw-ups going back to before I even joined the company by the time I was done speaking. I decide instead just to take the hit.

"I don't know," I say, trying to offer next to nothing. "I'll have to look into it."

"We've got to do better than this, Andy…"

And he's off. The dressing down has begun. He glares at me as he runs through his probably pre-prepared speech and I just have to accept it like a naughty schoolboy. It feels like it goes on for half an hour, but it's no doubt more like three minutes. I'm

215

surprised he doesn't end with, 'So, what have you got to say for yourself,' but it just winds downs with an action plan of how we're going to contain the issue.

I head back to my desk, my insides turning like the drum of a washing machine. I now crave a standard Tuesday. Booksy showed his true self in there. Did he care that I'm on my way back from having cancer or that I have MS? Of course not. For him it's all about this inconsequential business we spend too many of our waking hours fretting about. That and how much he can make himself appear god-like in this trivial cell of humanity in which we have to involve ourselves to earn a crust.

I investigate the job in question. The first question I always want answering in these circumstances is when did I check it? What day and which part of that day? Was it a Friday afternoon when I really couldn't be bothered or was it a Monday morning when I was struggling to care? I open the folder and look at the date and time that I burnt the files to CD, ready for the printer. Jesus bollocking Christ. It was a Monday but the afternoon. Rather more significantly it was the day I returned after the surgery, swinging my balls of steel. December 21st, the first of those three and a half days I came in when I really didn't have to. Well that makes me feel a whole load better about the situation. I hope you're proud of yourself.

When you make a mistake doing what I do you go through something similar to the seven stages of grief. I can't remember exactly what they are or in what order you're supposed to go through them, but shock and denial are definitely in there, as are anger, depression, guilt, arguing that you weren't to blame and ultimately acceptance, followed by shrugging it off, ready to face a new day. Currently I'm feeling sorry for myself but I try to remember that in the great scheme of things it really doesn't matter. I once heard an old actor talking about whenever he read a bad theatre review for one of his performances in the morning paper. He said it was OK to allow a bad review to spoil your breakfast, but don't let it spoil your lunch.

Speaking of which, it's now lunchtime and I'm still here to enjoy it. And Booksy is still – and will always be – a complete and utter wanker.

SUMMER 2010 – THE ANGRIEST MAN IN WEST YORKSHIRE

This is going to be good. I feel guilty about the pig that had to die to provide me with this small pleasure, but I bat these thoughts away by divorcing myself from the whole unsavoury process and focusing instead on the salty fatty delight that will soon be entertaining my taste buds. The bread is buttered, ketchup is at the ready and the meat is crisping up nicely, a few mouth-watering seconds from being ready.

I pull the grill pan out and check the bacon is cooked just right. I turn it over with a fork and bollocks! It drops through the bars and into the moat of grease below. Grinding my teeth, suppressing swearing, as E is in audible range, I try to retrieve it but I can't stab it without soaking it in the river of fat and god knows what else is living in the bottom of the pan. A tiny portion is poking out saying, 'You could grab me easily,' so I make that call, but instead of grabbing it, I feel the heat of the grill pan, which jolts my hand upwards and I catch it against the still red hot grill element. FUCK!

I reel back in pain, the rage erupting like Krakatoa. Something deep within me remains conscious of the child in my midst, so what comes out of my mouth is not, 'Fuck, fuck, cunting fuck fuck,' as would do if I was on my own, but merely a primal howl. I hurry across to the tap and run cold water over my burnt flesh. "GODSAKES!" I scream.

"What's wrong? What's happened?" Kate asks, her voice full of the type of alarm someone might have if she feared I'd just chopped off a finger.

"Just dropped the bloomin' bacon in the bottom of the pan, then I burnt my flippin' hand." As soon as I say it, I realise how disproportionate my response has been. Yes, a burn while cooking is painful, but I'm hardly going to require a skin graft and the bacon is more than salvageable. This is just the way my mood goes at the moment. If the smallest of first world problems dares to blacken my day, it will elicit an explosion of rage completely at odds with the minor inconvenience that has befallen me. I can't find my keys – rage, I trip over one of E's toys – rage, I left something upstairs that I meant to bring downstairs and my legs are already weak today – rage. The list of molehills that are taking on the proportion of mountains in my head seems endless.

I don't remember being like this when I still had a thyroid and it was going crazy. From memory, I was just tired and hungry all the time. Maybe it's something to do with the fact that the thyroxine flowing through my body is now coming directly from tablets, rather than a naturally present gland. Whatever the reason, the dose of Levothyroxine I'm currently on appears to mean I'm likely to blow up at any point.

It has to be the pills. It's all that's changed recently and my temper has shown itself more frequently in step with the increases in dose I've been ordered to take. I don't fully understand how it all works but they keep talking about keeping one level low, so my thyroid doesn't try to grow back, which means my thyroxine level needs to be artificially high, at the very upper limit of what's healthy.

In January, I started on 175mg. They weren't happy when they checked my bloods a few weeks later so in March I was put on 200mg. By June I found myself on 225mg. I started to notice a change in February when I was only on the 175, so it's predictable that another 50mg is killing me. Kate has started calling me Bulldog after the sports guy in *Frasier*, who regularly barks, 'This stinks! This is total BS!' In my impression of his tantrums I am failing, however, with the part where calm soon descends on the situation, as Bulldog realises almost immediately that he was getting irate about something imagined.

She may be able to laugh it off some of the time, saying Bulldog is in the house again, but our relationship is currently taking a good kicking. No one wants to live with a man who screams at you, "Why can't you learn how to load the dishwasher right?", "How could you spend so much at the friggin' supermarket?" and "I curse the day that I ever married you." OK, I made that last one up. If Kate has thought that occasionally this summer, though, I wouldn't be surprised.

I just hope she can see the irony. I've had fourteen years of Kate being usurped by some kind of sabre-toothed monster once a month, ready to bite my head off at the slightest of perceived transgressions. The monster seems to appear for about four days out of every twenty-eight and lives on a cliff edge, primed to push me over it at any moment. That's over a hundred and sixty months by my reckoning, or over six hundred and seventy days. From such experience I know it's not pleasant to be on the receiving end, but in the face of those figures can I not be afforded some allowance to burn my newly acquired short fuse? It's hormone based after all. What's the difference?

All I know for sure is that it's getting so bad, I find myself wondering which is worse – the cancer coming back or being controlled by my hormones. I don't want to piss Kate off so much that I lose her. I'd rather be dead than have that happen. I've already spoken to endocrinology about lowering my dose, but they won't budge. They say it's in my best interests. Procedures have to be followed. If they understood what it was doing to my marriage, perhaps they'd change their mind, though I doubt it. I mean, I've told them how it's affecting me but it looks like my only option is to not take the pills. I could take it back down to 200 or even 175 and see how I was. But if I self-medicate, it'll show up straight away on my next blood test and I'll be taken to task next time I have an appointment. I could handle a telling off from Dr Amalia Gonzalez if she were dressed up like a sexy teacher with mortar board, glasses and cane, but I doubt that is likely to happen. In fact, I have a feeling that she has moved on to quicken the pulse of sad, needy patients elsewhere. I haven't seen her this year and I didn't spot her name on any door on my last visit there. So that little pleasure is now denied. Just me, my 225mg of Levothyroxine and a ridiculous propensity to fly off the handle for the most trivial of annoyances in my life.

Kate, please try to find it in your heart to understand that it's not me, it's the drugs. I will try to count to ten more often. I seem to have more success controlling myself around E. I'm sure Mad Dad is a character in his life these days, but that shouty man is only generally heard in the next room. I mostly manage to bite my lip around him when he's acting up like six-year-olds sometimes do. I might have to chew my face off while I'm around Kate but I'm going to have to try to do something. The queue of women lining up to take on an angry, middle-aged man with multiple sclerosis is, I'm sure, a rather short one.

SEPT 2010 – CROSSING THE LINE

There's a line that no one should cross. I am the only one allowed on the other side of it. I plump my pillows and prop myself up against the headboard in this, at a guess, four by four metre room, probably glowing like the Ready Brek kid, kicking out a level of radiation that is potentially harmful to every living thing except apparently me, preparing for my week of splendid isolation.

There is literally a line drawn on the floor near the door. Blue and three inches thick, it acts as my shield against humanity. No person should be brave enough to breach it, as for the next few days I am going to be a dangerous man to know. The capsule I swallowed this morning was, I'm told, around eighteen times stronger than the one I ingested previously and Shit Superhero's thyroid should be well and truly zapped as a result, meaning the cancer has nothing to attach itself to if it was considering making a reappearance, while the thyroid levels set by the pills I now have to take every morning will be easier to measure.

So that's me for the next seven days. Billy no mates. No real contact other than hospital staff occasionally sticking their head round the door to check on me and a few brief family visits. Visitor chairs are of course beyond the line away from me and they can't stay too long and neither can the doctors and nurses. I'm going to be spending a lot of time on my own.

Bloody brilliant! I've been looking forward to this and every male friend to whom I described my impending situation agreed that it sounded great. Now I will discover if the reality matches the fantasy. As a married man with a child – as are all the aforementioned friends – the peace and quiet of a few days away from all the bickering, hassle and noise does indeed have considerable appeal. I can live without the joy for a short period. I'll create my own joy in this bubble in which I find myself. No sand, sea or sunbathing, but a restful holiday beckons and I can think of nothing I will enjoy more right now than a rest.

*

I have a go on the exercise bike while watching a DVD. I have the bike on quite a light setting, but I'm grateful that I can still do it at all. To say I've had MS for over four years (and that's not counting the years when it was beginning to make its presence known before my diagnosis) I remain capable of a decent amount of physical exertion. I'm still reasonably fit and I'm pumping away a good ten minutes into the episode of Peep Show that's on the TV. I guess the programme is partly responsible for helping me to ignore the weakness that is creeping up through my legs. I'm partly drawn to the comedy because I often see myself as a fifty-fifty mix of Mark and Jeremy. Uptightness and an over-developed sense of social awkwardness together with an interest in history (Mark), combined with Jez's fecklessness and dissolute nature. I was, I'm sorry to say, rather like Jeremy in my twenties. Now I'm a man with responsibilities, an everyday job, a wife, a son, a mortgage, a middle-aged man's car, a big TV, a dishwasher and a washing machine. Choose life. No thanks, I'll choose a nice break from it all.

The legs are holding up a white flag, reminding me that as well as all those other things, I'm in possession of a chronic condition. I watch the rest of the episode crashed out on the bed, then start the next. I'm interrupted by an orderly who wants to know my lunch choices. My mind must already have wound down to basic functionality because I have to ask her to repeat the options before I tell her I'll have the beef stew. What did Papillon do to keep his mind sharp? The film is my only real reference point for a long stretch of solitary. Should I pace the room, counting my steps? Would an exercise bike and some DVDs have been sufficient to keep him sane?

I continue to plough through the Peep Show series whilst I have lunch. My mind drifts off to wondering which DVDs Papillon would choose if he was confined today. *The Shawshank Redemption*? Undoubtedly a good film but perhaps he would want to steer clear of anything to do with prison, even if the heroes do escape at the end. Maybe he'd like something completely silly to give him a laugh like *Father Ted*. Why am I thinking about this? How should I know what he would like and why should I care? I've read the book, as well as seen the film more than once, but I can't pretend to know the guy and as far as idle daydreams go, this is a particularly pointless one, even for me. All I can say for certain is that I bet those coconuts sent by Dustin Hoffman tasted better than this hospital stew.

*

I've brought in some paper and my little notebook laptop. This is an ideal opportunity to develop some of my song lyric ideas, as well as make a start on that children's book I keep talking about writing. I realise at the age of forty-one that my teenage fantasy of making it as a songwriter/musician is wearing thin, but I still enjoy writing songs. I know it's time to look at other escape options from wage slavery, though, and as probably every other parent who's read to their child at bedtime, I think I'm capable of writing a children's book. So here goes. In *Misery*, James Caan writes a whole novel in a week or two when in what must be terrible pain from his mangled legs. Surely I can get a few thousand words out of my incarceration here.

What shall I start with first – my songs concerning the bottomless well we call the human condition or the story I have in my head about a boy who can't stop picking his nose? The book… I think. I suppose this is why I check pet food packaging for a living rather than enjoying the materialisation of my dreams. Lack of focus has always been my enemy. I suddenly have all the time I could wish for on my hands, coupled with a complete lack of distractions, and what am I thinking about now – what most men think about doing when they're left alone and at a loose end. I don't really have any material to feed my pathetic urges that out of the blue have come a calling. I have a laptop but no Internet access. I run through the DVDs I have with me. I do quite fancy that American hippy-chick Jeremy is with and then there is Big Suze. She would do nicely, but I can't. I don't think a nurse would like to see that as part of her working day. It'll have to be in the bathroom. I shut the door and turn on the lights. I'm back in the interrogation room at the Chinese Doctor's. The white glare bounces off the metal support bars around the toilet and there's also one of those, 'Help, I've fallen,' strings that you find in supported living. This is not creating the right mood, despite the face of that cute Chinese shop assistant flashing up somewhere in the memory/wank bank. And it suddenly feels wrong. I'm not quite sure why, but it does and I give up on the idea.

I sit back on the bed and draw the little table up to my chest and hover my fingers over the keys of my laptop again. I've only lost ten minutes but I'm pretty sure that this is not how you're supposed to write a book.

*

Day Three in the Big Brother House. Andy is coping admirably with his quarantine and has so far successfully resisted the inclination to practise onanism, not that he needs much practice. He has finished the lyrics to one song and completed over a thousand words of the first draft for his debut children's book, *The Boy Who Couldn't Stop Picking His Nose*. Andy is in the same room he has been in for the last two and a half days. He is upset because of the endless interruptions and was heard to mutter, "What is the point of being so radioactive that no one can come near you if people keep entering your room and bothering you." He is currently staring into space.

Yes, I've got myself into quite the routine here. Shower, breakfast, read, bit of work, bit of exercise, DVD, bit of work and so on, but people will insist on popping in to see me. Nurses and doctors asking after my well-being, orderlies asking what I want to eat, bringing me something to eat, taking away pots that food was eaten off and out of. No one ever crosses the line, but they are in the room and it seems to be an endless procession. I'm sure Papillon would have been delighted by these pleasant disturbances of the monotony, but I would be happy to dial them down a notch.

This is all in between my daily visits from family. I know this doesn't reflect well on me or perhaps my family either, but I find their social calls awkward. They are only allowed to stay for fifteen minutes and of course, they have to remain behind that blue line. With them at the other side of the room, just inside the door, I can't help feeling like an exhibit at a freak show. Conversation in such circumstances, even with those closest to me, is never going to flow naturally. I feel bad too that they keep making an hour round trip for the sake of these short, forced interactions. How would they take it if I said they didn't need to bother? Maybe they would be relieved or perhaps they would feel rejected and be upset. I don't want to risk finding out it's the latter, so the visits will have to be part of this weird landscape till I leave.

*

Is it my fourth day already? It feels like I've been here two minutes. Bet time didn't pass quickly for James Caan, Papillon or the other guy I've been thinking about often while I'm in here, Tom Hanks in *Castaway*. Three men pitted against their environments, without contact from the outside world. I've always enjoyed that kind of story and now I'm starring in my very own. The obvious difference is that they couldn't know if they would escape before they died. I can be fairly confident that I will be leaving on my seventh day and at the moment, time is flying towards that point.

Maybe I should give the exercise bike a name. 'XSF 500!' Doesn't really have the same emotional power as 'Wilson!' I'm not that fond of it anyway to be honest. Cycling and not going anywhere is boring and exercising without any fun attached just reminds me that I have MS. It's amazing what the brain can learn to overlook – mostly I can forget about the mild pins and needles in my feet for example, as I've possibly mentioned previously – but when the weakness in my legs shows itself, as it does much sooner than it should for someone who's reasonably fit, I'm all too aware and I'm back to being pissed off with my lot.

I wish I could be on a beach playing volleyball with one of Wilson's friends right now, like I sometimes do on holiday and

228

like I'm still capable of doing, at least to the low level at which I always played the game. Yes, when I get out of here I'll have to speak to Kate about organising another holiday. Being cast away on a beach for a week sounds like the kind of isolation from life that would suit me best.

A nurse appears. I have to say she has a better bedside manner than Kathy Bates, not that she can come anywhere near my bedside. Instead of a mallet, she has a sample bottle. They need to make sure Shit Superhero's radioactive powers are draining sufficiently through his bladder. Such is life in my current setting. She goes, I collect the bottle from where she left it and I step into the bathroom with a sigh heard by no one but me.

*

While my mum and dad are visiting today, a nurse appears that I haven't seen before. She has the flustered air of someone who is relatively new to the job, yet with a wilful demeanour that suggests she fails to listen when you mention the rules. My instincts are correct because after she has asked me a couple of questions from behind the blue line, she says to me, "Y'know, I'm just going to come closer."

With those words she penetrates the forcefield I have around me – well she strides across the line – and stands right next to the bed to continue the conversation. This is the first time a single person has been this close to me in days. I have to collect my food from a table just behind the door and return my pots there when I'm done. No orderly, doctor, or nurse has been within three metres of me since I swallowed my medicine. I'm slightly unnerved and look across to my parents with a 'what on earth is she playing at' look on my face, as they dutifully sit behind the line as they've been told to do. I mutter, "Erm, I don't think you're supposed to…" My words peter out as another nurse comes in and clocks the situation.

"Emma, can I have a word please." Judging by the presumably more senior nurse's expression, I fear for Emma, who marches back out of the room. I hear hushed, aggressive tones from behind the door, a pause and then a gunshot. A second later, what I can only imagine is Emma's body hits the hard floor with a lifeless thud. Another pause and then I can hear a bloodstained body being dragged away along the polished linoleum.

I'm starting to feel like I may have been in here long enough now. My mind is starting to explore strange places. Emma's punishment is of course no more than words can administer, of which we pick up most. The reason I'm in here and the purpose of the blue line are emphasised. What she was thinking, I really don't know. Bit thick that decision, I'm afraid, Em. You maybe need to ask yourself if nuclear medicine is the department for you.

*

My penultimate day. I'm enjoying writing the book, not that I've made it as far as I would have liked by any means, but I have to admit I'm getting a bit fed up now and just a touch bored. These feelings sometimes spread through me towards the end of a holiday. I start to wonder what's happening back home. What are people I know up to, is the house OK? If only we could spend a few minutes in our old lives, before returning to our present. That's usually all that's required for me to wonder why the hell I spent even a fleeting moment wishing a single second of my holiday away.

This might be one of those times.

*

230

I'm leaving today. I've packed up my stuff, checked the cupboards, the bathroom and under the bed like I do when I leave a hotel room and wait for Kate to arrive so she can take me home.

I've discovered that I'm the type of person who can live without people, even those close to me, for a short time without any bother. But I've also discovered that this number of days is about my limit. In truth, I knew this already, but it's been underlined. Now I'm looking forward to the old routine. In particular, I can't wait to see E and play football with him in the garden. I haven't seen him at all of course since I left the house. He's doing fine, though, and just getting on with it, like he always seems to do. We're very lucky in that way.

Kate arrives and after a quick debriefing from a doctor, I follow my wife to the door. When I reach the blue line I say to her in a croaking voice, "I... can't.... break... through." I stand on the line and attempt the classic Marcel Marceau-style mime of a man trapped in a box. I instantly regret it as I realise my mime skills are non-existent and I probably just look like a man trapped in his own personality. A roll of the eyes from Kate confirms that it did not go well and I step into the outside world with head slightly bowed.

I stride down the grey and shiny corridor, thinking about how out of control my life has been for the last few years. We always like to think we're the masters of our own destiny, but a few unexpected cards get dealt and suddenly you find yourself shut up in solitary, despite never having broken the law, because scientists have told you that they need to make sure a part of you is dead, in order to keep you alive. And that's before I get onto all the other business: having pins and needles in my feet every minute of every day, the weakness in my legs after low levels of exercise, the inability to pee like normal people, injecting myself with drugs every week, putting on a stone in just over a year because my appetite went mad, being radioactive for a fortnight, finding a

231

lump in my neck that could kill me if left untreated, finding a lump in Kate's neck that wouldn't kill her but was scary for a while, having part of my neck removed, taking a load of tablets as soon as I get up in the morning as a result of having part of my neck removed. All of it has been part of the stock car race that has brought me here to this moment.

I've probably forgotten a few things, so much has been going on. Is the finishing line anywhere close? Can we start a new race now for competitors that have MS and nothing else?

Time once more to dredge up that positive attitude from the very depths of my soul. I'm still married to a woman who makes my life better in so many ways (I'm mostly managing to keep a lid on my mood explosions, which has improved matters between us a little), I still get to watch my son grow up, I still live in a nice house, I'm still working and I still get to pursue the majority of the activities that make me happy.

And I'm still able to walk out of here, unaided, without any issues, normally. In fact, anyone who saw me in the street wouldn't know that I had a care in the world. As Papillon says at the end of the film, 'Hey you bastards, I'm still here.'

PART THREE

I like waking up after a bad dream
Makes it feel like life ain't bad
Little kids go out to play
They're just happy it's another day
It's up to you and me and who's to say
These could be the good old days

Eels – The Good Old Days

SPRING 2011 – THE GREAT UNKNOWN

When did he become this fast? Muhammed Ali said he could handcuff lightning, but even in his prime I bet he would struggle to catch E in this garden right now. Round and round the hedge we go, E's laughter trailing behind him, taunting me but not really taunting me, as I'm loving it as much as him. A simple game of tag is steamrollering all life before it, making me forget about all the shit, all the obstacles I've jumped and blundered through that are behind me, all the hills I might have to climb in the future.

I'm putting in a decent effort here. I nearly touch him but he's always just out of reach. I can still run fairly quickly for a short time, but he's able to dart and turn much more adeptly than me. I'm not too out of breath, but after a few minutes of sprinting after him my legs are saying enough is enough. I used to get this feeling if I'd been out on my bike for three hours or been made to do five laps of the football field by a sadistic games' teacher at school, but this by some distance was a more limited amount of exercise. I collapse in the centre of the lawn.

"You've beaten me."

E climbs on top of me, his gap-toothed smile evidence of a milk tooth falling out the other day. "Pathetic," he says, playfully beating his little fists into my chest. Seven years old and I know I'll never be able to catch him ever again.

"You must be the quickest in your school," I say, hopefully.

"Nearly. Fraser is quicker than me."

"Just give me a few minutes." Once I've rested for ten, I'll be good to go again. Papa Lazarou explained to me on one of my recent visits what happens to someone with MS after physical exertion. Of course, he couldn't help but be patronising, speaking as if I was the thickest of layman, but the information was useful nonetheless. He said that when a person without MS exercises, the muscles fill up with lactic acid and, as he put it, rubbish after a certain amount of time, depending on how fit he or she was. This is what made the person fatigued and eventually unable to continue. Someone with multiple sclerosis finds that the muscles fill up with this rubbish quicker and it takes longer for the rubbish to go again.

Something like that anyway. Maybe he should have patronised me a little more. What I know for certain is that my relationship with exercise of any kind goes like this: walk, run or cycle for a while, get so tired I can't continue as my legs take on the physical properties of barely set jelly, rest for a while, go again. I try not to complain. The situation could be much worse. I can still run after E on sunny days like this. I just get tired much sooner than in the past and need to rest more often. It's just a matter of resetting. Knowing my limits and adjusting to them. A bit like getting older, but prematurely.

"Why don't you practise your keepie-uppies?"

He's showing some promise as a footballer but struggles with kick-ups. He collects his ball from under a bush and proceeds to try and break his current record of eight. I lie back in the grass, thinking. First thought: the grass needs cutting. I'm finding I have to take the fortnightly lawn-cutting in stages. Thanks to Kate's foresight and talent in property development, we have a sizeable garden. It's as if a park backs straight onto the rear of the house, complete with trees, a small football pitch, two other areas of lawn. I'm sure this would be the envy of many and it is something to enjoy for the most part, but keeping on top of its maintenance when you have a chronic condition is beginning to become a problem. After cutting the main lawn, I have to sit down for fifteen minutes or so. I then cut the football pitch. Rest again. Then if I have anything left, I cut the small patch down by the compost heap before crumpling in a mess of wasted limbs on the sofa.

My contributions to the rest of the garden upkeep are limited. I'm not sure Kate fully understands why I can't do more. Maybe it's just frustration when she complains that she's having to do too much chopping and weeding on her own. Frustration is an emotion with which I'm all too familiar. I know that just because you express frustration, it doesn't mean you don't understand the root cause of your frustration, though I challenge anyone who doesn't have MS to fully understand. It's like weakness courses through every cell in your body. Having the will to overcome it is irrelevant. You will never win. You just need to wait for it to pass.

"Oo, so close. Seven." I continue to watch E's efforts, while my mind is elsewhere. I'm back in hospital consulting rooms, treatment rooms, wards, operating theatres. I reflect on my cancer scare, though Kate gets annoyed with me if I call it a cancer scare. It wasn't a scare! You had cancer. But I never felt in danger, except that time that Frewitt started talking about the possibility of it spreading to my chest. It all happened so quickly that I barely had chance to catch my breath, let alone my thoughts. The main episode that sticks in my head is still of Dr Amalia Gonzalez positioned in that chair with her round arse aimed in my direction, her looking over her shoulder and laughing in my direction. Is this a defence mechanism, or am I just a dirty get?

Hopefully, it's all behind me now (though I will hold onto that image of Dr Amalia's behind). Maybe this is why I've been spending more time contemplating – some would say brooding – on my prospects regarding the MS. I can now, so I do. I came across a statistic in some recent reading on the subject that I had heard before but had forgotten, or at least parked in a dark corner of my mind: 80% of patients with relapse remitting MS go on to develop secondary MS after two to ten years. Well it's five years since my diagnosis and nine years since I first experienced some symptoms. Can I expect things to start changing soon? From what I know, secondary means the disease is progressing irreversibly. There's no remission element to it. You're gradually becoming more disabled with each passing year and you're not going to claim any ground back. That ground is disappearing beneath your prickly feet and you best get used to it.

The rate at which it happens is the great unknown.

"I did it, Dad! I did it! Did you see?"

"Yes," I lie. Well I saw it, I just wasn't counting like I was supposed to be doing. "Nine, brilliant, well done."

"It was ten, wasn't it?"

"Erm... maybe."

"Dad!" He groans as it dawns on him that I may not have been paying full attention. "Watch. I've got it now."

Of course, he proceeds to demonstrate that he hasn't really got it and keeps failing for the next five minutes on five kick-ups or less. You will get better, though, son. You'll get stronger, fitter and your motor skills will keep developing for years to come. It's all ahead of you. For me, everything in that regard is heading in the other direction; how rapidly I don't know. Let's see how lucky I am as I head into the great unknown.

SUMMER 2011 – MS BLUES

I feel sick with nerves and have done for days. I'm only playing in a Wakefield pub at Henry Boons' Acoustic Night, but it's still enough to have left me sleepless and all too aware of the rivers of sweat that keep streaming from my armpits. Have I rehearsed enough or will bum notes pepper the set like fire alarms going off, signalling my incompetence? Will I forget the words at any point and have to rely on the back-up lyrics that I've had to employ in songs previously – mumbled nonsense that I hope is unintelligible but sufficiently comprehensible to be deemed English?

Why do I put myself through this every so often? There was something about these Thursday nights in Boons that I found irresistible I guess. The audience are music fans who have specifically come out to listen to local artists that they have never heard of. I am now one of those musicians and I suddenly feel like I have an awful lot riding on it. If even these people don't like my stuff, maybe it'll be time to call it a day. I'm too old to keep headbutting the door, hoping someone will take any notice.

Talking of which, where's Dave? He said he'd be here. I didn't even bother telling my other friends, as I didn't think they'd show much interest. I thought it would only add to the nerves too, being judged by my peers when my music isn't their kind of thing anyway. But I told Dave the time and place and he said he'd be there to support me. I give him a call. No answer. Bloody hell. I could do with seeing a familiar face here. Even Dionne isn't here yet. She's my former next-door neighbour who plays the cello. She accompanied me when I played songs at my wedding and she's agreed to reprise her role today. She said she'd be getting here around now, but so far no sign.

I'm standing at the bar, trying not to down my pint too quickly. It might calm me a little but too much lager will not be beneficial. If I'm remotely drunk, I'll sound like Shane McGowan and not in a good way. The first act is coming on to distract me. A singer-songwriter called Holly something or other with long blonde platted hair. She introduces herself, appearing natural and relaxed. Has she spent the morning on the toilet, sitting in a nauseous haze, wondering if this whole thing is really worth it? She begins to play her guitar. With just her fingers and barely looking at the strings. I have never been able to play like that. I'm strictly a plectrum guy and regularly have to check where my hand is going next. Not that I've ever had a single lesson or put much effort into learning how to pluck solely with my fingers. I've got to this point purely on my strong desire to inflict my lyrical ideas on a public who don't appear to share my vision. Maybe tonight will be different.

But watching this Holly woman, I suddenly feel like a fraud. She seems like a proper musician. I seem like someone who should have stayed in his bedroom, playing purely for his own pleasure, like thousands of other bedroom superstars across the country. And she can sing. She has a pure melodic voice. Easy on the ear and emanating from her throat without any obvious strain. That is certainly not me. I can carry a tune so long as there aren't too many notes in it. To put it another way, Mariah Carey is reputed to have a five-octave range. I can just about manage one on a good day. I take solace from the knowledge that if Ian Curtis, who I've been likened to before, went on *X Factor* he wouldn't get any further than the early rounds when they put on delusional nutjobs for the amusement of the populace.

Her song heads into the chorus. My spirits lift a little as I begin to realise that she isn't all that. Although there is a professional air to her performance, her song is a little boring, run of the mill, heard a thousand times before. If this is her first song, which you'd imagine was one of her stronger ones as that's how most sensible performers construct their set list, it doesn't bode well for the remainder. Still, the audience is quiet and letting her get on with it without interruption. They're probably like me, appreciating that she can play and sing and her song is nice enough, just unremarkable.

There's a decent smattering of applause. Enough to make me feel comfortable that I won't have rotten fruit thrown my way and hopeful that they may even clap a little harder as I give them something which to my ears is more engaging. Dionne arrives carrying her huge cello case. Perhaps the appearance of someone by my side sporting a proper in-your-face instrument will make a few of the people surrounding us sit up and take notice. 'This guy's set-up looks intriguing. If he attracts musicians of this calibre to his side, maybe he's worth watching.' It's good to have someone in my corner anyway. Dionne teaches other would-be cellists so knows what she's doing. True, this adds to my fraudster worries, but at least this bona fide musician will be underpinning my music, not undermining it. I offer her a drink. Just a sparkling water. No nerves to suppress for her, despite our very limited rehearsal time. She's written down genuine notes on proper staff paper, so any moves to the bridge or back to the verse at the wrong time are likely to be mine. Dionne playing the right notes in the right places is not one of my concerns.

Twenty minutes pass by and the first act's set is winding down. I'll be up next. My throat contracts to a level where I struggle to finish my lager. Still no sign of Dave. I give him another call. Godsakes, voicemail still. Clearly couldn't be arsed to come down to offer some encouragement to one of his closest friends. Oh well, if this is a disaster, they'll be no one I know to witness it other than Dionne and she'll be part of it, even if she isn't the reason for it. Holly packs away and clears her equipment from the small stage at the end of the room. Dionne and I take her place and get organised. Fortunately, the sound guy who runs the night is a friendly sort who is no doubt used to inexperienced bags of nerves like me and helps me get set up. Another draw for me was that he always seems to achieve a great sound. This has rarely been the case for me with the handful of gigs I've played over the years, so this will be a welcome novelty. I play a few chords to test out how it sounds and brave the microphone, singing a few lines till I'm happy with what I'm hearing. It's not the most extensive soundcheck, but I trust my soundman.

I look across to Dionne. Is she ready? It's now or never. She nods. Let's go.

We're starting with a short atmospheric instrumental. The idea is that it will help me to settle in. The chord structure is simple – just two of the tricky bastards – and any sound problems can be sorted before we begin the set proper. This is just the album opener to get things going, just something to calm my nerves and kill conversations among the onlookers. The cello kicks in and sounds just as I'd wish, eerie and full of portent. Time to shut up everyone. There's a new musical talent on the scene and you need to focus on this.

Everyone is now staring and I feel like they are there for the taking. Well, they've not experienced the full limitations of my singing yet, so enjoy the feeling while it's there. We launch straight into *Butterfly Crush*, a song about how apparently inconsequential decisions can have a monumental effect on your life. It's about the time in my late twenties when I was out on a pub crawl with the lads and we were trying to decide whether to stay in the place where we were or head to the Tut 'n' Shive. Pete advocated moving on, the line he trotted out, 'You're not going to meet your dream girl in here,' making it into the song. As we walked through the doors of the Tut 'n' Shive, a gorgeous woman with olive skin and a striking look caught my eye. When we got talking I discovered that her name was Kate.

Our performance is note perfect, I remember all the words and even feel like I sing them in a competent way. There's a respectable rumble of applause at the end. So far, so good. Let's try and enjoy this a little more now. It'll be over before you know it. Breathe. To slow the pace down I elect to chat with the audience, introducing the next song. It's one I've written recently called *MS Blues*.

In my head, I'm going to sound like Peter Ustinov, polished and confident as I explain the roots of this song I'm about to sing. What I actually do is blurt out the words, "So... guess the disease."

Some wag calls out, "Chlamydia."

I suppose I deserved that. "No, that was ages ago," I reply, which gets a small laugh. "No, I had some bad news a few years ago. I have multiple sclerosis. This song is about that."

OK, as spiels go, it's hardly going to be gain me admittance to the Guild of Raconteurs, but I think it's important to outline the source of the song, so no one is left wondering what I'm singing about before the subject matter becomes clear in the chorus. On reflection, I could probably have just given them the title, but maybe they'll be more on board now they know it's me who is dealing with this situation.

It has a country feel this one with a bum-tit-tit bum-tit-tit rhythm, the simplicity of the words juxtaposed with the indication of the mental struggle that comes with the territory, as the chorus kicks in along with the cello backing. We reach the opening lines:

> Pins and needles got hold of my feet
> And they won't let go
> Crazy legs got me in a twist
> When I say work they say no

> When I go to take a piss
> I can stand there for hours
> I know dear it's not easy for you
> Watching your man lose his powers

We're about to change into the bridge when the atmosphere is cut in two by the shrill ring-ring of a phone. I can't believe someone has forgotten to put their mobile on silent. Turn the bloody thing off will you! I'm baring my soul here. The ringtone continues to chime loudly. There's the odd quizzical look amidst the audience but no one is reaching in their pocket. I'm struggling to concentrate, particularly as the top of my leg appears to be vibrating. Oh God. The horrible truth dawns on me in a sickening instant. It is, of course, my phone that is disturbing the peace, it's ring all the more piercing for being in close proximity to the microphone. I could try to style it out, pretend that it isn't mine and hope that it goes dead in a second or two, but what if it doesn't? I don't know how many rings there'll be before voicemail kicks in and I'm kind of busy, so clarity of thought is in short supply.

I decide to make it part of the show. I stop the song dead and take out my phone. I see that it's Dave on the other end. I press answer and say, "Eh up, mate," which garners a loud cheer. I'm going to ride out this storm in another way, making it something to amuse. "Where are you? You were supposed to be here an hour ago." He says something about thinking I'd said half eight, which means he's still late. "Well I'm on stage now in the middle of a song." Another smaller cheer. I wonder if his embarrassed laugh and half-arsed apology are audible to the entire room thanks to the mic near my mouth. Whatever, I realise I need to end the call. "See you when I see you."

After hurriedly turning my mobile off, I try to reclaim a modicum of cool by throwing it onto the floor. This rather pathetic version of the rock star throwing a TV out of the hotel window immediately has me worried that I may have added a knackered phone to my pressing list of problems right now. Should I restart the song or continue where I broke off? I decide on the former and soon enough, the interruption fades into the distance. I have to get my head back in the game quickly. Regain my composure. Try to draw people back into the song.

It helps when I get past the point where the shit went down. At the second attempt, we make it to the bridge:

Will I still work
Or will I have to shirk
My responsibilities

Shall we have another kid
Or shall we just rid
Ourselves of these hopes and dreams

Chorus
Yeah I've got 'em bad
The MS blues
Yeah I've got 'em bad

The MS blues
Verse
We'll be OK in ten years' time
I know our love is for real
Just hope I'm not looking up at you
From a Stephen Hawking-mobile

Bridge
I might be a cripple
Or always walk tall
You'll just have to wait and see

If I lose my sight
Or talk with a slur
Will you be there to understand me

Chorus
Yeah I've got 'em bad
The MS blues
Yeah I've got 'em bad
The MS blues
Yeah I've got 'em bad
The MS blues
Yeah I've got 'em bad
The MS blues

As my words fade out, the cello takes centre stage, adding big spoonfuls of emotion. I play the chords for the chorus over and over and delve into the same place I hope the audience are now currently occupying. I'm lucky to have Dionne. This isn't a style of music she understands and her pay cheque has been lost in the post. But her gratis contribution is reminding me why I chose to do this. I glance up at the faces staring back at me and see what I've always dreamed of – absorption, or at least a level of attention that has stopped people from talking.

At the end of the song, everyone goes crazy. OK, that's some way from the truth, but most people clap. The phone incident already feels ages ago as I soak it all in and try to appear nonchalant as I double check my sheet of paper to see which song is next. I'm growing into this, which is appropriate as the next song is *Growing Up*. I introduce it, play it and it goes down all right. Not *as* well, but satisfactorily. I spot Dave sauntering into the room, which brings the phone disaster back into my mind. An unkind part of me considers pointing him out to everyone – 'There's the nobhead who helped to ruin *MS Blues* everyone' – but decide that it's best if I don't help everyone remember that. I introduce and play *Blue Dress* instead, which is a really quiet song. I'd say you can hear a pin drop, but what you can actually hear is the sound of the beer pumps being pulled and hissing back into position – a reminder that this is just the back room of a pub that I'm playing. Not to worry, it sounds just as I'd hoped otherwise.

We've reached the last song. I invite everyone to show their appreciation of Dionne. There's a loud cheer and mutterings of, 'Yeah, yeah,' in which I detect an undercurrent of sentiment. Am I being paranoid to think that the noises coming from them are suggesting that they think she's the real find here? 'Yes, that cellist is really good. She carried the songs in truth and you could almost ignore the fact that the guy couldn't sing.' I try to shake off this notion, knowing that our final song properly offers Dionne the opportunity to steal the show. It's a cover of *Lovesong* by the Cure that I played at my wedding. The cello dominates once more in the closing section. I have no choice other than to embrace the situation. The thing they may mostly take from this evening is their appreciation of Dionne's musicianship but who arranged all her parts, wrote all but one of the songs that she is accompanying? There'd be no part for her to play if it wasn't for the guy, the poor sap whose singing they politely endured because he has MS.

Whatever the source of the applause at the end, in the moment I don't particularly care. After years of utter indifference or having backs turned on me, hearing reasonably loud, genuine applause is balm to my soul. I already feel the approach of an anti-climax as I think of the days of rehearsal and shredded nerves and know that after a mere thirty minutes it's all over. We clear away our gear, join Dave and I grab another pint. Dionne shoots straight off. Job done for her.

"What did you think?" I ask Dave.

"Yeah, good. You must have been pleased with the sound you had."

Classic damning with faint praise.

I pretend to sort through some of the CDs I've brought along to sell. They're all the same so sorting them in any way is somewhat unnecessary. I just want to remind everyone that the CDs I mentioned halfway through the set are still here for sale. So far I've shifted a grand total of one, which was to Holly and certainly only because I bought one of hers. Dave offers to take one off my hands too, probably out of guilt for missing half the show. I know for a fact that he won't listen to it but I'm happy to take his money.

Five minutes go by and an old geezer, balding but grey hair straggling down the sides, appears at my shoulder.

"Enjoyed that, cheers," he says. "How much?"

I attempt nonchalance. "Five quid."

He starts to examine the front and back covers. "Been doing this long?"

"On and off for years," I tell him with a shrug.

"Right, yeah... I used to be in a few bands myself years ago."

"Right." I firmly resist any temptation to ask him about this period of his life. I don't want to get into any Les McQueen-type conversation about how his band's single was Peter Levy's record of the week on Radio Aire back in the eighties, like we're in an episode of *The League of Gentlemen.*

"Sorry to hear about the MS by the way. Good song, mind."

Again, I recall the apathy of previous audiences. It's just one old guy and one who possibly buys the CDs of all local acts as his way of supporting them, knowing from experience the loneliness of trying to get anyone to take notice of your music, but I'm not about to dismiss his comment as unwarranted.

"Thanks."

"Anyways, cheers," he says, holding up the CD. "I'll give this a listen."

He departs and I'm left with the hope that he is the beginning of a steady stream of customers visiting my corner of the bar demanding a copy of my CD. Of course, it doesn't materialise. In fact, no one else comes anywhere near me. I chat to Dave for ten minutes while the final act sets up. It's a four-piece band, which presents the immediate challenge of fitting on the tiny stage. They run through their set and they're fine. They play capably, the singer can hit the notes and is certainly more of a singer than me but there's nothing interesting about his voice. In truth, there's nothing interesting about their whole act. There's an acceptable level of applause at the end of each song, but you can tell that the general vibe in the room is mild boredom. They mention the CD they have for sale and jokingly appeal for everyone to buy it as they had to pool their scarce resources for the studio time involved. You can tell that they're going to struggle to beat my stunning level of sales.

I hear Les McQueen again in my ear. 'It's a shit business.' It is indeed, Les. To get anywhere, you need to be more than talented. You need to be relentless and lucky, two things I'm apparently not.

The talented part is open to considerable debate as well. All these years, maybe I've been as delusional as these four guys. It's easy to fall into the trap of thinking you just need to find the right venue, the right audience. Well this audience were the right sort. They had come out tonight specifically to listen to acoustic-based singer-songwriters and they were attentive and appreciative, even silent in the parts where I needed them to be silent.

With those circumstances, I'm left alone with my own limitations. I didn't mess up, other than the phone incident, though admittedly that was a monumental fuck-up, but if I'd played any longer I'd be amazed if I didn't make a major mistake at some point. And then there's the voice. I had very kind, high calibre reverb to work with tonight and I felt like I sang as well as I'm ever going to, but I know deep down that it's still not good enough.

I stare into the cardboard box containing the CDs, wondering what I'll do with the stack I have left. It is clearly never going to get better than this. It feels an appropriate time to call it a day. Like sportsmen say when they retire, go out whilst you're on top. OK, I've not won any cup with this performance but it's a narrow victory and that's good enough for me.

And I got *MS Blues* out into the world for it's one and only airing. That was the highlight. It also contained the lowlight with my phone going off in the middle of it, but for five minutes while I was singing those words, I felt a little better about the situation. Tomorrow, it's back to reality.

NOV 2011 – BALLS TO MS

For my forty-third birthday Kate is taking me to a Nazi death camp. Well to be precise she's brought me to Krakow for the weekend and, for me at least, Auschwitz was the must-see of the trip. I'm sure it's not what she would like to be doing on this of all days, but it's my birthday so she had to agree, albeit with a roll of the eyes.

You don't come to Poland in late November to bask in the sunshine and today the weather does not disappoint. The sky is a uniform grey and there's a bite to the chilled air as we arrive at the bus station. We debated for a good while how to get to the camp. Travelling there and back by taxi worked out at about sixty quid. The bus would be more hassle but considerably cheaper. As we skip up the steps outside the station, an old stubbly guy stops us and tries to persuade us that his taxi is a much better option. The bus will take for ever, he tells us, and will hardly save us anything. The figures he fires at us seem a little off, though, from what we've read, so we plough on past him.

We were already cutting it fine and that little delay has eliminated any margin for error we may have had regarding where to get our tickets or from which bay the bus is leaving. Fortunately, the queue at the ticket booth is short and the vendor speaks good English. Unfortunately, the bay we want is at the far end of the station. We have to run for it and I'm struggling for breath by the time we get there. I started playing football again recently but I'm still far from fit. Happily, passengers are still boarding and we are able to take our seats and let our heartbeats settle down to a regular pace.

We are soon motoring through the bleak Polish countryside. When we plumped for the bus I imagined a typical single decker but it's actually just a minibus and the driver is throwing us all around in the back like we're scraps of paper caught in a stiff wind. I remember where we are going and resolve not to moan to Kate. This isn't the day to be bellyaching about my problems, whether trivial or MS-based. I see a train on the horizon and redraw it in my mind as a chain of cattle trucks proceeding to one of Poland's many concentration camps, each carriage carrying a sorry cargo of people. Trapped in their wooden crates, they wouldn't even have had this featureless landscape to distract them.

No, I must not complain.

Having said that, there's nothing to stop me complaining internally and I do plenty as this journey begins to leave me longing for a taxi. Sardined in this tin can, we are apparently in the hands of a frustrated fighter jet pilot. Every time he sets off after dropping off and picking up passengers, we're slammed into our seats by the G-force created as he hits the accelerator, then unpinned again as he flies round every corner like his life depends on it and our lives are worth nothing.

I said there would be no bellyaching today but I now have to contend with a physical bellyache. For someone who has never been the best traveller, this is a severe test. As I spot a sign that tells me we're only a few kilometres from our destination, I begin to feel sickness wash over me. I groan as we go round another bend and pray that I can hold it together for the next few minutes. Feeling like you're going to throw up should surely be at the end of the night on your birthday.

For the benefit of the tourists, the driver calls out, "Auschwitz," before I can be given the award for Most Unpopular Passenger in Poland for Spewing in the Confines of a Minibus. I'm surprised that we are the only ones who alight. I'm guessing all the other tourists are not as tight as us and paid for a taxi. I sit on the kerbside for five minutes, breathing in the welcome fresh air till I feel better, then we look for the entrance. We were surprised that we weren't dropped off right outside, but after some gormless scanning of our surroundings we spy some coaches and people in the distance, so assume that this is where we should head.

It's a ten-minute walk down this straight, non-descript lane, which gives me ample time to wonder yet again why we didn't just get a taxi. We have another issue to contend with now too – it's lunchtime, we're both hungry and the likelihood of finding something to eat round here appears remote. We're in luck, though, as there is a single café next door to the building where you get tickets. The interior decorator apparently took inspiration from a tour of the camp and choice is limited, but the pizza on offer seems a safe bet. A woman whose Polish name probably translates as Austere grabs a pre-made one and bangs it in the microwave. Oh well, at least we won't be waiting long. Two minutes later we are eating a sloppy tasteless pizza but we're at Auschwitz and I'm very grateful that we're able to stuff our faces and know that this won't be the last time we eat today.

I must not complain.

Next door, we go to buy our tickets but there is a problem. We were planning on joining one of the group tours but although it's only half one, the last one has already left. We ask if we could not catch up with them but they left twenty minutes ago. We could go round on our own but will we get the full experience? Everything I've read suggests you need a guide to really understand the place. We're never going to be here again and the alternative of a personal guide is being dangled in front of us. I'd considered this option before we came but had dismissed it as too expensive. Kate makes noises like she's happy for us to explore on our own but it's up to me.

It pains me to part with the money but not half as much as it pains me when I do some quick calculations in my head. If we'd taken a taxi, thus avoiding the hellish bus journey, we would have been here in time to have done one of the group tours and been no worse off. If we'd forgone the culinary delight that was our microwaved pizza, we could also have caught the last tour too. Bugger.

I must not complain.

Our guide arrives, a woman wearing a purple beret about my age who introduces herself as Marika. She takes us first to the entrance where the infamous wrought iron gates reside. The words 'Arbeit Macht Frei' stare down at us – work makes you free. The Nazis are not noted for their sense of humour but maybe we underestimate them. What a crock of shit, particularly here. Apparently, the original gates were stolen a few years ago and these are a copy. Where are the original ones now I wonder? Are they at the end of someone's drive in Bavaria, someone whose back bedroom is stacked to the ceiling with an impressive collection of Nazi memorabilia? On our request, Marika takes a photo of us with the gates in the background. I enjoy the experience of no one telling me to smile for once. Yeh! I've finally found a place where my resting face fits.

Next to the fence that was once electrified, we're given lots of background information about the camp, who was sent here, what they were made to do. I soak in all the details of this historical horror story. Kate's interest in history generally is passing, but I can tell that she too is fully engaged.

We are then taken round the various barrack-style buildings, each illuminating a different aspect of the whole grim episode. In one dedicated to the medical experiments that took place here on the unwilling human guinea pigs, Marika tells us about Dr Mengele, surely one of the most evil men who has ever lived. I knew plenty about him beforehand, but here in Auschwitz you can somehow feel the chill of his hand on your shoulder. He was particularly fond of performing his barbaric and entirely pointless experiments on identical twins, but people with a physical defect of any kind were also fair game. However, I'm sure I would have been of little interest to him. Hans, you appear to have brought me a man who's gait becomes a little unsteady if he walks for an hour. Vot do you expect me to do with him? Sounds like he's going to struggle to do a fourteen-hour shift in the munitions factory, though. Send him you know where.

I feel uncomfortable for turning the spotlight on myself, even silently, but it's difficult not to imagine being one of Mengele's subjects while you listen to Marika's descriptions. We move on to the next building but not before she delivers the stinger to the saga: after the war, the Americans had Mengele prisoner and by rights he should have been one of the first given a one-way ticket to the gallows, yet due to administrative errors he was released and he lived out his days in relative comfort in South America. If you're ever looking for proof that bad things happen to good people and fortune shines on the worst that humanity has to offer, here it is. I step out into the light, ruminating on how everything in life is so random. You can create some of your own little victories but ultimately you have no control. Whichever way the wind blows is the direction in which you'll travel.

My trite musings lead to another internalised admonishment,

but any selfish thoughts immediately vanish as we are confronted with the large glass display cases in the next room we enter. One is filled high with a bed of human hair, shaved from the prisoners' heads when they arrived. The other contains a mountain of shoes, confiscated along with all other possessions. Marika says a few words then lets us take in the scene in silence. I glance across at Kate as she scans the vast cascade of shoes. There are scores of tiny ones amongst the adult boots and ladies heels. Her bottom lip begins to tremble and as she turns to me I see tears are falling from her eyes. I move closer and put my arms around her. She nestles her head in my chest and we stay like that for a good thirty seconds.

I look over Kate towards Marika. She's no doubt seen many reactions like this over her time as a guide. "We have a seven-year-old at home," I say to her, somewhat unnecessarily.

"Yes, it is very sad," she replies, rather robotically.

Matters don't become any more cheery when we visit the wall where prisoners were shot or one of the ovens where they were burnt. It's difficult to comprehend that this all happened as recently as my mum and dad's childhood years until you remember that similar things are still happening in some countries. It's certainly a birthday I'll remember.

The bleakness is set to increase further as well. Our time in Auschwitz 1, which has essentially been converted into a museum, is coming to a close. Now, Marika explains, we will be taken by bus to the other camp, Birkenau. This has been preserved purely as a memorial – the sole purpose of Birkenau was to be an extermination camp.

The bus ride is only a ten-minute one but we are on the type of long single decker I envisaged for our hour and a half journey from Krakow – and we are the only ones on this one. But I suppose many visitors will already have left, as it is getting late. Darkness is not exactly approaching fast but the light is starting to fade, perhaps partly as a result of a mist that is falling in wispy swirls.

We arrive at the camp and the first thing you notice are the train tracks that cut straight through the main entrance. Immediately recognisable from the many documentaries I've watched surrounding the subject, this is where the cattle trucks arrived from all over Europe. As soon as people were standing on Polish soil, they were divided into those that would be sent immediately to the gas chambers and those that would be worked to near-death before being sent to be gassed.

We're taken into one of the wooden huts where prisoners slept. Packed in three to each bunk, sometimes more, their only consolation must have been the body warmth of others. Back outside I'm struck by the icy promise of the forthcoming Polish winter. I ask Marika how low the temperatures can drop round here. She tells me that minus twenty is quite common. I pull my big coat around me. When the camps are discussed, people concentrate on the systematic murder, the starvation, the disease, but standing here in Birkenau, feeling the wind whip across the vast empty expanse and cut right through me, I reflect that the cold must have been one of the greatest hardships. Dressed in the thinnest clothing with no source of heat, how did anyone at all survive?

Marika invites us to head to the top of a watchtower. As I climb the many steps, I become ever more aware that my legs are starting to pack up on me. I've been on my feet for ages, traipsing all over the camp and the MS is instructing me that enough is enough. All the strength in my leg muscles has departed by the time I reach the top but I've made it, just. Kate notices me struggling up the last flight and asks if I'm OK. Yeah, no problem.

I must not complain.

As one would expect, you have a clear view from up here of

most of the camp. There is no sign of the seat that I currently crave, so I lean against the window, deep in thought. How would I have survived here? The Nazis were no fan of disabilities, genetic defects and the like. Would I have been sent to my death as soon as I arrived? If I'd been standing up on the train for hours, I might have struggled to stay upright for the inspection. But they would probably have thought this was just due to the conditions of the journey, as I would not have been the only one. Nobody would automatically know that I had multiple sclerosis. Maybe I'd be spared and could continue to hide my health problems. No one seeing me in the camp today would guess I had MS. It's nearly ten years since those first symptoms began to prickle in my legs and I'm doing all right. Still getting around fine for a while and even able to play football to a level above embarrassing. I'm sure I would not have been able to endure this life for very long at all, but MS would not have been the first adversary to knock me down.

I look across the fields, imagining the desperate scene below seventy years ago. There is a large group of students, all wearing white hoodies, tramping over the grass in a line behind their tutor. I note that one or two of the female students are rather pretty. Is it wrong for my eyes to point this out to me while in this place? Bad eyes! I shake this thought and focus instead on the fact that several of them are carrying large white flags complete with a blue Star of David on them. This act of defiance is visually striking and, as I watch the flags flutter high in the breeze on their poles, it brings a lump to my throat. Fuck you, Nazis. You didn't win. We are strong. Balls to you Hitler, or should that be ball to you, as you of course only had one. We are still here and you are not.

It's nearly time to leave. I have a lovely three-course birthday meal waiting for me back in Krakow. Talk about counting your blessings. My legs have recovered a little from their recent exertions and I descend the stairs no problem at all. Alone, we wander the fields for five more minutes. I give Kate a kiss and stare off into the distance across the great nothingness. We then get back on the bus.

JAN 2012 – REYNARD TO REYNARD

For some reason, the news hasn't made the back pages that I'm playing football again. True, I'm part of a Dad's Army of middle-aged men who are just thankful to make it through a match without dying, but it's definitely a mark in the good news column.

We've been having these kickabouts for the last few months at a football centre that has recently opened near to home. Getting enough players has not been easy. We've had to press-gang people into participating who have rarely broken sweat for years. This has meant that men have been falling like a Home Guard that has actually seen some action. Every week someone pulls or twists something, including one guy who came the first week, played for twenty minutes, injured his knee and has never been seen again. Despite this, we always seem to manage to rustle up at least ten men to do an approximate impression of running about on the 3G pitch.

I say men but not everyone is yet allowed to vote. The first week E came down with me to watch and I let him join in with the warm up. When we were ready to start I told him to watch from the sidelines, but the others said no, it's fine, stay on, perhaps thinking that even at seven years old he couldn't be worse than them. To be fair, E is a good little player and has recently been picked up by Huddersfield Town's academy, so I was confident he wouldn't embarrass himself or me. I was just worried that someone might fall over in a misguided attempt at a Cruyff turn and accidentally sit on him.

So far, he remains unscathed and happily, even with MS, I'm able to show him that some of the old skills were only slumbering. All that was required to rouse them was entering the arena again – and pitting them against less fit, less determined and less able adversaries. I can get around the pitch fine and at this level I would even say I'm one of the better players. I just have to go in goal for a while after around twenty minutes to recover. When play is at the other end I crouch down on my haunches, to take the weight off my legs. Ten or fifteen minutes later, I'm able to rejoin the outfield action. I can't last as long second time around and am back in goal for the end of the game, but considering it's six years after my diagnosis and ten since symptoms first began to appear, I'm happy that I'm able to be part of this at all.

It's my first stint in goal. I've made a couple of decent saves. Nothing wrong with my arms and my reflexes are still there. I'm kneeling on the pitch now, however, as the muscles in my thighs and calves feel like a big needle has been inserted into them and all the strength has been drawn out. My eyes focus on E. He's loving being allowed to play with the grown-ups and I'm loving playing alongside him. A straightforward case of father-son bonding that I strive to bathe in and not take for granted. I watch him dash here and there without a care in the world. I told him not to try anything too complicated. Just control it and play a simple pass, an instruction which for the most part he follows. He bangs in a few goals too. No one bothers to mark him, of course, so he often finds himself free in shooting positions. Every time he finds the back of the net, I experience a tiny murmur of pride.

I recall myself at that age. No idea what life might offer me or take away. Just the simple joy of managing to score against an older boy or adult and seeing the expression on his face. Even at that age you can tell that rueful smile is trying to conceal annoyance that a little kid has managed to get the better of him. I see that same expression now on Martin's face as he picks the ball out of the goal after E has slotted another one past him into the corner. The boy has a pretty hard shot for his age. Is it timing or a physiological thing? I imagine the strength in his young legs is similar to mine right now, only they're supporting considerably less weight and he won't have the sense that missing strength has been replaced in equal measure by weakness.

I stand up as the opposition is now on the attack. I feel a lot better for the rest and have to spring to the edge of my area to try to close down Simon as he bears down on goal. He beats me, though, and now it's my turn to retrieve the ball from the net. The break in play at least gives me the opportunity to swap goalkeeper duties with John and I trot back into midfield.

The match ebbs and flows with goals flying in all over the place, including a brace from the man with the scars in his brain and spine. Everyone is tiring rapidly now, not just those with defective central nervous systems, and defending is going out of the window. E picks the ball up in the left back area and brings it forward. A combination of fatigue and the fact that he's only just turned eight means that he is able to proceed relatively unopposed. Simon steps forward to offer cursory resistance, but E spots an opportunity in the shape of his dad who is standing near the centre spot. He plays the ball to me but doesn't, as football pundits would say, stand there admiring his pass. He continues to run into the attacking half and with one touch I return the ball to him. In a single move we've bypassed Simon's attempt to take possession from us and E is now approaching our opponents' goal. He takes the perfectly weighted through ball in his stride and easily slips the ball past Martin yet again.

"Get in!" I find myself shouting.

E skips back towards me, a huge grin on his face. I hold out my hand for him to high-five me and he obliges. A commentary has quickly formed in my head. 'Wonderful combination play there between the father and son duo. Reynard Junior picks it up and plays a quick one-two with Reynard Senior and the young man has finished with aplomb.' I hear Alan Hansen's voice chip in: 'What I like about this is the way Reynard doesn't stand around admiring his pass. He's on his bike ready to receive the return ball from Reynard and he shows nerves of steel to slot it home. I know I said you can't win anything with kids but…'

In the moment, I forget all about the enemy within that forces me to rest even when I'm not particularly out of breath. Reality soon retakes control of my thoughts, though. In truth, the reason why I gave E a one-touch return pass was because I was incapable of doing much else. After my latest stint of running, I can no longer move and the job of goalie once more beckons. I shuffle back to the penalty area and lean back against the crossbar – the goals are wide but only about three feet high – my arms stretched out either side of me along its length. Though I'm back in the grip of MS, I don't care much right now. It's been a good game, I've kept up my fitness, bagged a few goals and what just happened between E and myself is filling me with a joy more abundant than is probably warranted.

But fuck it. I'll take my pleasures wherever I can find them and hold onto them with whatever strength my body can still muster.

EASTER 2012 – DON'T TAKE YOUR LEGS FOR GRANTED

For our family holiday, I agreed to be repeatedly fleeced by the Disney Corporation in Florida. As I had insisted we visit Auschwitz on our last trip abroad, I could hardly argue with Kate if she suggested the next place we should go was Disney World, the self-proclaimed happiest place on earth.

Since being picked up off the floor after hearing how much it was all going to cost, I have tried to throw myself into the spirit of this adventure. Strolling around the parks, listening to the sunny music that's piped in from everywhere, even someone like me who is more than in touch with his miserable side found it impossible not to be carried along by the prevailing vibe.

Only I'm not in the happiest place now, and not because our tour of the parks is over. We've travelled south to West Palm Beach and Disney seems to have sucked me dry not only of cash. My body appears to have collapsed in on itself. I should be on the beach or sitting in a beachside bar with a cocktail, but instead I'm confined to bed. Just like that Christmas when I still had a thyroid and it decided to get in on the action by screwing me over some more, I'm incapable of movement. I've done far too much of it – movement that is – over the last week. The endless walking from one ride to another, in between the constant shuffling along in queues, has clearly taken its toll on a body inhabited by MS. I feel like I can't even lift my arms, never mind put one foot in front of the other to go anywhere. This is now my lot on this vacation, for how much more of it I couldn't say.

Kate and E have gone out to explore. I told them there was no point in them missing out as well. The martyr, however, is now marinading in his own thoughts. Rays of sunshine are creeping through the thick floor-length curtains but this is not delivering the joy it normally would. It just reminds me that I'm stuck in here, calculating how much money these hours equate to as a percentage of this very expensive break.

I try instead to focus on the fantastic time we had in Orlando. The smiles on E and Kate's faces infected me too and my natural aversion to theme parks took a beating. It helped that E is only taking his first forays into 'big ride' territory. When it comes to rollercoasters, I've always said I would rather be punched in the face than get on one. Fortunately, there's little that's too fierce in Disney and what there is of that ilk, E approached with similar trepidation to me. A few relatively tame rides and some visual treats. That suited me fine.

But I'm now being given a reminder that my body hates me. That blissful family time has now been kicked firmly in the family jewels. I feel utterly drained. I'm hoping I'll drift off and wake up a different physical specimen. I've been lying here like this most of the afternoon and so far sleep has proved elusive. I can't help wondering what I might be missing out on, what Kate and E might be doing right now, while I'm stapled to the bed by multiple sclerosis.

I strain to listen to the ocean in the distance. Waves crashing is one of my favourite sounds in the world. I imagine I'm the sea being pushed backwards and forwards, at the mercy of a force out of my control. The natural rhythm of the back and forth calms me. I have a vague sense of letting go.

*

I wake with a start. Not in that dramatic fashion where the character in the horror film sits bolt upright in bed – has anyone ever done that in real life? – but something happens in my dream that jolts me back to reality. I was running, trying to get somewhere, yet the faster I seemed to run, the further away my destination appeared. I'm not sure what made my brain spark back into consciousness but I know the precise source of my anxiety dream. Lanzarote 1998.

An unremarkable week in the sun, that's all we wanted. We had it all booked. Cheap hotel in a mediocre resort. Holiday reads at the ready. Two sun loungers with our names on them. My passport, though, was still in a drawer at my mum and dad's at this stage in my life so at the weekend I went to collect it. Whilst there, they gave me a holdall for my hand luggage. I didn't really want to take it as its style hardly fitted with the Seattle rock image I'd been cultivating since the days of Nirvana, but they were so proud of this bag that they used for their holidays, showing me all the useful zip pockets it had, that I felt obliged to take it. I'd decide later if I was really going to use it.

I got home that Monday evening after work, a week or so before we were due to fly, to find Kate waiting for me at the door of the bungalow we were renting at the time.

"Andy, you're here."

What a strange way to greet me, I thought. "Erm, yes."

"I think we've been burgled."

"Fuck, no," I groaned. "Have they taken much?" Part of me was wondering why she wasn't sure. She admitted to me later that her first thought was, had I left her? We had only been living together for four months, but even allowing for insecurities early in a relationship, I've always found this to be a strange notion. Would I leave in such a hurry that I would break a door handle and make my exit out the back? And why would I take all her CDs, including ones for which I'd professed disdain?

We assessed what they had taken. Besides the CDs, the TV had gone, along with the video recorder. That's how last century it was – if you ever got burgled in the 80s and 90s, they took the prized cutting-edge technology that was your VCR. We were insured, so we could just about cope with the fact that we wouldn't be able to tape *Friends* while we were away, but I wasn't looking forward to telling my parents that their beloved holdall had been employed as a convenient carry case for our CDs.

After the police had gone, we were busy being stoical as we climbed into bed that night. My head had barely touched the pillow when I sat bolt upright like a character in a horror film when they wake from a nightmare (I hadn't been asleep, if you happen to be thinking I'm contradicting myself).

"Oh, fuck, fuck, fuck, fuck, fuck!"

"What's up? What's wrong?" Kate asked, understandably alarmed.

"My passport was in one of the pockets of that holdall!"

"You're joking."

Now was not the time to wonder why the phrase 'you're joking' is automatically employed upon receiving all manner of news – I bumped into that guy you used to go out with in the supermarket, I think you should know I have a third nipple, your entire family has been captured by Somali pirates. Now was very much the time to fret about how I was going to obtain a new passport in the space of a very limited number of working days.

Some of the exact details are now sketchy in my mind but I

must have paid extra to Fastrack a fresh application, as I remember that the new passport had been processed and was on its way back to me with time to spare. Workers at the Royal Mail in Liverpool, however, had other ideas. They had heard that a man in Yorkshire urgently needed his passport and so called a lightning – and indefinite – strike. My precious package could be anywhere in the system and when it would be pushed through my letterbox was anyone's guess.

The day of the flight was fast approaching and there was only one thing for it – I would have to drive to Liverpool and pick up an emergency passport. As our flight was not till early afternoon, to cut down on travelling we decided perhaps and, as it turned out, definitely foolishly to travel to Liverpool, then Manchester airport on the same day. If we set off early enough in order to arrive as soon as the passport office opened, we had enough time. What could possibly go wrong?

Everything, just about. We were on the road early but hit rush hour traffic and the office had been open half an hour as we entered the building, so plenty of people were in front of us. When we were finally able to head back to Manchester with a fresh passport, we were cutting it fine but still felt like the clock was on our side, so long as we had a clear run. It was clearish but the check-in desk had been open a good while as we neared the airport so I dropped Kate off at the terminal with the cases while I sped off to the way off-site parking that I'd booked. Only problem was, I couldn't find it. I found out later that the road or junction numbers had changed round there recently and, in an age pre-satnavs, I was working from an out-of-date information sheet. Thus ensued a fruitless tour of the motorways that surround Manchester Airport, all the while the terror rising within me till my brain began to melt and I could no longer think straight.

I returned to the airport in a screech of tyres and dumped the car in the short-term parking outside the terminal building. No doubt the first task I'd have post-holiday would be paying a fine to release a wheel clamp. I dove into what I thought was Departures with ten minutes to spare, but I couldn't see where to go. I'd only just started wearing glasses and didn't really use them except for driving at night, but now I was finding it impossible to read any of the signs. In my extreme panic, I had probably forgotten how to read anyway.

For some completely unfathomable reason I soon found myself in the long stay multi-storey. How or why I've no idea but I remember running between the cars, trying to find the exit. This is the section of the drama that used to turn over and over in my head years ago, as I endured regular night sweats as a result of the whole distressing episode. As it plays out in the dream, as it has done just now, I'm bouncing over the bonnets of cars like I'm in *The Professionals*. How do I escape this labyrinth? Will I ever see Kate again? Have I any chance of making that plane?

The nerve-shredding anxiety often wakes me at this juncture, but sometimes I burst through a set of grey double doors, tumble to the floor and look up to see Kate standing at the checkout desk, drumming her fingers, saying, 'Where have you been?'. The actual events were not that much different. I happened upon her almost by chance after my unscheduled tour of the airport and she said to me, "Where the fuck have you been?" in a rather less chilled out voice than the calm one my dream gives her.

Apparently, they had been asking her for the last ten minutes if she was prepared to go on her own. If I'd been one minute later, they would have refused us entry through the gate and that would have been it. As it was, we were let through, but our problems were not over. As our current run of luck dictated, the plane was sitting at something like Gate 642, a distant crew regularly calling our name and growing angrier by the second.

We had to full-on leg it for what felt like miles and my hand luggage seemed to weigh every kilogramme of the 10kg allowance. Another part of my dream is coming back to me. I was running through the airport, this time with Kate alongside me. I had a large rock on my back, or was I carrying a suitcase? Whatever, it's interesting that both parts of the dream I remember clearly are where I'm running. I'm full of anxiety but none of my concerns centre on my ability to run. Despite the distance and the great weight I'm hauling down endless corridors, I'm sprinting without a second thought being given to the act. I'm only thinking about catching that plane.

If I could go back to that fool who assumed he'd be healthy all the way till old age, I would love to give him a shake – 'Stop taking your legs for granted!' He would no doubt stare back at me vacantly and once he overcame the shock that his future self was talking to him, he would probably say, 'What the hell are you talking about, don't take your legs for granted? What else am I to do? They've always been there.'

'But they won't always behave how you want them to!'

'How do you mean?'

Maybe at this point in the little play I've concocted here I would think it was better for me to live in ignorance. Would I really have liked to know what was coming? It was only another three years till that day when I walked into town after dropping my car off for its service, but seven till my diagnosis. That was seven years without the presence of MS in my life. Yeah, it was probably best to be ignorant of what was on its way.

'I said, how do you mean?' Pre-MS Self asks again.

'Oh, erm, well you know, legs are always there to support us and get us around. Don't you think that's amazing?'

'I thought I'd get wiser as I got older, but Future Self, you're an idiot.'

The scenario raises a smile in me but then it hits me again that I can't currently get out of bed. To be honest, I would have struggled to move another step when I finally collapsed into that aeroplane seat, absolutely dripping in sweat. I think I'd just about stopped breathing heavily by the time we began our descent into Lanzarote, but we'd made it. Somehow, we'd made it.

It was a good holiday too, perhaps enhanced by the awareness of what we had gone through to experience it. It was certainly not one that would have been improved by knowing, in a few years' time, multiple sclerosis would come knocking at my door.

2013 – HANNAH AND HER SISTER

I sometimes speak to Hannah at work. You may remember she's the woman who likes to rap on the big window in the studio whenever someone is doing something noteworthy on the other side of the glass, such as skinning up a joint or exposing their cock in the bushes. Hannah is the anti-me. Any observer would mark her down as the happiest person imaginable. If Hannah ever came into work with anything approaching depression etched on her face, we may as well all give up on life. She's relentlessly chirpy, a bit mad, not averse to the odd sexual comment in the workplace. As a birthday treat, Steve reckons she even flashed her bra at him in the kitchen, though he's not the most trustworthy source. Still, whenever I'm alone with Hannah in the kitchen, I make a point of mentioning to her that it's my birthday, whether or not it is.

Yes, nothing appears to get Hannah down. Just as well when you shine a light on her sister. Hannah's sister is one of our main topics of conversation. Her sister, you see, also has MS. But not like I have MS. Her MS is a rather different beast. Let's compare and contrast, starting with myself.

I have a list of annoying and frustrating symptoms. My feet feel permanently weird – a strange combination of numbness and pins and needles, which makes it seem like my socks are made from a fine grit and my feet are made of wood. These strange sensations can sometimes rise up my legs all the way to my waist and even infect my fingers. There is a limit on how far I can walk that is way below where it should be for a man of my age and build. I occasionally feel really weak to the point that I can't do anything for a while. This can last for several hours like it did in West Palm Beach or even a couple of days. I also have difficulty peeing. It's very frustrating that a simple bodily function is such a struggle every time, but it's just something to which I have had to become accustomed.

All these limitations on my bodily functions are seen through the prism of not knowing what the future holds. A version of Damocles' sword hangs permanently above my head. Try as I might to avoid ever focusing on how sharp the blade may prove to be, it's difficult not to when another episode of extreme fatigue visits me or I'm lying awake at night staring at the ceiling, mind grasping for any morsel of anxiety that can keep me awake some more.

On the bright side, I've never required any kind of walking aid. Maybe I would benefit from one after I've been walking for a while, but I'm not prepared for that kind of come down yet. I guess I should celebrate the fact that I have that choice this far into my relationship with the condition. And not only that, I can still run for a short time, even play football, though that is becoming increasingly difficult. So long as I can even consider stepping onto a football pitch wearing kit, I will strive to avoid complaining too much.

I also see a brighter side to it all when, perhaps unkindly, I think these words: at least I'm not Hannah's sister.

Relapse remitting MS – the type that I have – can be a bastard. Many people with it have it far worse than me. They acquire it at a younger age and head downhill quicker and further. Hannah's sister, though, has primary progressive MS. With primary, as soon as the first symptoms begin to appear, they steadily become worse. This can take a long time, but she was not so lucky.

Around the period when I was chasing burglars down the street in the midst of our hellish house renovation, Hannah's sister was on her hen do. In her early thirties, she already had a toddler but she and her boyfriend wanted to put an official stamp on their partnership. Towards the end of the night, she dropped her glass on the periphery of the dancefloor. Everyone assumed she was just pissed. Hannah must have seen something on her sister's face that suggested otherwise and went over to see her.

"I couldn't hold it," she was told. "My hand's locked up."

No more thought would have been given to it if normal service had resumed by the next day, but she still could not grasp anything with that hand and had to eat her hotel breakfast using the other one. If it persisted she would have to see the doctor, but in the meantime she had a great deal of life to plan. There were all the final details of the wedding to iron out. She tried not to let the problems with her right hand bother her and the wedding was a beautiful day, everything she had dreamed it would be. What's more, soon afterwards she discovered that she was pregnant again. It was a traditional path of contentment but one she was delighted to be pursuing. Everything was mapped out as her younger self would have hoped and all was as it should be.

Except for this blasted hand problem. She had visited the GP who suggested that it was probably the stress of planning the wedding and now the thought of a second child on the way that had caused it and it was likely to go soon enough. Had she tried any of the various relaxation techniques available? This she found unsatisfactory and being unable to use her right hand effectively was getting her down. She didn't feel particularly stressed. Hannah and the rest of the family had been a great help in organising the wedding and she really wanted this baby. OK, the first one was stressful but they knew what they were doing now. They had it covered.

The hand problem did not abate and soon her left hand began to mimic her right. They were more like the claws of a crab than hands. She couldn't work as that involved using a keyboard so she found herself at home, trying to look after her toddler despite really struggling to hold anything. She comforted herself with the knowledge that she would have been going on maternity leave in the near future anyway, but she desperately needed to get to the bottom of what was happening to her.

By the time she was diagnosed, she had a new baby in her arms. But those arms felt stiff and she was so tired all the time. She was a parent again and sleepless nights came with the territory but she was sure that the fatigue was mostly a result of the MS. She would just have to get through it the best she could. But this quickly became almost impossible as she often had no choice but to curl up in bed. This was beyond simple exhaustion. It was as if her whole body was shutting down.

Some periods were better than others but then the stiffness spread into her legs. She was spending more and more days in bed and very soon this became weeks at a time. Her husband and the rest of the family had to shoulder the responsibility of childcare and life was becoming a harsher place. She was now getting bedsores and other infections. She was in and out of hospital. This was the only pattern of events that her two young children had known. The elder was now at junior school and aware of all the other mums standing at the school gates, while hers was in hospital again.

Her husband needed to keep the money coming in and couldn't keep taking time off to look after her when he had two children to support. She was in hospital so often now that it was only a matter of time anyway before she became a permanent resident. The stiffness in her body was accelerating and bed was now her world. Her daily family visits were her only contact with any other. Days were long and getting through another was a triumph that gave her no joy.

She was taking all sorts of muscle relaxants to try to give her more flexibility but nothing was working. Her legs had now adopted an 'A' shape, permanently bent at the knee, completely resistant to being straightened. Eventually, it was suggested that the best course of action was to have them amputated. The health risks of having useless legs frozen in one position was greater than her spending the rest of her life without any legs. Even so, she and her family were understandably reluctant. It was a big step but in the end, they had to be guided by the doctors. It was horrible beyond words but if it gave her a few years more to see her daughters grow up, it had to be worth it, even if she could only observe and hear developments from a hospital bed.

The date of the operation was five weeks ago. Hannah has been off for the last two of those weeks because her sister died not long after surgery due to complications from the amputation. We all knew Hannah was on compassionate leave because her sister had died but I still stood there awkwardly as she discussed it with me just now. Should I hug her, I thought? Is that appropriate in the workplace with a colleague you don't really know all that well? Hannah always wears figure-hugging dresses and many of the guys in the studio have the hots for her. If I put my arms around her after she had just told me her sister had died, would it be misinterpreted by any bystanders? While I wrestled with social anxiety, the moment of opportunity quickly vanished and all I did as she prepared to depart was say, "I'm really sorry to hear that. Must have been awful." I was then left on my lonesome with thoughts of admonishment. Why did I have to revert the situation back to my feelings of embarrassment? And why, even as she told me about this tragedy, was I so aware of the dress she was wearing?

I'm back at my desk now yet I'm not getting much work done. I never met Hannah's sister but I feel her pain and that of her family. I try to feel it on a purely unselfish level, but as someone who also has multiple sclerosis, I can't stop imagining myself in that situation. I know how soon you can be wallowing in despair when you are a prisoner in bed. A couple of hours and I'm losing all hope; she had years of it. I've been able to do most things you would expect a father to do with his son. She was never a regular mother to her daughters. I wonder if the larger part of her was ready to go when the time came? It's an appalling part of the story to consider, but I truly hope so.

Rest in peace, Hannah's sister.

2014 – I'LL BE DOUGLAS BADER

I'm becoming an embarrassment and that kind of spoils the fun. It's around three and a half years since I started playing football again and in that time I appear to have lost the capability to play the game. My body has been powering down in such a gradual and even way that I have barely noticed but the evidence is now impossible to ignore. The joy of being able to run, chase and kick a ball in the direction I intended has been replaced by the strength and footballing skillset of a toddler – a toddler who is destined always to be picked last in games.

I swear I was good at this sport growing up. I was generally the youngest in my group of friends, made up mainly of neighbours and bigger boys we met up with at the cricket field. The local cricket club was where we usually organised any larger matches, much to the annoyance of the groundsman there. He generally tolerated us so long as we didn't stray onto the roped off square that housed the wicket. If the ball rolled beneath the barrier, it was as if the person sent to retrieve it was entering a minefield. He had to tiptoe across the sacred turf and scurry back to safety before any explosion from the groundsman as he noticed you trampling over the face of his baby.

I never had any trouble keeping up with the standard of these games with older, stronger boys. Quite the contrary. Ones that didn't know me well often became annoyed with me buzzing around them like an irritating fly, nicking the ball off them and firing a shot past someone two, even three years my senior.

When I was eleven I was made captain of the school team. Unfortunately, this was the peak of my footballing career. I've always joked that I could have been a professional if it hadn't been for my loss of form between the ages of eleven and thirty-five, but the truth was I was sent to a school that played rugby, not football, so spent my teenage years hiding on rugger fields, hoping that the surgeon's son with the ball wouldn't pass it to the shopkeeper's son, as he would probably then get flattened by the son of a solicitor.

Besides, my parents had no interest in supporting my love of the game. In fact, they actively discouraged me, pushing me to concentrate on my studies. I can now see their sensible reasoning, though it would have been nice if they had come to see me play more than once. I was so shocked when they appeared on the touchline at a gala when I was eleven and so desperate to impress them that I served up an absolute stinker, adeptly rounding the keeper on three occasions when running on instinct, but then missing the open goal each time as thought reared its head and anxiety took control.

After that showing they probably doubled their efforts to emphasise the importance of exams and getting a good safe job. Just as well, I suppose, as looking back I was nowhere near as good at the game as I thought. But that didn't stop me loving it, a love that has continued to this day.

Well, that's not quite right, as for the last few months I have been busy falling out of love with it. Now I'm just frustrated by it. Depressed even. MS has left me with a body that just cannot do it any longer. Certain players – I'm talking about you Craig – are pissing me off. He's not a friend as such, just someone who joined us after a Gumtree ad begging for more players, and is very competitive, to the point where he makes very little allowance for the fact that I have this condition. He shouts at me if I'm not running back to cover him if he ventures upfield, apparently averse to making any concession to the fact that it's clear I'm utterly fucked.

The only reason I wasn't already in goal when he was having another go at me just now was because I was too knackered to walk back there. He knows I have MS but probably just thinks I'm being lazy because I'm not as fit as him. It's the same mindset that gives rise to people suggesting that perhaps it's just an age thing, which as I've probably already mentioned, makes my blood boil. I realise I might not be able to do what I could when I was twenty-one, but I should be able to do more than collapse like a snipered soldier, once I've been running for all of ten minutes. Simon, for example, is older than me – he just turned fifty – and recently completed a half marathon. Completing half a mile would be way beyond me nowadays.

You'd think that Craig may have got the message from the last few minutes of play. Every time the ball has come near me, I've displayed all the grace and silky skills of Douglas Bader. DB may have been a war hero but I don't believe Brian Glover says, 'I'll be Douglas Bader,' in *Kes*. I've been spending ever more of the hour-long matches in nets and unlike Billy Casper, I'm not using the goal posts as a climbing frame – I'm holding onto the crossbar for support. Being keeper is OK – at least it's some involvement – but watching other people charge about at will somehow raises the level of sadness. With every darting run and shot I see other men making, I feel the death of my own abilities a little more keenly. The only exception is E. Viewing his development is always a thrill, a vicarious joy that transports me back to the cricket field and carefree summer evenings.

It won't be long before I can't even effectively go in goal, as a keeper who operates from a reclining position may be considered unconventional at best and more likely a liability. With legs that fluctuate between being like planks of wood one minute and jellied eels the next, that's the way it's heading.

The end feels very nigh.

2015 – VISIONS OF THE FUTURE... AND OF COCKS

I'm passing through reception when I spot Roger getting out of his car. He leans on the bodywork as he makes his way to the boot and opens it. What's he getting out of there? He's only coming into work to tap at the keys of a computer. Oh. Shit. A wheelchair.

I wait for him. Roger is a nice guy but a bit dour. I probably wouldn't make a point of talking to him but we have something fundamental in common. He too has MS. There are only about seventy employees here but one had a sister who died largely as a result of having it and there's another fellow worker with it. Some may say this is quite the coincidence, but last time I looked there were well over 90,000 people in the UK with the condition, a rise of around 10,000 in just under ten years since I first took any notice. I'm sure a statistician would say it's still a coincidence that there should be two people with it at a medium-sized company but I'm not surprised I get to compare current symptoms with someone at work.

On the whole, it's good to have someone to bounce the moans off, someone who understands and isn't regretting asking how I am. But there is a downside. Roger was diagnosed three or four years later than me but he is already worse. Watching him is like looking into a disagreeable crystal ball and this latest development has me reeling. At least he's carrying the chair through the front doors but he's now unfolding it and lowering himself into it with a grateful slump. It seems like yesterday that he was lamenting the fact that his days of being able to run were behind him, in response to my news that I had started playing football again. Soon after that he bought a walking stick. Last year I had the shock of seeing him limping along in the studio using crutches. Now this.

"How long you been using that?" I ask.

He looks up, startled, as it's clear he hadn't clocked me half hidden on the other side of the staircase.

"Oh, quite a while."

I've not seen him for some time as he's been forced to start working downstairs and I'm still on the first floor. I just come down here for the toilet facilities. He wheels towards me and we discuss issues surrounding our usual topic for a couple of minutes.

"Do you use it at home too?" I ask, hoping the answer is a firm no.

"Yeah, sometimes. Depends how I'm feeling that day. You know how it is."

"Aye," I nod, sagely I hope. "Do you have any trouble getting around at home?" I add. "Are your doorways big enough?"

"Yes and no," he tells me. "We're building an extension at the moment. I'll be in there."

"Right," I say, thinking, 'Well that's depressing. Sounds like he's moving into a granny flat.' He's a few years older than me but still only in his early fifties.

The slightly stilted conversation limps along. He asks me how I'm doing. I always feel a little awkward at this juncture in our interactions, as I'm always doing better than him, even though I've had it longer.

"Y'know, good and bad." Part of me is pleased to be able to

impart some bad news from my MS-shaped world. "I've had to give up football, which is annoying."

"Why's that?"

I would have thought this was obvious but he's going to make me spell it out. "Just couldn't do it anymore. Couldn't even stand up in goal long enough."

He doesn't say anything; just kind of sucks his teeth. What does that mean? That's shit – because it is, I'm gutted – or what are you complaining about? I've not been able to run for years, never mind play a sport. Probably the former. Like I say, he's a nice guy. He's never given the impression he was ever a keen sportsman though. Probably can't fathom why it is such a loss for me.

I start to back away, as a method of extricating myself from this exchange. It doesn't appear to be heading in any interesting direction. Certainly not any direction I wish to travel and besides, I really need to pee, having left it and left it in order to give myself a chance of emptying the bladder this side of lunchtime. We say bye and I enter the disabled toilet. We've moved building and here, for added humiliation, the disabled doubles up as a ladies toilet. Two plates on the door – one showing a stick man with a Kim Kardashian-size arse and another showing a woman with an afro and a single fat leg. Neither appears to be aimed at me, but how little people know or could understand. Firstly, there's the privacy. No one in the room or parked in the next cubicle making arse noises. Then there's the metal bar I often hold onto, as well as a cistern at the right height that my phone and I can rest upon. It's a bit of a walk and I have to descend the stairs to get here, which is ironic, but this is my sanctuary from a world that never has to give a second thought to the process of peeing.

Dark reflections have entered my sanctuary, however. Poor old Roger. Who am I kidding? Poor old me. Were his troubles just a vision of the future? Is that where all this is heading? I try to concentrate on the matter in hand while simultaneously relaxing but achieve neither. As usual, the first drop of pee is showing its usual reluctance to appear, even though I can feel the tank is nearly full, and this makes me think of Roger even more. From previously frank discussions, I know that his problem is the opposite. When he needs to go he really needs to go, otherwise he might piss himself. As a result, he once tried the old catheter as recommended by his MS nurse. The frankness continued as he described how the pain involved led him to giving it up as a bad job before the tube had made it halfway up, which made my mind picture his cock in HD, despite my best efforts to visualise tits and only tits. I wonder how he'll get on now he's using a wheelchair on a regular basis? When the urge comes will he leap from the chair and start pacing quickly to the bathroom? If he's in a public place, will it seem like a miracle, or will bystanders wonder if he's a malingerer who's just too lazy to use his legs most of the time?

I bore a hole in the white wall before me with my stare. When will this future visit me? Witnessing Roger in that wheelchair has got me thinking more clearly on the numbers and when it comes to MS, thinking clearly is the last thing I want to do. I'm unlikely to be retiring for twenty years. I've had MS for less time than that, so logic suggests... I want to travel more in my retirement. Where could I comfortably travel to if I'm on crutches or in a wheelchair? I wonder if this worms its way into Kate's thoughts? Does she ever consider that in her retirement she'll be pushing me rather than us walking hand in hand? At least I'm not Hannah's sister. At least I'm not Hannah's sister. But I could soon be a Roger. One major relapse, that's all it would take. Or just the passage of time, a few years of time.

Should I be crying? Part of me wants to cry, but I'm a million miles from doing so. It always feels so unreal. Even though I have MS, I still hang on to that most human of instincts – hope, or to be more precise, the sense that really bad things happen to other people, it won't happen to me. Isn't that strange, because when I look back on the last ten, thirteen years, lots of bad things have happened to me. Maybe it's useful to be a dreamer, living in my head, living in a sitcom of my own creation, instead of real life.

Real life. What will that be like in three, five, ten years? Will it be a steady progression? If so, at what pace? This one? Working it out, gauging how much better I was three, five, ten years ago sends a shudder through my soul. Ten years ago, I barely noticed anything was the matter. Five years ago, I was noticeably worse, but still fit. Still able to run, play football. Three years ago, tiny bit worse, but still not really any severe restrictions on what I could do. Just a need to be a bit cleverer about certain tasks. Do things in stages. Allow for the fact that MS will affect how long I can move before my body hits the brake.

Now? Well still no wheelchair, no crutches, no stick. But no football. And I did take a quick look on Amazon the other day, to see what was out there in the world of walking aids. It depressed me too much to form any strong opinions, but I know it's on the way. Just a matter of when. As I run these days, I creak, like the metal hinges that act as knee joints for my wooden legs need a bit of WD40. Running at all will be the next to go. The first rung on Roger's ladder. That's probably the wrong word to use. The correct term would be to say I'm on the head of Roger's snake. No, that just sounds wrong, like Roger has a huge shlong and I'm about to fellate him. Godsake, the point is a simple one. Sometime soon, I'm likely to follow the path that Roger started on before me and that path only heads in one direction – down. Can you have a path that heads down? Yes, course you can. Downhill. I was thinking of a vertical descent but a gradual slope down is probably more appropriate as a metaphor. It certainly works better for me; more palatable.

Is choosing the most apposite metaphor really the best use of my time here? Is that what is really important – how steep is this path? Something has just come to mind that is rather more pertinent. I recall now that Leezou once told me that after about ten years of living with relapse remitting MS, many (or was it most?) sufferers experience a progression of the condition, as it develops into what is known as secondary MS. Not as bad as the primary that Hannah's sister had but worse than relapse remitting. Secondary is a steady progression of the disease. It's what Roger has and, in all honesty, what I probably have now.

Bugger.

Secondary. Known in some circles as Roger's snake. No, stop it. You're thinking again now about Roger's cock. If you're going to think about anybody's cock, think about your own, the one that's dribbling piss into the toilet at a wearisome pace. My phone bleeps with an alert. Great, inconsequential bullshit that I could have lived without knowledge of and the jolt has made me involuntarily clench, halting the flow. This will require all my powers of concentration to get started again. Or maybe I'll use that other tactic, not think about it at all and wait for nature to take effect in all its fucked-up glory.

I open Kindle on my phone and begin to read the book I currently have on the go, a Bill Bryson. I wonder if when authors write a book they ever stop to wonder about the number of people reading their books on the toilet? Bet there's not many who can get through two or three pages while just taking a leak. But that's me. Phone propped up on the cistern, cock out, tinkling occasionally disturbing the peace.

I'm often in this position when the phone rings too. I usually ignore it, but sometimes it's important. So as well as reading, conversations go on with the cock out. And if it's important, that usually means something official, like E's school calling to tell me he's had a bump on the head, can someone collect him? Ah, modern life. Before the age of mobile phones, I doubt many conversations with officialdom went on with one party standing there with his cock out. Now these interactions are going on across the land, every day. And in this very moment, I'm standing here with my cock out, with the image of other men with their cocks out in my head. I try to focus on women with their trolleys down to their knees, everything on show as they discuss insurance claims with faceless individuals in call centres but I have to admit, it's not as arresting as the image of men with their cocks out.

Oh, thank God, the last few drops have crawled down my urethra and fallen into the bowl. I can put it away and stop thinking about cocks. Great, now I'm thinking again about what life might be like in ten years' time. Will it be a walking stick all the time, will I be asking Roger where he bought his wheelchair, if he got a good deal? Or will progression be at a pace similar to the one that regulates my visits to the toilet. Maybe I'll be hanging on to some semblance of normality. Maybe maybe maybe.

I exit the toilet. Fuck! Linda almost falls into me, as she was about to try the door handle. Does she know I have MS? Has she heard on the grapevine? Even if she has, she sees me walking around, apparently without any disability. Is she just thinking, why is this pervert in the ladies toilet? If I explain, it'll definitely sound like the protestations of a deviant caught in the act. Why can't there be a dedicated disabled toilet? I just have to step aside and hold the door open for her. Holding the door open to the ladies bog for a woman when you're a man who's currently standing inside the ladies bog is not a good look. A part of me is now eager to cry. A part of me at least is dying inside.

Perhaps I should buy that walking stick purely so I have a prop to brandish in this very circumstance. Would it be worth it to avoid this embarrassment? Probably a decision that will soon be taken out of my hands.

DECEMBER 2015 – THREE-LEGGED MAN ACQUIRES FOUR-LEGGED FRIEND

The thing about being a family of three is that you can be outvoted. I said no several times. I really didn't want a dog and made this abundantly clear. But Kate really did and so did E. She was relentless and E called me stupid and mean. In the end, you get sick of the eye daggers.

So we now have a dog. And that dog needs walking, which means I've relented on buying something else that I was far from keen on allowing into my life – a walking stick. Yes, I can still walk a fair way without anything to help me, but if our stroll lasts longer than thirty minutes, I'm struggling. The stick helps me to keep going when I start to feel weak and unstable. A third leg just to add a little balance and something from which to push off occasionally.

The dog is proving less useful. Yes, Kate is much happier, as is E, though being eleven he has, of course, already relinquished all responsibility for such noble duties as clearing up dogshit from the garden. It's not that I actively dislike dogs; it's just that I have no strong feelings towards them. Which makes the work involved onerous to say the least. The aforementioned poo clearance is the most obvious task any right-minded person would wish to avoid, but if only it ended there. A puppy, of course, sees your whole house as a lovely luxurious toilet and they're also so needy. The endless whining and howling when you leave it downstairs at night and the attendant relinquishing of my nice warm bed to go calm it after Kate has tried four or five times – well it's her who wanted it – takes me rapidly back to when E was a baby. Only this baby will never grow up. It'll be permanently anchored in the toddler years, house-trained but in a state of suspended development when compared to their human equivalent.

I guess it is quite cute, though. Maybe I'll get to like her. It just seems an inopportune time to be acquiring a creature that needs walking a number of times every week, just as my leg power significantly deteriorates. A walking stick will surely only paper over the cracks and to be honest, I'm not at all keen on being seen out in public with one anyhow. I found the thought of having a walking stick so dispiriting that I asked for it for my birthday, so someone else would have to search through those available and assess their various merits. This had the somehow unforeseen consequence, however, of me receiving a walking stick as a present on my forty-seventh birthday. Now that was depressing. I laughed it off and everyone in the room said, 'Well, you did ask for one,' and I had to admit that yes, I had. What a tit.

But I can't deny, it is proving pretty useful. For the majority of any walk, I carry it under my arm like a stuffed shirt major, looking like I might whack anyone who dares to ask why I have a walking stick tucked under my arm. I also sometimes twirl it like a marching band leader. But when the fatigue begins to take hold, it is there as my insurance, my trusty assistant to help me back to the car.

Like Ellie the dog (a Lhasa Apso in case you're wondering, which if you know your dog breeds would have a Rottweiler any day), there is no use in resisting the stick now. It's a part of my life now, so I may as well embrace it for what it's worth. It's not a proper old man wooden affair anyway. It's black, metal and adjustable. Cheap, as I instructed. I won't be using it much, with or without dog, so why pay more than the minimum. It will do the job.

As we progress around the park, I hear a familiar tap of cane on the gravel path that echoes the tap tap of my own.

'Eh up, Alf. Been lucky lately?'

'Nay lad, not bloomin' likely. Same old same old.'

'Look, I have a stick now just like you.'

'Aye, I see that. But you're nearly 'alf my age, son.'

'Yes, I'm well aware of that.'

'Bugger.'

'Indeed, Alf, indeed.'

SPRING 2016 – DIFFERENT COUNTRY, SAME ISSUES

Dave has persuaded us all that Torremolinos is no longer the archetype of the egg and chips, lager lout Brits abroad budget Spanish destination. He's assured us that it's gone upmarket and is now more a resort to which the Spanish themselves head.

'Do they still sell San Miguel? Yes? It'll do,' was the general consensus of the guys.

There are four of us on this short break. Besides myself, there's Dave, Steve and an old work friend, Mik, who I've hardly seen in the last ten years. He knows I have MS but probably thinks it still hasn't properly taken hold, as he is yet to see me walk any distance. Neither have I brought my walking stick. I thought long and hard about it but it somehow seemed an inappropriate piece of kit to take on a lads' holiday, even if the 'lads' are all over forty. OK, I admit it, I was embarrassed by the prospect. Surely, I won't really need it, I have told myself.

Mik is also yet to be introduced to the nature of my toilet proclivities, as becomes apparent before we've even left Malaga airport. Before we get in a taxi, I need to piss, as do Dave and Steve. While Mik takes the opportunity to smoke his first fag in hours, three of us enter the facilities together, but only one of the party slips into a cubicle.

I've been holding it for a while, which always makes the process more problematic. Knowing Mik is outside waiting and that he will soon be joined by the others makes it worse again. Anything that adds pressure to the situation is a stick in the spokes of this wheel. I spread my legs some more and try my best to relax but I know that his cig has now probably been introduced to the sole of his shoe and the group is most likely moaning about me. Why aren't we in a taxi already on the way to our first pint?

Imagining this scenario only adds to my anxiety. The anxiety is miniscule, but that is all that is required to derail my efforts to urinate. Come on, godammit! At least no one is in the neighbouring cubicles. I close my eyes, try to convince myself I'm completely alone in the world (which in these moments isn't such a stretch) and in my mind I conjure up the sights and sounds that accompany a successful evacuation of the bladder. Halleluiah! We're in business. If guttering was leaking at this rate, you probably wouldn't bother getting it fixed, but the job is eventually complete.

I rejoin the gang outside. Dave and Steve gloss over the fact that I was so long. They know the score and have been in this position before. This is Mik's first encounter with my toilet issues and a look of disbelief has taken control of his features.

"Fuck me, you didn't tell us you were going for a shit. Couldn't you have waited till we got to the hotel?"

"That, my friend, is me pissing. My brain signals don't work right, do they."

I can see the recollection that I have MS and the realisation that he may have made what could be considered an insensitive comment colour his expression. "Oh, right, yeah."

I'm glad no apology is forthcoming, as it is far from necessary. I don't want to be the odd one out in the group or for my health to be a topic on this trip. I'd like to forget about multiple sclerosis for three days as much as is possible. I just want to be one of four drinking buddies, out to soak up a bit of sun and a few cold lagers.

Without my stick, though, I hope there's not too much distance between the bars. Otherwise I may be adding extra meaning to the term pub crawl.

DEC 2017 – I'M DISABLED!

I try to concentrate more on the free parking and less on the official seal given to my steady descent into the disability underworld. I can't deny that this day has been on the way for a while. Once walking aids enter the equation, a blue badge is not likely to be far behind, or so it has proved.

My acceptance of the new order has been anything but sudden, yet I can point to one particular incident that certainly helped to crystallise my thoughts on the matter. In 2015, the Reynards were on a family holiday in Crete. We visited some town on, unbeknownst to us, the public holiday of Oxi Day. Every woman, man and child were out on the streets, celebrating when the Greek Prime Minister stuck two fingers up at Mussolini in 1940, so we were told in a roundabout way by a waitress once we finally parked ourselves in a café. Firstly, however, we had to park our car, which turned into a nightmare exploration of every single street in the town, as each possible space was already occupied by the local revellers.

One space we found early on was free, but it was marked out for a disabled occupant. I gave it little consideration for the next fifteen minutes, as we continued to tour round fruitlessly. I may have MS and be no longer able to play football, but I was obviously not disabled. The universal signifier of disability – a wheelchair – was so beyond my current sphere of thinking, despite my encounter earlier in the year with Roger, that the vision of that empty space was quickly dismissed from my mind. Even if I had possessed a disability badge then, I doubt it would have been applicable abroad anyway, but that was not why I pursued a regular space like a regular motorist, without cursing the fact that I didn't have an internationally recognised permit to park in a disabled spot.

We eventually found a place to dump the hire car, on the seafront, close to a mile from the centre. Maybe it was the endless heeling and toeing as we slowly explored every inch of tarmac in the resort, but whatever it was I quickly found myself unable to walk like an able-bodied human. My right foot turned inwards and locked up so I had little control of it and after only a short way I began walking like a more sluggish and uncoordinated Ratso in *Midnight Cowboy*, dragging the toe of my trainers along the pavement with every step. I took Kate's hand but this mainly had the result of putting her in a bad mood because I clenched her fingers too tightly, as I struggled to proceed and not fall over.

The journey from the car to the hub of cafés and bars was interminable. I'd never felt so disabled in my life and it's no coincidence that I acquired a walking stick not long afterwards. I also changed cars to an automatic around the same period, one of the best decisions I've made. It's like driving a bumper car and allows me to permanently rest my left leg.

Yes, that day in Crete, pushing down a stiff clutch over and over, then stumbling from our vehicle into a nightmare of weakness and instability, forced me to confront some home truths. It was time to face up to a few facts that I had been treating as fiction. I wasn't still fine, MS wasn't still something in the background, it had advanced unsteadily to the forefront of my life. OK, I was better than many with my condition after so many years, but there was no use pretending any longer that everything was fine. It was a bit shit and the forecast was for it to get shitter.

I have the stick, the disabled-friendly car and now what must be seen as confirmation of my worst fears, in the form of this blue plastic card that has just come through the post. Like everything else in this realm, I haven't entered lightly. Ever since Crete, the notion has resided somewhere distantly in my mind. Was I sufficiently disabled to warrant one? I knew I would benefit from one for those days when I was seriously struggling. On other days not so much. But what was the point of the whole system if you were excluded because you were having a good day?

So finally I filled in the application form, making sure it reflected the worst-case scenario of my current state, though nothing was a lie as I just described my worst Ratso days. One way in which I did portray myself in a more favourable light was in my photograph. I found a couple of passport-style photos in the back of a draw. I doubt the picture on the blue badge should strictly be ten or more years old but it still looks like me – just a cooler, younger version of me, from my long-hair rock star era. If it makes me feel better about being officially disabled, then surely the authorities can turn a blind eye.

"What's that?" asks Kate, as she sees me flipping over my new blue badge to stare at the photo and reminisce about a time before multiple sclerosis. That's the irony of the photo on the card. The condition had yet to show even its most tentative hand when it was taken. 'You poor, carefree fool,' I think to myself, as I look into the eyes staring back at me. Good looking and healthy. You had it all and pissed so much of it away, on bad fashion decisions and hangovers.

I turn to Kate. "I'm disabled!" I say in a high-pitched voice.

This is in reference to what in my opinion is one of the funniest sitcom episodes of any series ever – when Roy in *The IT Crowd* has to pretend to be disabled because he has used the disabled toilet and tried to flush by pulling the emergency cord. As usual when there's something I'm not eager to deal with in my life, I resort to turning it all into a big joke.

Kate looks at me quizzically, then as she works it out says, "Oh, you've got your disabled badge through. Nice one, Roy."

Instead of confirming that she is correct, I simply repeat, "I'm disabled!" in the same silly voice.

As well as quoting lines from sitcoms, I comfort myself with the knowledge that I can now park right outside the doors of shops and my days of feeding coins into meters in the town centre are over. True, I'm not looking forward to the accusing stares that may come my way. If I've been having a lazy morning, it is more than possible that it will appear for all the world that there is absolutely nothing wrong with me as I alight from my vehicle in the supermarket car park. If anybody confronts me, I will have to say, 'Well, wait till I come back out and see how I am then,' and point to the shiny new square of blue plastic on my dashboard.

Failing that, I can always just play dumb and cry, 'I'm disabled!'

SPRING 2018 – A LES McQUEEN MOMENT

I've started a blog. Yes, I've become one of those people. The urge to create is always there and since my epiphany at Henry Boons, the impulse to make music has collapsed, which I suppose is more evidence that I was never of the right stuff to make it in that particular arena. As E is fourteen and I'm now unable to pursue my love of playing various sports, I have more time on my hands too. Something had to fill that void.

In my bloody-minded pursuit of the smallest audience possible for my artistic endeavours, the subject is my hometown, Wakefield, and its history, looking for any interesting and little-known stories from its past. *Wakefield – Hidden in Plain Sight* is its name and I don't suppose it will be of much interest to anyone not from the city. In fact, my casual friend from the Torremolinos trip, Mik, was distinctly forthcoming in his feelings on the subject matter. "I couldn't give a fuck about Wakefield," were his actual words, which I had to admit would no doubt be the attitude of anyone who didn't consider Wakefield to be home.

But I am enjoying researching it and writing it. I've always been interested in history and am aiming for a Brysoneque style. Don't skim read that and think it's dark and louche in the manner of Lord Byron. I refer in fact to the king of humorous travel writing, Bill Bryson, who wanders the globe drawing the reader's attention to interesting stories from the places he is visiting. This has taken him all over the USA, Europe and Australia. I strive to emulate his approach, only I won't be travelling further than five miles from my home.

Balls to having an audience of any significance. I've discovered all sorts of fascinating details about my city that I never knew previously and it's been a great way to develop a voice that is my own. The notion of the blog may have formulated as I read a Bryson book, but I believe it stands on its own feet now. One aspect that is particular to it is the way I have introduced my walking difficulties into the descriptions of my wanderings around Wakefield. Rather than keeping my condition a secret, I have made a feature of multiple sclerosis and my attendant disabilities.

This led to a Les McQueen moment. Some might call it a lightbulb moment, but I prefer my term, as there is a subtle difference. The bulb lighting up in one's brain is likely to be a moment of inspiration or insight, where the solution to a problem suddenly becomes apparent. A Les McQueen moment is when a bright but probably foolish idea abruptly comes to mind, in a triumph of hope over experience. At some point as I read through one of the first blog posts, I metaphorically put my finger in the air and said, 'Heeeeey!' as the thought came to me that maybe I could write more directly about my experiences with MS. Maybe there was even a book in it, if I could make it funny and interesting enough. I had all that thyroid and cancer stuff to throw in the mix too.

Like all the other projects in my life, it will probably go the way of a crème brûlée left out in the rain, but I'm going to write a few chapters and see how it shapes up. Who knows, someone may read it and enjoy it one day. If they do, they'll have the Les

McQueen that lives in my head to thank, the voice that always imagines there will be an unlikely victory for success over reality. Poor old Les has taken a beating these last few years, but thank God he's still capable of donning his lamé suit and going one more time. Otherwise what's left to say about life? It's a shit business? Downbeat Les is never far below the surface, but the one that says, 'Heeeeey, we can do this,' is easier to have by my side.

I use my phone to take a video snapshot of the current scene, as it perfectly captures where I am. I focus first on the Trabant that is on display high above on a hydraulic platform, then slowly pan across to the section of high, white and graffitied concrete wall that surrounds much of this outdoor bar and which used to surround much more. Next, the big screen comes into view, showing the World Cup match between Germany and Sweden. The locals are going nuts, as their team has just come from behind to draw level. To put the final tick on the checklist, I lower my phone to zoom in on the leaflet that is fluttering on the ground near my feet. I can only make out two words on it – 'Hitler' and 'Bunker'.

Yes, there's not much doubt about the fact that we're in Berlin. This is the third of what has become our annual male jaunts abroad. Torremolinos was the first, then last year we toured round the First World War sites of Flanders and northern France and now we're in Germany's hippest city.

Looking back on the trips, they have become markers of my continuing steady decline. When we went to Spain, I didn't even take a walking stick. I would probably have benefitted from one occasionally, but another sit down in a bar was never far away, so I coped with getting around the resort with little bother. In Belgium and France, I had my stick with me, but it never left the hotel room. I realise it probably should have had some use, but I guess embarrassment was still winning the battle with my developing disability. Our visit to Pozieres cemetery was a low point. I had to ask my companions to wander up and down the mass of graves trying to find my great-grandad's stone, as I was incapable. Not only did an odd part of me feel like I was dishonouring the memory of my great-grandad by not finding him myself, but I also had to face an awkward exchange with the rest of the party as, after fifteen minutes of fruitless searching, I remembered that he did not actually have a headstone. Mum had told me that her grandad just had an inscription on the surrounding wall, as the cemetery had soon become too full due to its proximity to the killing fields of the Somme. As it was, no one complained. Perhaps in the same way I tried my best not to gripe when visiting Auschwitz, they felt it would be inappropriate to moan when surrounded by so much tragic and pointless death.

Now, beneath my wooden bench, lies my brand new walking stick. Bought today in a Berlin outdoor pursuits shop, it is a cast-iron necessity if I am to have any chance of exploring the city. I brought my stick from home, of course, but when I went through security at the airport, I unscrewed it and squashed it down as far as it would go. When I tried to put it back to its correct length, I couldn't get it to hold together in that position. As soon as I leant on it, it would slide back down again, like it was one of those comedy whistles. The result was that it would only have been any good to assist the progression of a small disabled child.

I managed to make it to the plane OK, but come evening I was in our hotel room frantically trying to put my walking companion back to how it had been pre-airport. I only wish I could say this was the first walking stick I had broken. In Mexico, almost exactly the same thing happened. I compressed it so I could fit it in one of the plastic trays at security, then when I tried to extend it again, its two halves came apart completely and I couldn't get it back together again. Thus my holiday in Playa del Carmen was spent swaying over tiled walkways, banging into walls and occasionally reaching for Kate's hand before crumpling onto a sunlounger. If she knew I'd broken another one in very similar fashion, she would be trotting out her oft-used phrase, 'Monkeys learn quicker.' I prefer to say that monkeys don't buy cheap shit off the Internet.

As we headed into an area of Berlin that we heard was known for its high density of bars, I was on edge, knowing that if we had any trouble finding this quarter, I would soon start to display the gait of someone who had already downed several steins. Sure enough, we were soon roaming the streets, thirsty and clueless, one with legs that craved a long sit down. My companions noticed my developing struggles and doubled their efforts to make sense of Google Maps on their phones. Dave had the best solution, however, offering me a shoulder to lean on, in a literal way. Mik and Nick were too tall to have provided a comfortable level of support, but my shorter friend was just the right height for me to position my left hand on him like an epaulette and stroll beside him, utilising him as a human mobility aid. I was reminded of the few times I have been on a horse and you can feel the bones of the creature moving under their warm skin, but I guess it was fine. A little weird, but appreciated and essential.

But it was hardly a long-term solution. By the next morning, I felt like my hand was becoming an unwelcome guest on Dave's shoulder and before long Google Maps was again being scrutinised, this time for any shop that might sell walking sticks. "Camping and outdoor supplies!" someone excitedly cried. "They should at least have some hiking poles," and Dave's pace seemed to quicken.

As it transpired, they even had normal walking sticks. It was a little more expensive than my former purchases, but I have much more confidence in this German-made model. Green and grey, I think it looks better too, more like an aid to power-walking than mobility. When Kate took one of the previous walking sticks from me while I hunted for the dog's latest present in the long grass of the park, I returned to her and just for a second thought she had wandered off somewhere. There was just an old woman where she had been, leaning on a walking stick. Then came the realisation: 'Jeez, is that what I look like when I'm using it? Do I really look that ancient?' It depressed the hell out of me, as I couldn't help thinking about what Kate saw when she looked at me now. She has always made jokes about my age, as I'm over four years her senior, but having seen her with that stick, her jibes about my age have taken on added bite. How will she ever see me as hot and desirable again? Am I now just an old gibber, ready for the scrapheap? But what can I do about it? Absolutely f all. It's just the way it is. Old before my time.

We drink some more, then Germany get a late winner and the place goes wild. As an England supporter, I'm supposed to will Germany to lose every match ten nil, but it's impossible not to be carried along by the atmosphere and be happy for our hosts. I'm not going to start hugging people, though, and dancing round in a circle like some fans are now doing. My dancing days are over.

*   *   *

In the airport bar, I watch my friends down their last pints on German soil. I have resisted the temptation to join them, as I want to keep the liquids in my system to a minimum before we get on the plane. Relaxing the bladder with my head pushed back by the curve of the fuselage is, I have learnt, far from easy. Yes, our Berlin excursion is coming to a close. Three nights is always the limit for these trips. Laughs and banter abound early on, before being replaced by fault-finding and irritation. But it's been good overall. I say overall because it was not quite as good as Flanders. I put hours into organising the hell out of that one. I even brought along the schedule on a clipboard, for which much piss was taken. I guess it was deserving, but my attention to detail paid off, as we always knew which museum, cemetery or town square we were heading to next and when.

Berlin has been a bit more random, by which I mean we have wandered vaguely or aimlessly on many occasions. Thank God I had my new stick, as we have ventured all over the city. I think Dave would have become rather fed up of me if my hand had been stuck to him wherever we went. And we did find the site of Hitler's bunker, as advertised in that discarded leaflet, which was exciting for a history enthusiast like me. Why are so many middle-aged men fascinated by the Nazis? I search them out now, but I would have been hiding from Hitler and his cronies if I had been in Berlin back then, as they would have been eager to round me up and pack me off to a death camp. I would have been able to cover up my disability when I visited Auschwitz, but they would certainly notice it now.

Everyone drains the last of their drinks and all except Dave go in search of the nearest toilets before we make our way to the gate. In the cubicle I adopt my usual position of legs apart, with one hand on the back wall to support myself. With nothing of interest to occupy my mind, my thoughts flit to this and that. I'm still yet to go when one particular thought leaps up with its hand in the air and says, 'Erm, this is probably fine, but it might be worth raising.' On arriving at the airport, I had my man bag on my shoulder with my passport and wallet in it and was pulling my small wheelie case behind me. Try as I might, after going through security, I cannot visualise having the man bag still on my shoulder. Surely I must have done? But if I'm so sure, why am I panicking ever so slightly? I put everything away – there's no chance of anything happening now – and call Dave, back in the bar.

"What's up?"

"My grey bag is there with you, isn't it?"

"Your gay bag, you say?"

"Yeah, yeah. The gay one. Is it with my case?" I hear the alarm escalating in my voice.

"Can't see it, no. Have you not got it with you?"

Oh yes, silly me, of course. That's why I'm calling you, clearly in a state of heightened anxiety. I end the call abruptly and head back to the bar, my heartbeat significantly quickened. It'll be there, I tell myself, Dave just hasn't looked properly. But I already know the real truth. I've left it in a plastic tray at security. What's more, our flight is going soon. If I could run, or even walk quickly, I would be able to make it back there and be on that plane no problem. As it is, I'm not even sure I can walk all that way back to security. But I can't send one of my friends to collect it. The staff are unlikely to hand over a bag to someone purporting to know me. Oh God, oh God, oh God, oh God, oh God, oh God.

I rummage through our hand luggage in the bar like a rabid sniffer dog but there is no salvation. Of course it's not there, 'cause the missing bag is currently back at security, probably spirited away to some lost property vault, possibly to be destroyed in a controlled explosion, just in case it's a security risk. I like that bag but I would put losing it down to experience, the experience of a complete idiot, but the contents are rather important. I've heard airport staff are generally reluctant to let you board a plane without a passport, and all my cards are in that wallet. Oh God, oh God, oh God, oh God, oh God, oh God.

To their credit, the guys don't give me a load of shit. I'm certain that will be delivered further down the line, but for now the gravity of the situation springs them into action.

"I'll go," Nick offers.

"But they're not going to give you my bag."

"Hmm, well I'll go with you. Make sure you get there OK."

We set off and it's not long at all before Nick is some way ahead. A certain amount of panic has clearly entered his gait too and he can't bring himself to move at my laboured space. This expedition has two major problems before we even reach security. One, the route from there to the bar was a circuitous one and at one point we emerged from a corridor through a side entrance that will be very easy to miss as we try to retrace our steps. We only took note because it seemed a very strange place from which to exit into a main concourse at a major airport, like we had just been searching a broom cupboard for a mop. Two, my legs are already knackered. My new stick is struggling to help me continue and we haven't even reached the door to the broom cupboard yet, I don't think.

"Is this it?" Nick calls out in the distance. He disappears through the thin entrance before I've reached him, so I hope he's right. Memories of Manchester to Lanzarote and that mad dash through the airport flood my mind. Twenty years ago exactly and the emotions are similar, but the physical realities of each event could not be more different. Even with a heavy bag, I ran much of the way that day. Now I'm moving like the Elephant Man when he's being hounded in the train station and trying to get away from the baying mob. I'm not sure I'm going to make it, even though I'm certainly not weighed down by a bag because I'm a complete halfwit. (Can you be a complete halfwit? No, now is not the time!) Only the consequences of not making it are projecting me forward. I have no other choice, even if I have to crawl on my hands and knees to get there.

I follow Nick. Yes, I think this is the correct route. My relief at this small victory, however, is offset by the sight of a flight of stairs that I now need to descend. The notion of sliding down the handrail enters my head but is rapidly followed by the image of me slumped in a heap at the bottom of the steps, a steady flow of blood emanating from my broken skull and pooling on the white tiles. With the stick and handrail to support me, I just about manage. I'm encouraged also by the sight of Nick, waiting at the doorway before you get to security. I thought it was a little further but here we are. Will they still have my bag? Will they just hand it to me if they do? Funnily enough, I'm not in possession of a great well of experience to draw on for this eventuality.

I'm about to storm past Nick, if indeed an invalid can storm past anyone, when he holds his arm across me to prevent my passing. "I'd be careful, Andy."

"God, yeah."

His wise warning has reminded me that some of the staff have guns and might not take kindly to a weirdo limping back into security babbling about a lost bag. The vision of me lying on the floor with my blood discolouring the tiles again comes into focus, but this time it's the result of a flurry of bullets.

So I enter the area cautiously and in a manner that I hope appears pathetic and unthreatening. The pathetic part is easy to pull off after the journey from the bar, as I'm about to fall over. I search for a friendly face. Fortunately, no passengers are currently queuing to come through, so the staff are mostly standing around unoccupied. I explain my situation as best I can and a smile appears on the face of the guy. He calls over to his colleague. His workmate goes one further and laughs as he retrieves my bag from behind him, under the counter. They exchange some words in German between them that has them both cracking up. I laugh too and slap my palm against my forehead in a what-am-I-like gesture that I hope is universal. Their demeanour comforts me, as it seems to say, 'Don't worry about it, this happens all the time.' Yes, I'm sure they encounter titheads every day, and now it's one more. But they seem uninterested in checking that it is actually my bag and pass it to me without a fuss. After a quick feel of it to check my passport and wallet are still present in the inside zip pocket, we are on our way.

*

I fasten my seatbelt, sit back and close my eyes. Having a couple of Germans laugh at me was a small price to pay for the sensation of relief that mainlined its way to my brain when I took my bag from them. Making the plane was the next obstacle, but somehow my legs overcame that one too. Maybe I should ask my neurologist if injections of adrenaline are available on the NHS.

How did I possibly manage to leave a whole bag behind? Now the relief is wearing off, the internal chastisement is dominating all other thoughts. Nobhead, wanker, stupid arsehole! My friends have been surprisingly reticent in joining in with my internal monologue since it all worked out. Perhaps hangover fatigue has saved me from that particular public flogging. I again run through the pattern of events that led to my act of gross stupidity. In a moment of forgiveness, I blame it on the walking stick. I was so intent on smoothing it over with the guard to allow me to put the stick through without squashing it down that I was only thinking about that. Is it reason enough? Of course not, but it's all I have, together with scars in the brain. I've been asked a few times by various neurologists if I have trouble with memory or concentration. I've always said no, putting any issues down to age, but maybe this aberration suggests otherwise. Yes, let's go with that. MS is to blame for everything else bad in my life, so why not.

We begin to taxi along the runway. Soon the jet engines will fire up and we'll be in the air. Not long after that I'll be basking once again in the warmth of my little family.

AUG 2018 – THE BOUNCER

After the meal, we decide to grab a drink at a new bar around the corner. I say new, but refurbished and renamed would be a better description. I remember it as the Buzz Bar nightclub and before that, in the eighties, it had the very eighties name of Sloanes. Some of my formative experiences with the opposite sex took place in those establishments. Teenage parties in Sloanes, praying a girl might be interested in a pale, moody goth, and in my grungy twenties, hunting the three floors of Buzz Bar for talent, like a horny Kurt Cobain. I'd slip away from my mates for ten minutes while I raced up and down the stairs in a shallow examination of the female clientele, scanning the room for a potential love match. In a pre-Internet age, my rapid circumnavigations of Buzz were, I suppose, like an early version of Tinder, just one that involved a lot more leg work.

Thirty odd years later, here I am heading for the same place, only now I'm hoping there won't be any stairs and that I can make the short distance from the restaurant to the bar. I clutch my wife's hand tightly, as I've left my walking stick at home. I still don't like being seen with it on a night out and we had no intention of walking anywhere tonight anyway. But the meal took less time than we expected and we thought we would check out what they had done with the old Buzz Bar/Sloanes, as it was nearby.

Nearby for your average person is not my nearby, however. We're only halfway there and I'm struggling. Whenever my legs pack up on me and I'm walking hand in hand with Kate, I'm put in mind of the chimps that you used to see on TV variety shows in my childhood. Dressed in a tutu or similar, it would be walking upright, holding the hand of someone, or on occasion another chimp, who would be dressed in dungarees and also walking upright. Their bowlegs and awkward swaying gait would have the audience howling with mirth, as if we had not evolved one iota from the crass behaviours of the Coliseum crowds. But I fear that's what I look like in these moments. I will often make a couple of chimp noises to try and deflate some of my frustration with humour, generally with limited success.

At least the chimp and his handler have now arrived. We approach the bouncer on the door, ready to nod, 'Evening,' but events take an unexpected turn. As Kate lets go of my hand and brushes past him with a smile, the guy places his arm across my path. "Sorry, pal. Not tonight."

"Eh?" I squeak.

"Sorry, pal. I think you've had enough for one night."

I laugh and roll my eyes, as it dawns on me what is going through his mind. I hope my expression is disarming, but the way his eyebrows are knotting on the bridge of his nose suggests otherwise.

"I can explain..." I say, about to explain, but he cuts me off.

"No need, not a problem. I just can't let you in. I'm glad you've had a good time tonight but it's not carrying on in here."

Part of me is feeling like I no longer want to enter anyway. His manner is overly aggressive and is not putting me in the mood for relaxing with a beer. Kate then turns round, wondering what the cause of the delay is.

"What's going on?" she asks, as she sees the bouncer and his broad arm barring my way.

"He thinks I'm drunk. I was just about to tell him..."

"He's got MS!" she blurts out, laughing, preventing me from explaining for a second time. At least she didn't say M&S. She used to work for them and I'd been diagnosed five years before she broke the habit of calling it M&S. "He has problems with his legs," she adds, flashing a smile that is no doubt considerably more disarming than anything I could ever manage.

I expect he'll feel pretty foolish now and I wait to hear him apologise profusely. I will of course be magnanimous, as I tell him it's no problem at all, no really, don't worry about it, it's fine. I am therefore somewhat surprised when his face emits further hostility.

"Well how am I supposed to know that?" he spits.

I'm so taken aback that I find myself still spouting the words I had prepared. "Don't worry about it, it's fine, not a problem," but my sentiment is not imbued with the same level of magnanimity. He finally stands down and I step past him. Kate is certainly seeing the funny side and, in a way, I am too. But mostly I am just puzzled. It was an honest mistake that anyone could have made, but his reaction to the truth of the matter was bizarre. Maybe he's full to the eyeballs on steroids and is incapable of reacting to any situation with anything other than belligerence. Existing on the cusp of a verbal explosion due to chemicals in the system is something to which I can relate.

"Can you believe that guy?" says Kate. "Trying to bar chimps, in the twenty-first century!"

I bow my legs and curl my arm over my head like I've seen chimpanzees do on TV. "Oo, oo, oo."

She shakes her head. "Don't do that in here please."

I stand up straight and scour the bar for a free stool, chair or sofa. The place is packed and sitting down appears unlikely. If I had come out with my walking stick, I would have waltzed, OK limped past the bouncer without any issue and now someone may well be offering me their seat. As it is, I'll just have to lean all my weight on the edge of a table.

Yes, maybe I'll come out with the stick from now on. Maybe it's time for me to accept that I'm disabled.

AUG 2019 – ROCK BOTTOM IN BERWICK

A gale is raging and the rain is horizontal as we park up at the B&B in Berwick-upon-Tweed. Kate and E make a run for the door and I follow them, at a somewhat slower pace. The owners have already greeted my wife and son as I dive inside, dripping and shivery.

"Hello!" they both say in my direction.

"Hi. Good Scottish weather out there!" I reply. This attempt at polite small talk is somewhat misjudged, as of course Berwick is actually in England. It may be very close to the border and we will be in Scotland tomorrow – we are on our way to the Edinburgh Festival – but for the time being the weather is entirely English. I realise what I have said straight away and see their faces drop ever so slightly, but they let it pass, before returning to talk to Kate, who I'm sure knows which country she is in.

I'm still cringing approximately every five minutes when I'm getting ready for bed that night. After completing all the bathroom tasks associated with a healthy person, it's time for me to fish in my bath bag for the signifier that I am in fact not a well man. I lay the packet containing the injection I must now self-administer on the side of the bath and sit down on the toilet lid. I remove the needle from the packet and hold it up to the light. I think of Trainspotting, attempting to instil a little junkie chic into proceedings. Maybe it's because I'm in Scotland that Renton and his pals have popped into my head. Nooooo! Not that again! My toes curl once more as I remember my arrival downstairs. Scotland tomorrow, you idiot.

I twist and remove the cap from the syringe containing a drug known as Brabio. I've only just started on this one. It's been a meandering path I've followed to get to this point. I was injecting Avonex for several years before Papa Lazarou's successor assessed my downward trajectory and suggested trying a different medication. I was certainly amenable, as one I was offered was purely tablet-based. I had become accustomed to my weekly injections, but I never once thought, 'Oh good, it's injection night.' So I was merely taking a daily pill for a few months, but my body said, 'Nah, this is too easy for you. I'm going to suppress your white blood cell count to a dangerous level,' so I was taken off that one. For a while I was on nothing, then they tried a lower dose of the tablet, but my body was still having none of it.

Now it's the turn of Brabio. I'm still holding out for a miracle cure, but in the meantime this will have to do. Since Leezou's retirement, I've been under the care of various neurology consultants, but when I ask how research is coming along into medication that can actually reverse the damage already done, every last one has said it's about ten years away. Always ten years away, yet if you believed numerous newspaper articles, the miracle cure is no more than ten minutes away. One in particular that garnered a great deal of attention a few years ago appeared to offer much promise. The treatment is severe – akin to chemotherapy – but results were being described as remarkable, miraculous even. My neurologist of the time, however, played down the reports, saying it was still very early days and besides, I would be at the back of the queue for that one, as it was for MS sufferers who were severely disabled, not patients like me in the disabled-lite classification.

Another time, my sister called, very excited about a new treatment she had come across. Faecal transplants are where they take bacteria from a healthy person's gut and introduce it to the gut of someone not so healthy, such as someone with MS. Some research suggests that the body could reboot as a result and repair itself. So I mentioned this to my latest neurologist. Imagine my shock when he told me that research in that area was probably around ten years from delivering anything of worth.

So Brabio it is, which only slows down the progression, and I'm struggling to get to grips with it. Shorter needles but you have to inject it three times a week. As soon as one injection is out of the way, it feels like the next one is due. And it stings like crazy when you remove the needle, just like you've been attacked by a wasp. After each evening performance, I sit there staring into the space that the TV occupies with an ice cube pressed against my stomach, wondering if it's all worth it. Should I bin it off and just let nature take its course? But I have a plan. There are various options for which body part you would like to attack with the needle. So tonight, instead of the stomach, I am going to try pushing it into a thigh. Avonex was going in there for years, so maybe my legs will cope better than my stomach has been doing.

I force the needle through the skin and slowly push down the plunger. On removing the needle, there is a spot of blood, mixed in with a clear liquid that I assume is some residual Brabio, ready to sink back into the open wound of the injection site and burn like acid. I quickly mop it up with some toilet paper, in the hope I can avert the worst of it. Still holding the paper in place on my thigh, I then hobble into bed where Kate is waiting for me.

"How was it?" she asks.

"Still stinging, but not quite as much."

"Good..."

"Ahhh!" A sudden pain spreads through my thigh. "Ow, shit that hurts!" It feels like the liquid I have just sent burrowing into my leg muscle is attempting to spread its wings and there is nowhere for it to go. The pain abates for a few seconds then hits a second time. I let out another yelp. Did it sound like the groans of a soldier severely wounded in the field, or like the whine of a toddler who's just grazed his knee? The latter probably, but I can't help it. The sensation is horrendous. The medication is forming a fist where there is only room for a fingernail. A persistent spasm that arrives every few seconds. I'm aware of Kate's concern at my shoulder, but equally aware that there's nothing anyone can do. This is my life now. Crying out in pain every other night as I try to reduce the pace of my steady decline. Not stop, or strive for improvement – just to prevent the inevitable happening quite as quickly.

I rub the area around the injection site, but with limited effect. The pain explodes through the muscle yet again. I drop back into the pillow and screw up my eyes. Kate kisses me on the cheek, which briefly transports me back a few years somehow, before the fist forms once more. But this time the pain is ever so slightly less. I await the next one, hoping we're now heading in the right direction.

"It's easing, I think," I say.

And it is. It takes another ten minutes till I'm out of the woods, but I can finally start to look forward to sleep. First, though, I assess the experiment of injecting in the leg, rather than the stomach. Overall, all things considered, it was a roaring failure. I can't go through that level of pain every time. The stinging I get in the stomach is nothing compared with that. I could always try the backside. That's another option. But I would struggle to self-administer. I would have to get Kate to do it. If life had dealt her the shit hand instead of me and she asked me to stick a needle in her curvy bottom, I would be in position like a shot. Try and stop me! She, on the other hand, may be somewhat less eager to stare at my hairy arse.

For a moment, I stop thinking about how crap things have gotten. I'm distracted, lost so deep in a reverie that I barely know where my thoughts currently reside. Then the mist evaporates and I realise I'm now focused on nothing else but Kate's peachy behind. She's already asleep in the dark but it's as clear as day in my filthy mind. I would of course have to push my hand on that lovely smooth skin to remove the needle. And we would have to put bright lights on too, so I could see what I was doing. In those circumstances, I may indeed look forward to injection night.

I avoid considering the fact that all this would mean that she had MS and not me, though the thought that someone, anyone, other than me has it is one that rolls pleasantly around my head, providing me with a momentary uplift. Because make no mistake, this is shit and I'm fed up with it all.

*

I check my phone. It's 4.12am. I fell asleep easily but I've been woken by my bladder telling my brain that it needs emptying. I reluctantly surface from the warm bed and I'm immediately confronted by the sensation that I need to pee with an urgency that is deeply troubling. The bathroom is across the landing and my pace quickens. There is just enough illumination coming through the window to negate the need to put on the light which would blind me, but I need to locate the toilet without delay, as I really think I'm going to wet myself. I virtually run the last few paces, which isn't easy as I'm hurriedly lowering my shorts as I go.

What's going on? This isn't me. I actually think I'm going to be too late. I aim from a half-stride further away than I would like, but I hear the collision of piss against water that reassures me, though the seat is still down, so who knows what kind of spillage may have signalled the beginning of this eruption. It's coming out at such speed that I'm struggling to control the direction, like a firefighter manning a hose single-handedly. I'm wishing I'd put the light on now, but there was no time. I'll just have to continue to use my ears. How long is this going to go on for?

The rapid expulsion comes to as sudden a stop as it began. I finish off, wash my hands and crawl back into bed. What the hell just happened? The only time I've peed like that in living memory was the last time I had a bladder infection. Ah. Not again. But it's the only logical explanation. That kind of urgency can only mean one thing. Bugger.

Henry Miller apparently once stated that to relieve your bladder is one of life's greatest pleasures. You could never say that if you had MS. For the majority of my bathroom visits, urination is the greatest pain in the arse of my entire existence. Every visit is like attempting to get a telephone connection between Timbuktu and Outer Mongolia through one of those ancient plug-in exchanges. Cables have been nibbled by the MS mice and it's the telephone girl's first day.

The process begins with some enthusiastic flicking of the head – yes, that one – in order to encourage some kind of muscle memory. Then I begin to stimulate nerves in the vicinity, which entails lightly running a fingernail over the skin. This can be pretty much anywhere between my waist and undercarriage. A favourite place used to be either side of the upper reaches of the bum crack, but I seem to have mostly worn this out now, and it takes some searching to find where the connection resides. In the meantime, I will use the other hand to grab the sink or whatever is nearby and at an appropriate height, or I will just lean against the wall in front of me – Kate is always complaining about dirty finger marks on the bathroom paintwork.

The final piece of the jigsaw is perhaps the strangest of all. I have to throw my head back, but not directly, at a slight angle, otherwise the messages from my brain can't get through to my urethra. And I have to open my mouth in a slack-jaw kind of way, like I've been given a heavy dose of ketamine. My expression is exactly like Lou Reed's on the cover of his lesser-known album, Ecstasy.

Then, if I'm lucky – it's always worse when I've just woken up or it's the middle of the night and I'm still half asleep – I might manage a single drip, like when Neil is trying to piss in Simon's mouth at the end of the second *Inbetweeners* film, only this isn't the prelude to a torrent about to enter the fray. It just means I'm finally out of the blocks. More concentration to fully relax, as well as some continued and varied nerve stimulation is required at this point. And we're now in business a little more. There's something akin to a flow, but it could come to an end at any point. If I change position by a millimetre, or someone or something disturbs me, my bladder could shut it all down again. If none of that happens and I continue to run my fingernail over the skin of my bum or the top of my thigh, I might get somewhere close to emptying all the contents in one go. If I don't and I only get close, I'll try to get going again, but sometimes this isn't possible and I have to leave a little in there. Which means I'll be doing this all over again sooner rather than later.

So that's it. I've spared you the explicit details up to now, but this episode has left me in the mood to lay it all out there. Does anyone reading this fancy going through this routine every time they need to pee? I mean every single time, four or five times a day? It's a motherfucker, as Eels once sang, though that was a romantic song about someone longing for the presence of his girlfriend. I just long for the days when I could piss like a normal human being.

Another song comes to mind – *Uncle Joe* by Red House Painters. 'I'm staring at the ceiling with an awful feeling of loss and loneliness...' That pretty much sums up the situation. Loss for the state of my health, loneliness because who can truly understand without being the one who has to deal with this shit. That's one of the reasons why my book is becoming so important to me. Writing everything down from the last twenty years seems the only way that anyone could come close to understanding. Knowing that one day someone might think, 'Huh, so it was like that, was it,' feeds me a crumb of comfort. I'm trying to make it funny too. Throwing some humour at it helps to douse the flames of the whole burning shitstorm.

The latest issue I have to deal with is a strange twitch I sometimes get in my hip. It's always when I'm tired, either when I'm trying to relax in front of the TV or more usually when I'm in bed. It'll start as soon as I try to get to sleep or in the middle of the night. It's like a very slow metronome. For three or four beats, my leg will shake, led by a weird pulse running through the nerves around my hip joint, putting me in mind of the last episode of *Blackadder* series one, when everyone's been poisoned and their last death throe is for their leg to wave uncontrollably in the air. Then you can count the seconds till the twitch arrives again. Generally between twenty and twenty-five seconds, but always the same number of seconds for the occasion in hand, regular as clockwork.

I've been given muscle relaxant pills to help control it, but that's all they do – help. Often, I take my permitted dose and the twitching continues, along with my sleeplessness. So, as well as MS fatigue, I'm suffering from regular tiredness. I've been referred to the spasticity division of the physiotherapy department at the hospital. When I was growing up in the seventies and eighties, spaz was a regular and unquestioned playground insult aimed at anyone considered deserving, for a wide variety of perceived misdemeanours. Happily, the term is now on the banned list, but as part of that generation, I can't help thinking of myself in those terms now. I have been put under the care of the spasticity team, therefore I am a spaz. Of course, I would never use the word out loud, and I'm only applying the name to myself, but still, that's what I now hear dropping like a slab of concrete inside my head.

To make it all the more poignant, the specialist physio I've been referred to is an old friend I know from my twenties, when the only health issue I had to contend with was my eczema. I was in a band with Adam back then, attempting to bludgeon an indifferent world into liking a genre of music I would term Cure-vana. Back then, my lyrics were brimful of mental anguish, but what did I really have to worry about? If only I'd known what would befall me thirteen or so years later, that glib phrase, 'At least you have your health,' might have meant something to me.

Reflections on my life, both then and now, continue to bounce through my mind like a cross between Tigger and Eeyore. When you're tired is the worst time to focus on your concerns and worries – that's something that took me far too many years to realise – but it's still difficult to avoid. For perhaps the first time, the thought that this just isn't fair enters my head. The downward slope has been such a gradual one that I think I've not fully grasped how bad everything has become. I imagine what my attitude would be like if I'd been completely healthy for the last what, eighteen years. If last week I'd had an accident or virus which had left me in this state overnight. Would that have been better or would the resultant fallout be too much to bear? If I was like this now without any warning, just bang, this is your life now, surely that would be doubly hard to take. But that thought makes me realise just how bad things have become.

It's not fair, but what ya gonna do. Shit happens and then, after a frustrating hour of hip twitching, so does sleep.

*　　*　　*

After my disrupted night's rest, Kate is the first one to the bathroom in the morning. When she comes back there's a look of puzzlement on her face.

"There was blood all over the toilet seat," she tells me.

I describe my panicky night-time visit. If there had been any doubt that I had another bladder infection, this information puts it to bed. Blood in the urine is a new one, though. I can't deny that for the most part I'm thinking, 'Sod it, do what you will to me. If it makes the MS symptoms worse, so be it.' I'm struggling to care anymore or perhaps I'm just eager to bury negative thoughts on the subject, as per usual. I'm on holiday and that's all I want to focus on. I'll sort out the infection when we get back home.

This MS thing has taken up too much of my life. I have two days to come of sitting next to my 15-year-old son, listening to comedians liberally use the C word. I just want to laugh, not think.

CHRISTMAS 2019 – ROUNDABOUTS AND SWINGS

I have always had a curiosity about the expression 'it's swings and roundabouts'. It struck me as a strange way of saying that there are as many gains as losses with whatever is being discussed. I always assumed it was rhyming slang, as whenever I heard the phrase it seemed to be coming from the mouth of some Cockney wide boy. But I never knew what it might rhyme with and never bothered to look it up.

Until now, for the purposes of this chapter. It seems its origins are sketchy but nothing to do with East End types. Many sources suggest it derives from the little-known poem Roundabouts and Swings by Irish writer, Patrick Chalmers. Published in 1912, it details an encounter with a travelling carnie, who explains the economy of the fairground thus: 'What's lost upon the roundabouts, we pulls up on the swings.'

The poem probably helped to popularise the saying but it certainly didn't originate with it. Six years earlier, PG Wodehouse used it in Love Among the Chickens and the saying was presumably already old. In the story, the protagonist decides to forget about the girl he's been fixated on and instead get on with writing his novel. These lines struck a chord with me:

'A man must go through the fire before he write his masterpiece. We learn in suffering what we teach in song. What we lose on the swings, we make up on the roundabouts.'

The fact that for Wodehouse the roundabouts are profitable, rather than the swings as in Chalmers' poem, belies a truth in the expression, but this was not what particularly interested me. What drew my attention was the first two sentences. Of course, the word 'masterpiece' would never cross my mind as I described my nascent book, but I have been through the fire and this has inspired me to write about the experience. And my ordeals made it into a song too, in the form of MS Blues.

All this put me in a more positive frame of mind – any frame of mind would be more positive than the one that afflicted me in Berwick – and set me to thinking about the advantages of having multiple sclerosis. Yes, there are some swings alongside the roundabouts, if you strain every sinew to find them. Here are my top eight benefits of having MS:

1. I can get out of doing all sorts of jobs that I don't want to do. Household chores, DIY, gardening... no, sorry, no can do. I'd love to but I'm just not physically up to it.

2. If I was capable, I might have it in mind to raise money for charity by running a marathon or climbing Kilimanjaro, pushing myself to the limits of endurance. Well that's not going to happen, but I have nothing to feel guilty about.

3. I have a Blue Badge. I can always get parked, I'm straight into the shops and in most places it's free.

4. I'm able to appreciate not having other conditions. There are scores of horrible medical problems that I don't suffer

from.

5. Similarly, I'm able to appreciate what I am still capable of doing. For example, due to serious hip problems, my brother-in-law can't comfortably put his own shoes on. I'm disabled but I could be far more disabled.

6. I was able to negotiate better working hours than my colleagues and I'm allowed to work at home for some of the week.

7. My peeing problems are frustrating, but at least I'm living in the age of the smartphone. It gives me the opportunity to catch up on my emails, Instagram or even read a few pages of a book.

8. Having my thyroid removed means that I am now entitled to free prescriptions. Not directly relevant to MS, but it's a benefit of my health difficulties (OK, I admit, at this point I was struggling to think of anything else that was good about having MS).

I try to focus on the above when MS knocks heavily on my door. And on the positive side, the bloodshed in Berwick does not seem to have had any detrimental effect on my health. I sorted out the infection on my return home and I seem no worse than before. Also, the Brabio injections have just become another part of the mundane routine. It took several weeks of distress, but everything has calmed down now. No pain, not even the slightest sting and no side effects. It's amazing what your body can become accustomed to.

On the negative side, every few months I seem to be able to walk a little less far and my balance becomes a touch worse. Some days I stumble through the house, bouncing from the walls like a ball bearing in a pinball machine. My greatest fear is that I won't be able to walk at all in my retirement. The image of being pushed out into the garden, a tartan rug over my knees, so I can enjoy some fresh air for an hour, pierces my thoughts every once in a while. If I'm ninety, fine. Sixty-five and I will be somewhat disgruntled, particularly if I'm also attached to a catheter. Are my peeing problems steadily worsening or am I just becoming more fed up with all that each passing year? Both probably, but it'll be a dark day when someone is shoving a tube up my cock. If that time ever comes to pass, I think I'll have to accept that resistance is over.

Besides the plusses and minuses I sometimes list in my head, the weirdest notion that crosses my mind is my fear of a cure. If all this could be wiped away and I was suddenly fully functioning once more, how would I feel? I identify now as someone with MS. I have MS, therefore I am. I hate to admit it, but it makes me feel a tiny bit special. Part of me would struggle with having that taken away.

Having MS removes choices too. For most, that appears to be a black and white issue. Having choices – good, having them removed – bad. But I remember my twenties. I had unlimited options and it left me in a paralysed state of anxiety. With so many directions I could take, each one possibly affecting my whole life, I felt unable to take any of them. MS gives me a framework within which to operate. It provides a level of certainty, to rub alongside the mass of uncertainty that it also introduces into the arena.

The brightest, most genuine light of all is being offered by the book I am writing. I've tried various working titles but *Balls to MS* is the one that has stuck, as it is the one that sets the correct tone most succinctly. I'm really pleased with how it's developing. In my more self-deprecating moments, I tell people that it's my best creative endeavour since my last creative endeavour but I really think it has a decent chance of being published.

Yes, I think this might well be it; there could be big changes afoot in the coming months. 2020 could be a good year.

2020 – THE FINAL WORD

Bugger.

So that was my story. Did you enjoy it? More than I enjoyed living it, I hope. If you made it this far, I'm guessing you at least didn't think it stank the place up.

Christmas 2019, when the last chapter of any length is set and when I was trying my hardest to look to the following year with optimism, was the last time the world would be blissfully unaware of Covid 19. By the last day of that year, reports were starting to emerge of a new type of pneumonia. And so it began. As global societies imploded, multiple sclerosis, like all other diseases and conditions, found itself suddenly and most unexpectedly, chucked in the back seat. In the boot, even. No longer talked about or considered, except by those directly affected by it. Even for those like me who carried that cross, we had to put our complaints to one side. I felt I had to anyway, as deaths began to rise and much misery ensued.

As for getting *Balls to MS* published by a regular publisher, lockdown of course encouraged a whole slew of people either to write that book they never found the time to write beforehand, or finish off that story they hadn't touched for years. The result? Agents saw a massive increase in submissions, adding to an already massive mountain, meaning an already slim chance of piquing their interest virtually vanished altogether.

I had more pressing matters to deal with during lockdown however. Seemingly the second WHO declared Covid a pandemic in March 2020, Kate caught it. We are fairly confident that Kate had it anyway. She wasn't particularly ill, but she did have some of the well-reported symptoms, mainly a really hot feeling in her chest and at the top of her back, followed by weeks of feeling drained and breathless.

Although I seemed asymptomatic, it was clear to me that I had caught Covid too; it was just that my body only told me by heightening my MS symptoms. My walking difficulties in particular became worse in a short space of time. Maybe it was coincidence but it was a massive one if the month or two after Kate thought she had Covid, I went significantly further downhill.

My leg strength has continued to deteriorate at an alarming rate. I wouldn't say the differences have been dramatic, but the decline has been steady and pronounced these last eighteen months. I'm still getting around without any aid within the house and still only use a walking stick when Kate and I take Ellie out, but for how long will this be the situation? Which brings me onto my encounter with Ron.

Recently, we had to take on a gardener. I can only manage to cut a small bit of lawn now before my 52-year-old body collapses back onto the patio furniture. This constitutes around 2% of what needs to be done. It's unrealistic to expect Kate to pick up the remaining 98%, as evidenced by vegetation spiralling out of control, so needs must.

Ron is fitter than me. And he's seventy-odd. He makes your average dour Yorkshireman seem like Russell Brand, but he's a hard worker. Of course, on his first visit guilt quickly raised its head. I was bringing drinks to a septuagenarian like I was the lord of the manor and he was some kind of Mellors character whose shagging days were long behind him. My feelings of awkwardness were exacerbated by it being a scorching hot day. During our verbal exchange on account of me delivering a cold drink to him – it was too stilted to call it a conversation or even chat – I quickly had to slip in the information that I have MS and this was why I couldn't do the work myself, not that I was too moneyed (definitely not true) or too lazy (OK, partly true) to do it myself.

Ron sucked in this information like Boomhauer in *King of the Hill*. I waited for him to reply with, 'Yup,' like the taciturn friend of Hank Hill, or maybe he would go with a loquacious, 'Can't do much then?' But no. Ron offered a nugget of information I wasn't expecting to hear.

"Hmm, my daughter has MS. Terrible disease."

"Oh right,' I said. "When was she diagnosed?"

His face contorted into a pained expression. I wondered if I shouldn't have asked, as maybe he was still coming to terms with it, but soon realised that he was just delving deep into his memory bank to remember.

"Must be, erm… around twenty years now. Maybe just over."

What he told me next got my attention.

"Can't walk at all now… Terrible disease."

"I'm sorry to hear that," I muttered.

And I truly I was, but not for entirely unselfish reasons. If you cast your mind back to the first chapter of this book, it's rapidly coming up to twenty years since symptoms first made their brief and barely noticed announcement that multiple sclerosis was on its way. That means I'll be catching up with Ron's daughter soon in terms of timescale. Just two or three years. I tried not to panic. MS can of course affect people in vastly different ways and employ varying time sequences. Maybe Ron's daughter had secondary, or even primary. Maybe she'd had a major relapse, if it was of the relapse-remitting type. I did a bit of digging, though not the type for which Ron is known.

"Has she been like that a long time?" I asked.

What Ron proceeded to tell me sent a shudder through me that has been keeping me awake at night. The pattern of his daughter's MS has matched mine like the most terrible mirror image (think Ann Widdicombe staring at herself with self-loathing the morning after her latest bender) – she's just been a couple of years ahead of me, even by age. For the first few years it barely affected her life. She had strange sensations in her limbs but was still able to get around fine and was even playing sports for a good while. But then she started to go downhill. Fairly gradually, but then in the last two or so years, everything's accelerated and now, now she's presumably in a wheelchair. I didn't get so far as to ask. I guess I was too busy reeling from this summary of the woman's life, a woman I had never met but whom I felt I had because her life is basically my life, at least if you hang it on these few details.

I tried to gather my thoughts, which wasn't a pleasant experience in the circumstances. "I'd quite like to meet her if possible." I was thinking some more details directly from her would be useful. Maybe she could somehow make the terror more palatable. Ron, however, quickly retreated back into his shell.

"Aye," he said, in a vague, non-committal way. What was I to make of that? Maybe there would be no point in meeting her anyway. Maybe she'll just be a junior, female Ron and I'll garner few, if any insights from her. Alternatively, she could be open and talkative and tell me lots of things that I don't want to hear.

I'm giving it some thought on whether or not to pursue it, in between the waves of panic, depression and hope. The way my symptoms have progressed up till recently I was optimistic that I would at least get to retirement age before my legs completely packed up. But the last couple of years have seen an acceleration of my disability. Just like Ron's daughter.

I've tried to raise my new concerns with some of the people close to me but been met with the predictable lines of empty reassurance, 'You don't know it'll go that way. That's just one person. Your situation could be completely different.'

I know, I know, but listening to Ron's description of the way things have gone for his daughter made it clear that it's a distinct possibility. My walking days may be numbered. And in years that number might be two.

Or to put it another way, there's an episode of *Frasier* when Frasier befriends a guy in a wheelchair. He soon regrets it because it turns out he has nothing in common with this dullard who's obsessed with barbecuing. He lives in fear of the approach of his disabled acquaintance in his favourite coffee house, an approach that is always announced by the squeak of one of the wheels on the guy's chair.

That's how I feel right now. I can hear the squeak in the distance and dread its approach. Unlike Frasier, I won't be able just to scarper when this level of disability shows itself because I'll be physically incapable.

Sorry if I'm trampling on those flowers of optimism I planted in *Roundabouts and Swings*, but I've striven to tell the truth throughout the book, so that's what I'm going to continue to do. Maybe I'm just tired. I spend most of my time tired these days. Not just because of MS fatigue but because of the spasms in my leg that were a relatively new symptom when I mentioned it in *Rock Bottom in Berwick*. It's continued unabated and I'm taking around fifty tablets a week just to keep it under some kind of control. But it's rare that a part of my time in bed isn't significantly disrupted by this irritating twitch in my legs. And who remains in a positive frame of mind when they're tired?

I'm fifty-three this month. When my dad calls and tells me how drained he feels and how frustrating it is that he can't do what he used to, I try to be sympathetic. During these conversations, however, I'm always drawn to the same thought: I understand that frustration, Dad, but you're in your eighties. I'm in my early fifties. Try that one on for fairness.

I fear I'm lapsing into self-pity. As Ron said, it's a terrible disease, but there are lots of others to go round. One of my favourite comedians, Sean Lock, died recently from cancer and he was only five years older than me. Despite everything I've gone through and have to deal with to this day, I'm still here, and Sean Lock, very sadly, is not. Neither are millions worldwide as a result of this pandemic which hit the moment the *Balls to MS* story ended. So positivity, come here. I've not finished with you yet.

A few brief thank yous. To be honest, I didn't get a lot of help with anything regarding this book but a special shout-out must go to Annabel Port. Some readers may know that Annabel was on *Absolute Radio* for years, as the comic sidekick to Geoff Lloyd. The pair of them now have their own podcast, *Adrift*, the theme of which is social awkwardness and the embarrassing interactions we have as humans negotiating life. In a section of the podcast, they read out stories from listeners – the Drifters – and a number of my tales of woe have made it onto the show. Writing these helped me to develop the style I use in this book and on the back of this success, I contacted Annabel to ask if she would read an early draft. She very kindly agreed and her encouragement – let's face it, mainly the fact that she assured me it wasn't shit – and her willingness to provide an endorsement spurred me on to complete the project.

Another thank you goes to Nik at Book Beaver who designed the book cover. He did a great job and I can highly recommend him as someone to work with if you need a professionally-designed book cover. Thanks also to Ethan Reynard for taking the photo that's featured on the cover. He agreed to help me for utterly selfless reasons. And the fact that he didn't have to buy me a Father's Day present if he did.

A final thank you goes to you (I hope I'm addressing more than one person here but whatever). The thought of people reading my book and appreciating my prose has been a major factor in keeping me ploughing on, so thanks for purchasing and even more thanks if you go that extra mile and tell the world what a great read it is. If you were underwhelmed by it or, for some unfathomable reason, didn't like it at all, feel free to keep your opinion firmly lodged inside your head.

If you really can't get enough of me moaning about my plight, drop in at www.ballstoms.com where you'll find more stories and comment about my current situation. Have I or have I not managed to continue to outpace the approaching wheelchair? It's a real cliff-hanger. There is lots of other stuff on there too, such as photos and a list of the stories I've had read out on Adrift and other podcasts.

If you or someone you know has MS, I hope he or she has found a way to deal with the situation. Just saying out loud, 'Balls to MS,' is a good starting point. But for now we've reached an end point. This really is the final word.

Andy Reynard lives in West Yorkshire, loves books, music, history, popular culture and football and is a regular contributor to a number of podcasts. For more information visit his blog, where you can also drop him a line.

www.ballstoms.com

Printed in Great Britain
by Amazon

86402705R00205